"Someone's gonna die tonight!"

At The Kettle restaurant, twenty-six-year-old Robert Fry became more and more agitated. When Fry was this intoxicated and angry, he was a danger to everyone around him. His friends knew this all too well. Now as Fry's verbal confrontation with another restaurant patron grew more heated, Fry's buddies worried that things were about to slip out of control.

One of them asked, "What's wrong, Bobby?"

In response, he muttered, "Someone's going to die!"

In a desperate atte⋯⋯⋯⋯⋯⋯⋯⋯d into another night⋯⋯⋯⋯⋯⋯⋯⋯e friend told Fry, "L⋯⋯⋯⋯⋯⋯⋯⋯"

Finally co⋯⋯⋯⋯⋯⋯⋯⋯w more insults with ⋯⋯⋯⋯⋯⋯⋯e restaurant. As he a⋯⋯⋯⋯⋯⋯ove away in a blue Ford Aspire, ⋯⋯⋯⋯⋯at a large knife he owned, which he'd named "Bubba the Butcher Knife." He growled, "Someone's gonna die tonight!"

MONSTER SLAYER

ROBERT SCOTT

PINNACLE BOOKS
Kensington Publishing Corp.
http://www.kensingtonbooks.com

PINNACLE BOOKS are published by

Kensington Publishing Corp.
850 Third Avenue
New York, NY 10022

All Kensington Titles, Imprints, and Distributed Lines are available at special quantity discounts for bulk purchases for sales promotions, premiums, fund-raising, and educational or institutional use. Special book excerpts or customized printings can also be created to fit specific needs. For details, write or phone the office of the Kensington special sales manager: Kensington Publishing Corp., 850 Third Avenue, New York, NY 10022, attn: Special Sales Department, Phone: 1-800-221-2647.

First Printing: January 2005
10 9 8 7 6 5 4 3 2 1

Printed in the United States of America

*This book is dedicated to Matthew, Joseph,
Donald, and Betty.*

ACKNOWLEDGMENTS

I would like to thank many people who helped me in the preparation of this book, including Debra Mayeux, Joline Gutierrez Kruger, M. B. Libbey, J. Quattrin and F. Zolfo. Special thanks go to Sheriff Bob Melton, Detective Tyler Truby and all the clerks at the San Juan District Court. Once again, I'd like to thank my wonderful literary agent, Damaris Rowland, and editor Michaela Hamilton.

A Note About Terms

In the Four Corners Region, where this book takes place, the terms "Native American" and "Indian" are often used interchangeably by the locals. The term "Anglo" is used for anyone of European origin who is not of Hispanic ethnicity. I have used these terms in the book much as a person living in the region would.

Go as far as you dare in the heart of a lonely land, you cannot go so far that life and death are not before you.

—Mary Austin

Prologue

Farmington, New Mexico, Thanksgiving, 1996.

A cold wind blew down from the snowcapped La Plata Mountains, scattering fallen leaves along the icy banks of the San Juan River. They whirled around the ruins of multistoried Salmon Pueblo, now a jumble of broken walls and empty windows beneath the pale glow of the autumn moon. A one-time thriving center of Mesa Verdean people, the adobe and stone enclosures had once echoed with the sounds of family life. Farmers tilled the rich alluvial soil along the river for maize and beans, and artisans created beautiful pottery and turquoise art objects. It was a proud outlier of the grand pueblo complex atop Mesa Verde.

Several kivas ringed Salmon Pueblo, underground domains of secret societies that gave thanks to the gods for the bountiful harvests. The societies told and retold the ancient stories of heroes and monsters who inhabited their homeland. These heroes and monsters were a living presence that dwelled amongst the mesas, mountains and very bluffs across the river.

One of these bluffs ended in the shape of a scorpion's tail. At the center of each kiva was a *sipapu,* a hole in the floor that symbolized the place where the first people had ascended from the lower worlds into the present world.

Dressed in brilliant finery and jewelry, the members of the kiva societies sent up prayers for the continued prosperity of Salmon Pueblo. Their prayers, however, went unanswered in the thirteenth century, and around 1250, the last of the villagers simply gathered up their household goods and wandered away; they left behind mute testaments of their passing, in mortar and stone. They may have abandoned the pueblo because of continued drought or the advance of enemy outsiders, and their passing left behind a mystery. Did they proceed to the Jemez Mountains to found Zia Pueblo? Or travel on even farther to start one of the pueblos along the Rio Grande River? No one knows for sure. In their wake, they left behind an empty village of silent stone.

Another mystery was about to unfold on the cold November night of Thanksgiving, 1996—a mystery that would encompass its own pantheon of slayers and victims, heroes and monsters. It was a mystery that would baffle local law-enforcement agents for years to come and lead down a winding trail of bloodied victims and improbable murder weapons. It began not in the desiccated ruins of thirteenth-century Salmon Pueblo, but in the nearby modern city of Farmington, New Mexico, on a night that most American families celebrated with joy and fellowship.

Thanksgiving began in the traditional way for twenty-three-year-old Robert "Bobby" Fry of Farmington as he sat down along with his parents to a table brimming with food. A large bearlike man, weighing 250 pounds and standing six feet tall, Fry had a shock of dark, thick hair, a full mustache and very pronounced five o'clock shadow. Even one of his friends, Larry Hudson, alluded to Robert's bruin image. Hudson said, "He was slow to move at the beginning, but then he would come on like a bear."

Foremost on Fry's mind—after the turkey, dressing and pumpkin pie at his parents' home that evening—was the thought of diving into bottles of beer with his drinking buddies. When it came to alcohol consumption, Fry had a formidable reputation.

It wasn't far from his folks' house to an apartment of a friend down by the Animas Valley Mall, Farmington's largest retail outlet. When Fry arrived, his twenty-three-year-old buddy Harold "Harley" Pollock was already there, along with some other friends. Fry immediately started pounding beers. He could literally drink five beers for every one the others took out of a six-pack, and as always when drunk, Fry became boisterous and agitated. His stories were loud and often included tales of violence and bloodshed.

Pollock remembered that particular night very well. He said later, "We all partied and kicked back. I'm not sure how much I drank, but I wasn't sober. Bobby, at one point, offered to find a prostitute and bring her back to the apartment."

Pollock wasn't particularly keen on the idea. He knew that the combination of Robert Fry and prostitutes often spelled trouble, but Pollock went along, mainly because Fry insisted that he drive. Fry, by this time, was so inebriated that he could barely walk straight. They both climbed into Fry's blue Ford Aspire and hit the streets of Farmington in their quest for ladies of the evening.

It was not a good night to be out looking for a hooker. The nearly deserted streets of Farmington were cold and frosty as the winds whipped down from the mountains to the north. The regular hookers had either taken the night off, wrapped up in their own Thanksgiving festivities, or been discouraged by the lack of clients. For the most part the streets were dark and empty.

As Pollock and Fry approached downtown Farmington, the area was practically a ghost town. In fact, it was the kind of night when traditional Navajos of the region were sure that ghosts made their way silently through the gloom. It was for just such occasions that they kept "ghost lights" burning near hogans and sheep pens, silent beacons to keep evil spirits of the dead away.

Like ghost beacons of their own, only one set of lights was burning in the interior of a building on the 100 block of North Allen Street. The building with the lights on was The Eclectic, a store dedicated to selling occult items, crystals, Dungeons & Dragons games, gothic items, role-playing booklets and ornate knives and swords.

The building itself wasn't much to look at, just a plain brown exterior that bordered Allen Street with a large plate-glass window. A sign on the front wall stated: "Eclectic: a. selecting at will; n. a thinker who selects and reconciles principles, opinions, belonging to different schools of thought. Pl. a cool store on Allen Street." On top of the building was a pink-and-white Pegasus.

Both Fry and Pollock knew The Eclectic very well. It was one of their favorite hangouts and they had gathered there many times with other adherents of role-playing games. Some fans of the games even wore costumes that conjured up images of witches, wizards and the occult. When Fry saw the lights on in the store, he suddenly told Pollock to stop the car. He needed to urinate, and The Eclectic was the only place available at the moment. Fry normally would have urinated in a dark alley, but the warm interior of The Eclectic was much more inviting on such a cold night. He knew that a young man in the store, Joseph Fleming, would let them in. Both he and Fleming were friends and security guards for a company that often patrolled the Animas Valley Mall and did security work at local events.

Twenty-four-year-old Joseph Fleming was at The Eclectic that night, not so much to guard the place as to hang around and play video games on one of the store's computers. Eighteen-year-old Matthew "Matt" Trecker was also there that night, asleep in one of the back rooms. This was nothing new— Trecker, Fleming, Pollock and Fry had all stayed overnight at The Eclectic at one time or another. It was almost their home away from home. The store manager, Alex Seifert, was very loose about such things and a whole flock of teenagers and twenty-year-olds hung around the premises on a constant basis. In a town as conservative and middle-American as Farmington, The Eclectic was as alternative as they were going to get.

Fry pounded on the front door and Fleming let him and Pollock inside. Fleming talked with them for a little while and then returned to his computer game. Fry used the bathroom and then he and Pollock drifted into the main showroom and gazed at the merchandise. Fry immediately gravitated to a display case containing ornate knives and swords. He was absolutely crazy about knives. Fry already owned more than a dozen—everything from jackknives with turquoise inlay, to a huge bowie knife with a wicked blade, which he had nicknamed "Bubba the Butcher Knife." He'd told his friends stories that Bubba wasn't meant for cutting animals, it was meant for cutting human flesh. He bragged how he'd ripped open opponents in bar fights. Most of his friends took the stories with a grain of salt. Bobby Fry was known for his outlandish embellishments of the truth.

The display case was unlocked and Pollock saw Fry pick up and admire the knives. While they were there, Joseph Fleming was so engrossed in his computer game, he didn't keep tabs on Fry or Pollock. They were his friends, after all, and besides, Fry was a security guard just as he was. But Fleming didn't count on Fry's inebriation or his lust for knives. Fry turned to Pollock and said, "I'm gonna steal some."

Pollock didn't think it was such a great idea, but he didn't object. In fact, he was afraid of Bobby Fry. Pollock weighed only about 160 pounds, at least ninety pounds less than Fry. He knew how enraged Fry could become when he didn't get his way, especially when he'd been drinking to excess. Pollock reluctantly helped Fry gather up several thousand dollars' worth of expensive knives and they let themselves out of the store without Fleming being aware of what they had done.

By now, Fry was feeling sober enough to drive his car. As they headed northwest out of town, he also became sober enough to realize that the theft of the knives might not have been such a good idea. Fry determined that Fleming was certainly bright enough to discover that merchandise was missing, and the first people he would suspect would be himself and Pollock. Afraid to take the stolen property home, Fry headed up to Chokecherry Canyon.

Chokecherry Canyon, often called "the Glade," was a favorite hangout for locals, especially partying teenagers. Both Fry and Pollock had been there in the past, especially Fry. He knew the dirt road into the canyon very well, even on a dark night. The road wound past rocky cliffs and drip tanks, pipelines and well heads of the gas and oil industry. By night these looked like silvery giants among the darkened rock walls. Despite being such a short distance from the city, Chokecherry Canyon was extremely wild and isolated, the domain of coyotes, bobcats and an occasional mountain lion.

As Fry's headlights illuminated large boulders, fallen from the cliffs, they looked like enormous tombstones amongst the drip tanks. In the summer months, the canyon might be filled with groups of partying teenagers, but on this cold November night, there was no one there except for Fry and Pollock. The entire canyon had a stark, haunted feel about it, and, in fact, it was haunted by one of the region's worst and most famous crimes.

In 1974, three local teenagers beat, mutilated and burned to death three intoxicated Native American men in Chokecherry Canyon. It became known as "the Chokecherry Massacre." The boys had taken a teenage rite of passage, "rolling drunken Indians," to murderous extremes. In their fury they pummeled the men with fists, boots, rocks and glass shards. They purposefully had pulled the men's pants down and set fire to their genital areas— graphic testament to their contempt for intoxicated Native Americans.

The arrest of the teenagers and their trial brought Farmington to the boiling point. When the boys received fairly lenient sentences because of their ages, many Native Americans in the region were outraged. Almost every Saturday there was a march of protestors down Farmington's main street. At one point things developed into a near riot. This was in the most strident era of the American Indian Movement (AIM), and up on the Sioux Reservation that very year, there were shooting deaths of two FBI agents and gun battles between pro- and anti-AIM adherents. Things never got that out of hand in Farmington, but the aftermath of the Chokecherry Massacre left a deep scar on the region.

If Robert Fry had any thoughts about this incident, so famous in local history, he didn't share his thoughts with Harold Pollock. Fry had other business to attend to at present. He grabbed a short-handled shovel he always kept in the back compartment of his car. Now, under a half-moon, it became very handy. He and Pollock dug a hole in the earth and buried the stolen loot amidst the boulders and sagebrush. The ghosts of the murdered Navajos were almost palpable in the icy air. Bent over his shovel like a tomb robber, Robert Fry began to concoct his own murderous plans. Fueled by anger, alcohol and fear, they took shape and transformed themselves into a bloody scheme.

The drive back to Farmington was not a pleasant one. Fry and Pollock discussed the theft and Pollock was sure they were going to be caught. Fry, by this time, felt the same way. Suddenly, to Pollock's surprise, Fry turned back toward the downtown area and said he had to use The Eclectic's bathroom once more. Pollock wondered if that was all he had to do. In the pit of his stomach, Pollock felt that something very bad was about to happen. He dreaded going back into The Eclectic.

Robert Fry pounded on The Eclectic's door once again, and Fleming let the pair inside. Fry used the bathroom; then Pollock took his turn. Pollock was feeling sick by now, not only from all the alcohol he had consumed, but from the fear of the theft and possible retribution. This was not the first time Pollock had been involved in a burglary, and the previous encounter had ended very badly for him with jail time.

As Pollock was washing his hands, he heard an altercation break out in the main part of the store. What happened next was revealed later by Pollock, and he told several different versions of the encounter. His first version was terse and graphic and he explained what he initially saw. Stumbling out the bathroom door, Pollock discovered Fry and Fleming wrestling around the display cases. Fleming was a big man, but so was Fry, and Pollock could see that Fry was enraged. In Pollock's later words, "He seemed almost possessed."

The two men battled between the knives and swords, beneath books dedicated to warlocks, dragons and vampires. They clawed and scratched like two wild beasts themselves, locked in deadly combat—Fleming trying to save his own life and Fry trying to kill him. Fry eventually got the upper hand. He placed his hands around Fleming's neck, choking him, and pushed him to the floor. Fleming was already bloody and bruised from several wounds, and his face turned beet red under the pressure of Fry's hands. Little by little, his struggles became more erratic and less defensive.

Fry stood up and stepped on Fleming's throat. Fry wore heavy work boots. Pollock heard a strange gurgling sound from Fleming's throat; then Fleming lay still.

Pollock looked directly into Fry's eyes. They held an array of conflicting emotions—wild and triumphant, enraged and fearful. Fry wiped blood from his hands and arms. To Pollock's gaze, he looked demented.

The commotion had awakened Matthew Trecker from the back room and he stumbled sleepy-eyed and half awake into the showroom. The sight he beheld must have seemed like a nightmare of unreality. His friend Joseph Fleming was dead on the floor, and Bobby Fry, a person he knew well, was standing nearby, wiping blood from his hands and arms.

Taken off guard, Trecker didn't stand a chance. Fry pounced on him like a wild tiger, hitting him in the face with all his might. "It was the hardest I've ever seen anyone be hit," Pollock recalled later. Matthew Trecker tumbled to the floor and ceased moving.

Pollock quivered in shock from this sudden turn of events. He never forgot the wild and exalted look in Bobby Fry's eyes. The look was like that of a wild animal that had just slaughtered its prey. Fry returned to Joseph Fleming and unsheathed his knife—the one he called Bubba the Butcher Knife. Then he bent down and slit Fleming's throat with the knife. Harold Pollock looked on in horror as a pool of blood spread across the floor.

Dripping with blood, Fry lurched toward Pollock and handed him a sword from one of the display cases. Even though Matt Trecker was his friend, having played many sessions of Dungeons & Dragons together, Fry said to Pollock, "Let's cut his head off." As he said this, Fry grabbed a samurai sword.

The urge for a decapitation was more than just Fry's blood lust, it was symbolic. Fry adored the movie and television series *Highlander*. Its hero, Connor MacLeod, in ancient times had become immortal by cutting off the heads of rivals. The very act of doing it increased his energy and longevity. Now here was a chance to do the same within modern Farmington, New Mexico. Ancient rituals and the modern world would become one, and Fry would be on his own way to becoming immortal.

According to Pollock, he reluctantly took the sword from Fry and stared down at Matt Trecker. He'd always liked Matt, but what was he to do? If he didn't kill Matt now, Fry was sure to kill him. Shaking and nearly crying, Pollock bent down and placed the sharp edge of the sword against Trecker's throat. Then his hand began to move and the blade slipped into flesh.

Chapter 1

Heroes and Monsters

In the 1990s and even into 2000, all of the victims and all of the killers would bring their tales of heroes and monsters to a collision point of violence and death in the northwestern corner of New Mexico. Just as genetics, schooling and environment were a part of their being, so were the cultures and landscapes of their origin. The interconnection of victims and killers was entangled at a crossroads of inevitability and mere circumstance, bound together by the ferocious urges of the killers and the vulnerability of the victims.

Joseph Fleming, Matthew Trecker, Harold Pollock, Donald Tsosie, Leslie Engh, Betty Lee and especially Bobby Fry would intertwine their lives and deaths until the story of one could not be told without the other. None of them lived in a vacuum. They made choices, for ill or good, that affected them individually and all their friends and family as well. To some degree, they were all products of their ethnicity and the landscape of their homeland. And these elements were very powerful in the Four Corners Region of New Mexico.

The landscape around Farmington is dramatic, to say the least. The bluffs south of town often glow with a golden light at sunset along the banks of the tree-lined San Juan River. To the west, the Hogback, a large wall of red sandstone, runs for miles in a nearly impenetrable barrier. The Animas River flows down from the north to join the San Juan, as does the La Plata River. Near Morgan Lake, the Navajo Mine gapes like a huge caldera, the largest open pit mine in the western United States. To the south of town, the Bisti Badlands comprise a wilderness of fantastically shaped stones, painted bands of rock and multicolored cliffs.

Dramatic as all of these features are, they are overshadowed by the towering lone sentinel of Shiprock, thirty miles west of Farmington. To the Anglos of the region, the rock seemed like a magnificent clipper ship in full sail, hence the name. To them, it was an emblem of their journey across the wide Atlantic in tall sailing ships, to debouch upon the wild and untamed shores of America. The first settlers had set out in the sixteenth century to obtain that which they could not get in Europe from overlords and nobles—land they could call their own. While in America, this quest for land spurred them on, year after year, ever farther westward—until by 1875, the first settlers hovered on the margins of what would become Farmington.

The Farmington area in the early 1870s was a no-man's-land. The Pueblo Indians had been gone for centuries, only their ghostly ruins, like Salmon Pueblo, marked their passage. The area had never been part of the Hispanic domain. Their outposts were farther to the east and south in Taos and Santa Fe. In 1874, President Grant, by executive order, set aside the area for the Jicarilla Apaches to create a reservation, but the Jicarillas did not want to be settled so close to their traditional enemies, the Navajo. They opted for a reservation farther to the north and east, centered around a beautiful valley below Archuleta Mesa, in a town that would become Dulce. The region at the junction of the San Juan and Animas Rivers remained empty, belonging to no one.

In 1875, the Hendrickson brothers of Animas City, Colorado, went to investigate the state of affairs at the river junctions. They found the land to be good for grazing, farming and orchards. In 1876, President Grant put the area back into the public domain, and with the doors wide open for settlement, the Hendrickson brothers were the first to file claims, followed by a myriad of others. These were mainly farmers and a few ranchers. In their first vote for a town name, they chose Farming Town. This was later shortened to Farmington.

The settlers dug irrigation ditches from the rivers and planted corn and fruit trees. Before long, the junction of the rivers truly lived up to its name. Apples thrived in the region, and by the turn of the twentieth century, an incredible 110 varieties were grown in the area. In the midst of the surrounding arid wilderness and desert, Farmington was termed a "New Eden."

Just how isolated this pastoral paradise was can be glimpsed by a poem, written by an unknown author around the year 1900.

Beyond the San Juan River,
are paths that lead to death
To the desert's scorching breezes,
that feel like Satan's breath.
Beyond the white man's outposts,
where the poisonous reptile waits
Are the Devil's own possessions,
his original estates.

Beyond the San Juan River,
'Tis said the story's told
Are paths that lead to mountains,
of purest virgin gold.
But 'tis our firm conviction
whatever else they tell
Beyond the San Juan River,
all paths lead straight to hell.

To the Anglos and Hispanics, Navajo land to the west was a brutal place, a domain of mystery and death. Even today, it seems devoid of life on first glance, a landscape of arid valleys and mesas. Yet it is to this very region that the Diné (the Navajo people) moved to create their homeland.

Very recent archaeological evidence points to the Navajo as being centered more in the area east of Farmington until the coming of the Spanish. Then in a conscious effort not to be dominated by the Spanish in culture and religion, as had happened to the Pueblo Indians of the Rio Grande Valley, the Navajo moved westward to chart their own destiny. They became shepherds, farmers, raiders and fine horsemen in the process. They became the masters of their own world in Dinétah.

In the very heartland of Dinétah, what looked like only jumbles of rocks or craggy peaks to the white man were often sacred sites to the Navajos. Almost directly north of Farmington, in present Colorado, is Mount Hesperus. To the Anglos, it is nothing more than a beautiful snowcapped mountain with a modern ski resort; to the Navajo, it is Dibéntsaa, Sacred Mountain of the North, and it is attached to the earth by a rainbow. To the east of Farmington, Mount Blanca is Tsisnaajiní, Sacred Mountain of the East. It is attached to the earth by a bolt of lightning. To the south of Farmington, near Chaco Canyon, with the help of Talking God, the Navajo were able to defeat the evil gambler Nohoilpi, who made slaves of men and women.

Of all of these sacred sites in the Farmington area, none became more significant or sacred than Shiprock to the west, or as it was known to the Navajos—Tse'Bit'Ai (Rock with Wings).

Towering to 7,178 feet above sea level, a full 1,500 feet above the plain, the "Rock with Wings" appears as some Gothic cathedral turned to stone—a beacon for one of the Navajo heroes and his most daring and significant exploits. It was here that one of the Hero Twins conducted a feat of memorable valor. The Hero Twins in Navajo religion are as important as Moses to Judaism or Peter and Paul to Christianity.

Changing Woman (Estsanatheli) gave birth to twins, and the Sun and the Water were their fathers. The elder brother went on to slay many monsters, and one of the most fearsome lived at the Rock with Wings. As the story goes, the elder of the Hero Twins, Nayenezgani, who would become Monster Slayer, set out to destroy Tsenahale, a large eaglelike creature that lived atop the Rock with Wings. Tsenahale clutched men and women with its claws and took them home to be fed to its young. As Monster Slayer was walking across the plains, he heard a whooshing sound overhead like a whirlwind. It was Tsenahale.

The great bird seized him in its talons and bore Monster Slayer off to the Rock With Wings and dropped him onto a ledge of the cliffs. For ordinary people this fall was fatal, but before setting off on his journey, Monster Slayer had been given a "life feather" by Spider Woman. The feather broke his fall.

When the young of Tsenahale went to eat their new victim, Monster Slayer said to them, "Shhh!"

They halted and cried out to their father, "This thing is not dead. It says, 'Shhh' to us."

"That is only the air escaping from its body," Tsenahale said. "Never mind that. Eat it." And then the great bird flew away to snatch more victims.

When the old bird was gone, Monster Slayer asked the young, "When shall your father return? And where will he sit?"

"He will return when a he-rain (thunderstorm) comes and sit on that point."

"When will your mother return, and where will she sit?" Monster Slayer asked.

The young birds said, "She will return when the she-rain (gentle rain) comes and sit on yonder rocks."

Monster Slayer had not long to wait until a thunderstorm approached and Tsenahale returned out of the dark clouds and tempest. Tsenahale flew right toward the Rock with Wings, and Monster Slayer shot it with a lightning arrow. Tsenahale fell to the plain below, dead.

Soon a gentle rain came, and the mother of the young birds returned with a dead Pueblo woman in its claws to feed the young. Monster Slayer pulled another lightning arrow out of his quiver and shot the mother bird dead.

"Oh, will you kill us, too!" cried the young birds.

"Stop your wailing!" Monster Slayer told them. "If I let you stay here, you would become evil things who prey upon my people. I shall now make you things of use for when in the days to come, man increases in the land."

Over the next years, Monster Slayer and his twin brother, Naidikisi (He Who Cuts Around), slew many monsters and helped the Navajo, but they did not kill all the monsters in the area. They left some to be the arbiters of death, lest mankind grow overpopulated and despoil the land.

Matthew Trecker, who would live and die in Farmington, New Mexico, victim of Robert Fry's fury, had his roots in the Southwest, by culture and ethnicity. His forebears could trace their lineage on his mother's side to a long walk out of Mexico, in the footsteps of the original pioneers of 1598 with legendary Juan de Oñate. Their trek was one of heroic proportions. Across the Río Bravo, through the Jornada del Muerto (Journey of the Dead), Juan de Oñate led one hundred thirty men of fighting age and five hundred women, children and servants to found a new empire for Spain. Oñate told the king of Spain, "I shall give Your Majesty a New World." The "New World" became in time, New Mexico.

In a long, thin line of heritage and Catholic religion, Christina Trecker, Matthew Trecker's mother, could trace a connection back to Imperial Spain. The twin lions of Aragon and Castile floated on flags above the world of her ancestors, testaments of explorers and conquistadores.

Christina was raised in the mountain border community of what had once been New Spain— Cuba, New Mexico. It was a region of grasslands for cattle, and forests, the very limit of civilization in the Hispanic world of Nuevo Mexico. To the west lay the Bisti Badlands and eerie ruins of the lost culture of Chaco Canyon. It was dominated to the west by the Peak of Cabezon (the Head, or Big Head), to the Spanish, or Tsenajin, to the Navajos. In the Navajo tradition Tsenajin was the clotted blood of a monster's head. One of the Hero Twins cut off the monster's head and its blood ran along the Puerco River. Matthew Trecker began his life in the shadow of Cabezon, and his fate bore an eerie resemblance to the ancient stories.

Christina and a man with the last name of Frank had a son, Matthew, in 1978. Before long, however, their union dissolved. In the mid-1980s, Christina met Jeff Trecker who had moved to the area from Chicago. Jeff was pleasant, handsome and kind. He not only adored Christina, but her son, Matthew, as well. Before long, Jeff and Matt became great friends.

In 1988, Jeff and Christina were married in Cuba and Matthew served as their ring bearer. It was a happy marriage. Matt loved his new stepfather and Jeff was generous with his time and affection. One of young Matt's favorite activities was their vacations to Chicago, where Jeff grew up. Matt was absolutely crazy about flying and learned everything he could about airplanes and aeronautics. Christina related, "He knew everything about planes from World War One right up to the Gulf War. He could tell you all about how they performed and this and that. He was a whiz on the subject."

When Matt had an opportunity to take a helicopter flight at the Farmington fairgrounds, he jumped at the chance. Jeff recounted later, "He wasn't a bit afraid. It was something he really loved. Flying meant adventure. Flying meant freedom."

Besides airplanes and flying, Matt also loved country-and-western music. By his teenage years he seemingly knew every song by heart. Jeff said that Matt could listen to the first few chords of a song that began to play on the radio and could tell him what the song would be. "He'd stay up into the late-night hours listening to one particular station out of southern California. He really liked the songs they played and the deejays there. He was such a loyal fan that he wrote them letters and phoned in with requests. They eventually sent him an autographed photograph of the whole crew and signed it saying, 'Thanks for staying up.' "

Matt was also an avid reader. He read on all subjects, but especially about science and aeronautics. He surprised his mother at an early age by telling her he had read the Bible from cover to cover.

Matt may have been a voracious reader, but he was not a stay-inside introvert. He was nimble and strong and loved rock climbing and rappelling. Larry Hudson, a friend of Robert Fry's who knew Matt, saw that he was a tough customer. Hudson said, "I saw Matt once out at the fairgrounds at a rodeo. He had just been thrown by a bull coming out of the chutes. He was all banged up and limping. But he walked it off and didn't complain."

Matt was just as kind as he was tough. He often took flowers and blankets to a senior assisted-living home in Farmington. No one told him to do it, he just did it on his own. He eventually wanted to become an emergency medical technician (EMT) and work with the county's search-and-rescue team. He told his mother, "I like helping people."

There was one more attribute to add to tough and kind—Matt was brave as well. One afternoon he and a friend were out at Farmington Lake, a local hangout for teenagers. They spotted a group of Anglo teenagers giving a Navajo boy and girl a rough time. It was obvious that things were about to get out of control.

"Let's get out of here," Matt's friend said.

"No," Matt replied. Instead, Matt walked up where the altercation was about to take place and told the Navajos to get into his car. Then he drove them to safety. Jeff Trecker later said, "He probably saved them from a beating or worse. Most kids would have followed the friend's advice. They'd say, 'It's not my business.' But not Matt. He was a brave kid."

Despite Matt's avid book reading, he had trouble in school. It wasn't that he was not intelligent, it was a matter of not being adept at taking tests or enjoying the dull routine of many classes. He had so much energy, he had a hard time sitting still. His grades suffered accordingly and by high school he was not doing well.

One of the administrators at Farmington High brought Christina Trecker in and told her, "Matt's not going to amount to anything."

This made Christina very angry. She knew just how smart Matt really was. When Matt dropped out of high school and took his GED, she approved. Matt's scores in the GED test proved just how intelligent he was. He scored very high in math and science. So high, in fact, it garnered him a scholarship for the coming year at San Juan Community College.

"That GED test made that person at the high school eat his words," Christina said. "Matt was a smart boy."

He enjoyed playing Dungeons & Dragons, a role-playing game that involved intellect and strategy. This brought him into contact with Joseph Fleming, or "Jovial Joe," as Jeff Trecker called him. "He was a big jolly guy," Jeff said. "Very mellow. I don't think I ever saw him angry. He and Matt were good buddies."

Joseph Fleming's roots ran back through another part of Farmington's history. It led directly to the "oil patch." In the 1920s, large amounts of oil were discovered in the region, followed by discoveries of natural-gas fields. These natural-gas fields would prove to be the largest in the United

States. What had once been a small farming community suddenly turned into the "metropolis" of northern New Mexico.

Things really took off in 1940 when Claude Carroll discovered a huge gusher, followed by huge gas wells in the Ute Pasture and Baker Dome areas. By the 1950s Farmington was known unofficially as "Boomtown USA." Housing was hard to find, and schools had to go to double sessions to accommodate all the children.

This new wave of immigrants came mostly from Oklahoma and Texas, veterans of the oil fields there. They were roughnecks and roustabouts, men familiar with the dangers of drilling and working under harsh conditions.

The oil patch workers brought in their own set of heroes, individuals who had gambled everything on a hunch and struck it rich. These were men who gambled with their fortunes and their lives. It was no wonder they became known as wildcatters. Their ethos ran back to such legendary characters as Pecos Bill, a mythical figure as important in his own way to these men as the Hero Twins were to the Navajo people. Pecos Bill typified rugged individualism and daring.

To accommodate this influx of "oil field boomers," another layer of society was added to a bustling Farmington—city and county workers who serviced the oil patch citizens. Among this group were the Frys. Robert Fry's father, James, moved to the Farmington area in the 1960s and began working for the city on a maintenance crew and later as an animal control officer. Robert's mother, Gloria, became a probation officer for the county, mostly dealing with misdemeanors by adults.

According to *Farmington Daily Times* reporter Debra Mayeux, "Gloria was in the public eye a lot.

She was very outspoken about women's issues and crimes against women and children. She became the director of a family crisis center and safe haven for women escaping a domestic violence situation. She essentially built the center from the ground floor up. She was very involved in this work and the person to go to about domestic violence issues. Everyone in the system around Farmington knew her."

The women's shelter had a family-counseling program, children's programs and something called a Gateway Program. In the Gateway Program a male offender took a twenty-six-week course to try and stem his anger and abuse. It was ironic in the extreme that Gloria Fry's own son would undo everything that Gloria worked for. His treatment of women at times would go from appalling to murderous.

Robert James Fry was born on August 18, 1973, into a blended family. He had an older stepbrother, Jimmie, and an older stepsister, Vickie, who were his father James's children from a previous marriage. Sister Jeanne was born into the family in 1969, and Robert became the last child of Gloria and James Fry.

Gloria said later, "We loved them all. When I found out I was going to have Bob, I called my father and told him I was pregnant. He joked and said, 'Okay, I'll let you have him if he's a boy.' And it was a boy, born on my birthday. I was also born on my dad's birthday. So we had three generations on the same day. It was very special and Bob was very special. I remember an article in the paper when they gauged the odds of that happening was one out of eight million."

Just what Robert Fry's early childhood was like depended on whom you asked. Next-door neighbor Daphne Habaugh said, "He was a very happy little boy. He played in the yard with the other kids. He got along very well."

Gloria Fry remembered later, "Bob was a good baby. He was every woman's thought of how a baby should be. He cried when he was wet or when he was hungry, and that was it.

"Bob played alone a lot outside. He liked his cars. He reminded me of my brother when he was growing up. They'd take sticks and branches and make towns and roads in the dirt and run their cars up and down them. They had an imaginary kind of play environment. Bob was loving. He was only three when my mother died. We had a tennis racket and when he was three he played it for her like it was a guitar. He was singing 'Rhinestone Cowboy.' And my mother thought that was the most wonderful thing she had ever seen.

"Bob got into Scouts and played football. He was on a junior team called the Cowboys. And he was in baseball. He was a normal, active, average child."

Sister Jeanne recalled, "Bobby had an innocence about him. A carefree attitude. He loved animals, especially puppies. He never fought with other kids and he wasn't prejudiced. To him, people were just people. He treated everyone the same."

According to Jeanne, when Bobby learned there was a bit of Mohawk blood in the family tree, he became very interested in that. She said he wanted to write a book about it someday.

Robert Fry could be very entertaining and a bit of a ham at times. He concocted wild stories of adventure and daring. In fact, he created his own fantasy world of heroes and monsters with himself as a hero. He loved television cartoons, especially Scooby-Doo. Scooby-Doo's tales were always filled with ghosts and monsters, who ultimately were vanquished by four teenage heroes and their intrepid sidekick dog, Scooby. Bobby Fry loved dressing up in homemade costumes and emulating his cartoon heroes.

There was a flip side, however, to Bobby as happy-go-lucky kid. He apparently became agitated when stressed, and he took Ritalin for a year with no obvious improvements. According to a psychiatrist who spoke about him later, Fry had low self-esteem and lack of acceptance by his peers.

Dr. Roy Jacob Matthew noted that Robert Fry was a skinny child who was often picked on at school and was beaten up by others. Even Robert's older brother would pick on him, and his school grades suffered. He mostly got C's and D's in school.

In fact, Gloria Fry spoke at length later about Robert's trouble in school and the reason she thought it occurred. Gloria said, "When Bob was in the first grade, he was left-handed. He went through kindergarten okay and got into first grade. I can remember him coming home and saying, 'I was tested today and they said I'm right-handed.' And he was very disappointed.

"Anyway, his teacher had laid a pencil on the desk and whichever hand the child picked the pencil up with, that was her test. But because Bob had something in his left hand at the time, he picked up the pencil with his right hand.

"From then on, Bob had a problem with the written part of academics. Orally he could do anything. He could do his tests, he had absolutely no problems, but he didn't do his homework if it was written. And I can remember going to the principal because the first-grade teacher thought Bob should be held back because he wasn't doing well in school. And the kindergarten teacher and second-grade teacher-to-be said that was not correct. They thought he was academically okay to go on to second grade.

"All of this created a problem. Writing was like a foreign language to him. He'd hear in his own language, have to interpret it and go into the other. He would have to do some kind of procedure in his brain to process the information."

And there was a very dark episode in Robert's youngest years, hidden in the recesses of his mind. Gloria recalled the episode later. She said, "There was an incident when Bob was three years old which didn't come to light until much later. My husband and I had gone out for the evening with some friends, and we had the friend's older daughter watching Jeanne and Bob. We came home and nothing was said except that the next day Bob was very different. Noticeably different.

"Before that day Bob was a very secure child. He would go outside by himself and it wouldn't bother him, even if it was dark. From that point on, he was afraid to go to bed at night by himself. He didn't want the light turned off. He didn't want to be alone. He was very insecure.

"I can remember one time him telling me that he wanted someone with him. I, in my great wisdom, said that you have Jesus with you. He said, 'Yeah, but I would like somebody with skin on.'

"Jeanne told us much later what had happened. She was frightened to say for a long time because she had been told not to tell. The baby-sitter had two younger brothers over that night. They were standing at the end of the hall with the lights turned off. And they poured ketchup over their heads. They said for Bob to go to the bathroom and he went down the hall. It didn't have any lights on. As he got to them, they turned on the light and they were covered in ketchup. It looked like blood. And Jeanne told me later Bob screamed and screamed and screamed until he couldn't scream anymore. From then on, he was frightened to be alone."

Aloneness was a real problem for young Robert Fry. He sought acceptance from the other kids at school, and instead he was made fun of and picked on. As a young teen his weight began to balloon upward, and it didn't make things any better. Now he was picked on for being overweight.

As a safety valve Robert Fry began to invent fantastic stories to tell the other kids. They were so outlandish and detailed that they began to have the desired effect. As Dr. Roy Matthew said later, "They were fantastic stories, so you would admire him or you would feel sorry for him."

Robert Fry finally began to gather a collection of friends around him at school, something he desperately wanted. And at some point he crossed a line and quit being the bullied and started becoming the bully. Perhaps it was revenge for all the years he had been picked on. He could now literally throw his weight around, tormenting those who had at one time been his tormentors.

Gloria Fry did not approve of some of Bob's new friends. She said later, "He picked these friends especially when he got into junior high and high school. They seemed to be the kind that didn't have any drive or ambition. Bob was very giving and he had almost a desperation to belong and be part of a group. He would give up his own wants and needs to just be accepted. That always bothered me because I would tell him how bright he was and he could be anything that he wanted to be. But he seemed to be willing to give up a part of himself to be with this group of people."

There was another strange insight presented by sister Jeanne about Bobby's character. She related that at one point he wanted to become an actor, but then she said he decided too many actors were homosexuals. Just how he came to that conclusion, she didn't say.

Robert Fry did not become an actor, but he did become an accomplished storyteller. In a group of teenage boys who bragged about their exploits, in what they called "bullshitting," he was the best bullshitter of the bunch. His stories took on fantastic details and flamboyant embellishments. They were the stuff of legends, except in this case the legends were about himself.

One friend, Jae Williams, recalled, "He was creative with his stories. But most of them were so unbelievable and there was nothing to back them up. Fry would try to make you believe he could jump from a building to another one across the street."

Larry Hudson was another friend of Bobby Fry's and he also knew Matthew Trecker. Hudson and Fry met in the fourth grade. Hudson later became such a good friend of Fry's that he considered Bobby to be his brother. He even called him that, and called Fry's parents "Mom" and "Dad." Hudson recalled, "I spent a lot of time at his house. We hung together all throughout junior high and high school. Played a lot of video games and that kind of thing. Driving all over the place. Went out hunting and fishing."

Robert Fry enjoyed the outdoors and went camping and fishing with his dad. For one who hadn't had many friends in his early years, Robert had quite a few now. At this point in his life, Robert Fry was at the juncture of who he would become—the bright, loving boy that his mother spoke about, or the big bully that many kids at school knew him to be. For a while, his better nature tried to assert itself. According to Gloria, "At eighteen, Bob became a volunteer firefighter and he loved it. He went out on some very serious incidents. Within a period of a few months, he traveled out to four fatalities.

"I remember Bob riding with a young man who was in a very serious accident and Bob had ahold of his hand and kept telling him he'd be all right.

"So, when he was doing that, it really impacted him, because there was a lot of blood at the scene. And the boy kept saying, 'Am I going to be okay?' Bob had a real hard time with that. And I think it made Bob think about the time when he was three years old and the boys had put ketchup on themselves and it scared him."

Despite Robert Fry's term as a volunteer fireman, the rowdy side of his nature started becoming more and more prevalent in his high-school years. He was part of a loose-knit group of teenagers who eventually coalesced into a band that called themselves "The Wild Bunch." They drove around Farmington in the late-night hours, playing the game CB tag. CB tag was a version of tag using citizens band radios in vehicles. The point was to drive all over the area and try to figure where the others were by use of the CB radios.

Eventually Bobby Fry and the others grew tired of CB tag and started playing Dungeons & Dragons. Despite his being one who didn't do well in school, Fry became adept with the arcane rules of Dungeons & Dragons. He took the game very seriously and played it to extremes. It held a fascination for someone who already lived in a fantasy world half the time.

It was around this time that Matthew Trecker and Joseph Fleming bumped into Fry. They, too, were Dungeons & Dragons aficionados who took the games seriously. The fantasy aspects of it were stimulating. It could take them thousands of miles and hundreds of years into the past, away from the Dairy Queens and Burger Kings of Farmington. They could inhabit a domain of witches and wizards, instead of gas stations and strip malls.

One thing became apparent as the group coalesced around Bobby Fry; many of those he hung out with were either a lot younger or a lot skinnier than he was. Except for Joseph Fleming, Fry weighed almost a hundred pounds more than all his buddies. And Matthew Trecker was five years his junior. As time went on, Bobby Fry dominated the others by his sheer weight and age. He also began to dominate them with his sudden outbursts of anger.

Even the teenage girls who hung out with them were, by and large, much younger than Fry. In the parlance of the region, some of them were "jailbait." Michelle Hearn knew Robert Fry from the time she was sixteen years old. At various times she and Bobby were girlfriend and boyfriend. Unlike some others, she said that he was always good to her.

"Bob was my best friend," she recalled later. "We would talk about our hopes and dreams. He was always there for me, unconditionally."

Yet during this same period, Fry once again showed his Jekyll and Hyde nature. He was also friends with Alexis Diego. Even though Fry was much older, she liked hanging out with him and his crowd. He bought her alcohol and she hung out at their parties. One night things went too far. According to Diego, "I was pretty drunk and must have passed out. When I woke up, I knew that

Robert had raped me. I couldn't believe it. He was supposed to have been my friend."

Christina Trecker also remembered Bobby Fry very well from this period and she recalled the games they were getting into. She said, "At first it was just fantasy role-playing games, like Dungeons and Dragons. Pretty harmless stuff. They would fight with make-believe swords and cast make-believe spells. But then it began to get more real. More violent. I think a lot of that had to do with Bobby Fry. He seemed like an angry young man."

According to Christina Trecker, "The games began to go way beyond their original intent. It started to scare Matt, especially the way Bobby Fry was acting. He said that Bobby wanted to fight with real knives and swords. He wanted people to cut themselves and drink blood. It got way out of hand. And there were all those young teenage girls, too. Fry was too old for them. I wondered what was going on. He was drinking beer and I'm sure sharing it with them, even though they were underage."

In fact, Fry was starting to have a real problem with alcohol. He would drink to excess and become agitated and belligerent. His stories to the others in his circle of friends became more graphically violent. He talked more and more about beating people up. He even said he had murdered someone. No one believed him at the time.

Darrell Hare recalled, "Bobby was a real heavy drinker. He would become more hyper. More aggressive."

And Jae Williams recalled, "Most of his stories were about him fighting. Sometimes it was about killing this guy or that guy. He would say something like he shot a guy and dumped the gun in the river. I'd check the newspaper and there'd be nothing there. So we wouldn't believe most of his stories. It was all bullshit."

Topping it all off, Robert Fry started using drugs as well. He tried marijuana, cocaine, methamphetamine, LSD and mushrooms, but his drug of choice remained alcohol. Perhaps even he knew how out of control he was becoming. In an attempt to change his life, Robert Fry enlisted in the U.S. Navy right after high school, in 1992.

After boot camp, Fry was assigned to the submarine tender USS *Holland*. Built in Pascagoula, Mississippi, in 1963, the ship was 599 feet in length and carried a complement of 1,346 personnel. In 1992, it sailed from Charleston, South Carolina, to its new homeport of Apra Harbor, Guam. It was here that Robert Fry joined its crew. The *Holland*'s motto was "Fixer, feeder—WESTPAC (western Pacific) leader."

Guam was not a bad place to be stationed. Palm trees lined its beautiful harbor and green hills surrounded the island with tropical flowers and trees. For recreation in off-hours, Fry could have chosen from swimming at the local beaches, an Olympic-size swimming pool, large gym or tennis courts. But as always, Robert Fry's recreation of choice was drinking at the bars in the nearby city of Agana. Interestingly enough, Agana in the Chommoro language meant "blood."

Once again, drinking to excess got Fry into trouble. He often overslept and was late for assignments. He was surly and too often hungover to perform his tasks well, even when he did show up on time. And when Fry got into a fight with a man on the island and broke his nose, that was the last straw as far as the navy was concerned. They booted him out of the service with a dishonorable discharge.

Back on the streets of Farmington in late 1994,

washed out of the navy and with even fewer prospects for good work in the area than when he enlisted, Fry began a series of low-paying jobs. He worked for a while as a bouncer at a downtown bar. At least his height, weight and tough appearance gave him an edge in this. So did his proclivity for fighting.

He even worked for a while out in the oil patch with Larry Hudson at various menial jobs. Then Fry drove a van for a halfway-house program that dealt with juvenile offenders. It seemed that his mother had helped in getting him this job.

Eventually Fry got a job as a security guard alongside Joseph Fleming. It was around this time that he bought a blue Ford Aspire and moved into an apartment with Larry Hudson. Hudson had been in the U.S. Navy, like Fry, and had been married. But the marriage ended in divorce with good reason. Hudson discovered that his wife had been cheating on him with quite a few men, including his own brother. When Hudson shared an apartment with Fry, he brought the divorce papers home one day and announced to Fry, "I'm finally rid of her!"

Little did Hudson know at the time, Robert Fry was one of the men who'd had an affair with his ex-wife. Hudson always considered Fry a good and loyal friend, but there were obviously some things he didn't know about him.

After the navy Fry changed residences almost as often as he changed jobs. He lived off and on at home with his parents, and for a while in different apartments with different friends. One thing he did maintain was a routine of sitting in late-night coffee shops with friends, telling outrageous, loud stories of mayhem and murder.

Jae Williams recalled, "The conversations at the coffee shops were always loud. They were about anything and everything, from cars to stupid things we had done. As time went on, the stories got more and more outlandish. Bobby Fry was one of the biggest bullshitters of them all."

Larry Hudson agreed, saying, "The Top Deck was one of our favorite places. We'd drink beer and shoot pool. Bob would become louder as he drank. The stories would become more outrageous. Especially if he was telling them to the ladies. He told them he had been a Navy SEAL. I had been in the navy and didn't believe his stories. I told him, 'Don't insult my intelligence.' But he would just go on and on. He would drink as much as people would buy for him."

On top of all these stories of mayhem, Fry and some of his other friends began playing a game called Vampire: The Masquerade. Vampire: The Masquerade was a role-playing game of intricate rules. Each player took the role of a vampire character and had to stay within the bounds of that character. A "storyteller" was in charge, making sure that rules were followed and the game moved along. In many senses it was improvisational theater, with each person taking on a role as an actor.

Each vampire had different strengths and weaknesses, depending on what type of vampire clan they were in. For instance, a Gangrel was nomadic, feral and wild, while Toreadors were lovers of art and aesthetics. Ravnos were deceivers and masters of illusion, while Ventrues were fallen aristocrats.

Perhaps the most appealing to Robert Fry were vampires who belong to the Sabbat. They included such subgroupings as Lasombras (shadowy and wicked) and Tzimisce (fearsome fleshcrafters). The one thing they had in common was that they were vilified by other vampire clans as brutish, monstrous and addicted to blood.

There was little loyalty among the Sabbat, who would often turn on each other in frenzied blood lust. When they did work together, they formed packs that roamed through the desolate parts of cities, sating their blood thirst on humans. According to the rule book of Vampire: The Masquerade, they were strongest in Mexico City, Detroit, New York, Montreal and Miami. Interestingly enough, they were also strong in United States border lands, such as New Mexico.

To be initiated into the Sabbat was bloody and gruesome. Supposedly, they had their heads bashed in with a shovel and were then buried, only to crawl out through the cold earth to the world above. One of the rituals of the Sabbat was a mockery of the Catholic Eucharist. Instead of drinking the blood of Christ from a chalice, they opened up each other's veins into the cup—then they drank the blood, which was supposed to make them stronger. Unlike other vampire clans, the Sabbat often practiced Devil worship and paganism. They were noted for brutality, blood rituals, torture and ceremonial killing.

Of course, all of this was supposed to be only a game, and the book had a disclaimer right up front: "Part of maturity is realizing that Vampire is only a game and that the situations depicted in these pages are strictly imaginary. In other words, you are not a vampire. For the 99.9999 + % of you who are sufficiently well-adjusted, there is no need for such a ridiculous disclaimer."

Unfortunately, by 1996, Robert Fry was slipping into that .0001 percent who could not discern reality from fantasy.

Matthew Trecker, in particular, was becoming concerned about Fry's erratic and violent behavior. He wanted nothing to do with Fry's penchant and desire to draw blood. Trecker also disapproved of the underage teenage girls hanging around The Eclectic. They were often taken advantage of by older boys with lures of alcohol and drugs. Apparently, manager Alex Seifert didn't take drugs. According to Harold Pollock, Seifert didn't like the stuff around and was even allergic to marijuana smoke. But it didn't mean the others weren't using illegal drugs.

Don Ogle, a man who lived in the neighborhood of The Eclectic, didn't like what he was seeing around there. He noted the group of teens who hung out in the area and knew what kind of items the store sold. He also guessed that there was drug use and underage drinking going on near the establishment. Ogle began a crusade to get the city of Farmington to have The Eclectic shut down.

Ogle also knew Robert Fry. Ogle told a reporter later, "Fry would brag about who he had beaten up and tell about incidents until you saw people moving from their seats (at restaurants) in order to get away from him."

Matthew Trecker also began telling these stories about an out-of-control Robert Fry to his mother. Christina warned him to stay away from Bobby Fry and The Eclectic. Matt was only too happy to break away from Fry, but he would not give up his friendship with Joseph Fleming or quit going to The Eclectic. He liked the games there and Fleming's company as well. This may have led to part of the argument he had with his mother just before Thanksgiving, 1996. Christina gave Matt one more lecture about staying away from The Eclectic, but he told her he was now eighteen years old and would go wherever he wanted. "Not if you're living under my roof," she said. In response, Matt moved out and went to stay at The Eclectic.

A short while later, Christina said to her husband, Jeff, "I don't like it. Something bad is going to happen there."

Chapter 2

Bloodbath at The Eclectic

Some of Robert Fry's friends had a checkered past when it came to the law, and one of these friends was Harold Pollock. Twenty-four years old in 1996, he and Fry had worked for a while for a company called Drake Drilling. Pollock was a roustabout out in the oil and gas fields. Pollock's trouble with the law began back on January 8, 1991, when he broke into a house owned by Bill Pace and stole some guns and video equipment. Pollock didn't have long to enjoy the items. Nine days later, San Juan County detectives Jim Cherie and Gary Mulligan detained him at Aztec High School, in Aztec, New Mexico. The detectives already had a probable-cause order written out and Mirandized Pollock on the spot before arresting him.

With search warrant in hand, the detectives recovered all of the stolen items at Pollock's residence. He was charged with one count of aggravated burglary and four counts of larceny of stolen firearms and was booked into the San Juan County Detention Center.

The judicial and law enforcement complex at Aztec was not far from the original pueblo, which dated back to the 1100s. Even more impressive than the Salmon Pueblo, Aztec Pueblo once had a great kiva that supported a roof that weighed ninety tons. Called Wide House by the Navajo, the name "Aztec" is really a misnomer, used by the early Anglos who thought the inhabitants must have had ties to the Aztecs of Mexico because of the immensity and sophistication of the structures. In fact, the inhabitants had been tied to the great commercial center of Chaco. There was even a mysterious road that led from Aztec to Chaco, more than seventy miles away. Without wheeled vehicles, it has never been determined what purpose the road served. It may have been ceremonial in design, somehow aligned with the planets and solstice. The more imaginative speculated that it was a landing strip for extraterrestrials—and the city of Aztec holds an annual UFO event.

Harold Pollock's own road led straight through the judicial system at the city of Aztec. Assistant District Attorney (ADA) Nicholas Cullander presented the charges against Pollock in the spring of 1991. By this time, Pollock saw how things were stacked up against him and agreed to a plea bargain. In the agreement, Pollock said he understood that he had a right to a jury trial and a chance to confront witnesses. He waived those rights and pleaded guilty instead. Judge Paul Onuska took everything into account on the charges and wrote, "On the basis of these findings, I conclude that the defendant knowingly, voluntarily and intelligently pleads guilty to the above charges and accepts his plea."

Harold Pollock caught a break from the judge. Onuska stated, "It is hereby ordered that imposition of sentence is deferred for a period of eighteen months and the defendant is ordered to be placed on probation. He shall obey all rules, regulations and orders of the Probation Authorities. The defendant is further ordered as a condition of probation to pay restitution in the amount of $887.68 to Bill Pace. It is further ordered that the defendant complete 200 hours of community service, fifty hours of which shall be with the Environmental Recycling Center."

Apparently, Harold Pollock did not like sorting aluminum cans, plastic bottles and cardboard. Nor was he a person who "willingly obeyed all rules, regulations and orders of the Probation Authorities." Pollock was advised by his probation officer on July 15, 1992, and August 4, 1992, not to contact a woman named Rona Metcalf. Defying the admonition not to cross state lines, Pollock went with Rona Metcalf to Durango, Colorado, on July 28, 1992, and called her at her brother's residence on August 10, 1992. The trip out of state was a particularly bad move. Pollock was supposed to tell his probation officer about any planned trips out of state. He did not comply with this order.

For disobeying a direct order, Pollock was shipped off to the Western New Mexico Correctional Facility for sixty days. After serving this time, without incident, Judge Onuska ordered him released on December 18, 1992, and further ordered that Pollock's probationary period be extended to July 30, 1993.

Harold Pollock seemed to have a hard time staying out of trouble. In July 1994, he had several warrants out on him, the details of those not readily available now. On July 24, 1994, at 11:38 A.M., Officer R. Anderson spotted Pollock's VW bug and recognized the license plate of someone with an outstanding warrant. Officer Anderson pulled the

VW over at a trailer park on Gila Road and asked Pollock to step out of the car. Pollock complied without raising a fuss.

Officer D. Bair arrived to assist as Anderson handcuffed Pollock and began to search his pockets for weapons. While Anderson was doing this, Bair discovered what appeared to be marijuana seeds on the floorboards of Pollock's car.

"Have you or anybody you know been smoking marijuana?" Bair asked Pollock.

Pollock answered, "No."

It was not good timing, however. Just as he said no, Officer Anderson discovered a substance that looked like marijuana in Pollock's front right pocket. He asked Pollock, "If you don't use marijuana, why is there some in your pocket?"

Pollock's answer did nothing to help his cause. He said, "I have to make extra money somehow."

This remark made him look like a dealer, which was even worse.

Officer Anderson further searched Pollock's clothing and found a small container that looked like it could store aspirin. Once Anderson opened the container, he discovered substances that appeared to be like methamphetamine and cocaine.

The officers called for a tow truck, and Officer Bair stayed with Pollock's vehicle as Anderson transported Pollock to the Farmington Police Department (FPD) holding cell. Anderson called in on the way and had the Farmington Police Department send a narcotics officer to meet them. Officer Jerry Cottrell of the New Mexico State Police came to the station and did a field test of the substances. He found positive results for cocaine, marijuana and amphetamine.

Charged with the possession of illegal drugs, Harold Pollock soon found himself working his way through the court system of San Juan County once again. This time he was represented by attorney Scott Curtis, and Pollock opted for a jury trial. At the end of his trial, he was found guilty for the possession of cocaine. The judge decided that even though Pollock could be incarcerated by the state corrections department for eighteen months, he would allow Pollock to serve only six months at the San Juan County Detention Center. Once Pollock was through, he was to be on probation for six months.

Pollock was never really a nuisance, nor was he a troublemaker behind bars. Released in December 1995, he walked out of the detention center with all his worldly possessions: a bandanna, a lighter, three T-shirts, three pairs of socks, three shorts, five games, three books and $12.75 in his wallet.

If Harold Pollock wanted to keep "a clean nose" after getting out of jail, the last person he needed to be hanging around with was Robert Fry, but that is exactly what he did. By 1996, Fry was drinking more than ever and hitting the local bar scene as often as he could. He had been a bouncer at The Top Deck Lounge, and he enjoyed its honky-tonk atmosphere. He also liked Gators Bar and Chelseas in Farmington. More than ever, his stories at the bars were loud and outrageous, filled with tales of beating up people and causing mayhem. Michelle Hearn, his ex-girlfriend, remembered him saying that whoever hit first and hardest with a sucker punch was sure to win the fight. And Robert Fry had no intention of losing any fights.

In many ways the party at the apartment near the Animas Valley Mall on Thanksgiving night, 1996, was nothing out of the ordinary for Robert

Fry. There was plenty of beer, booze and bullshitting, as usual. The music of choice was loud, raucous and raunchy. A group called the Misfits were one of Fry's favorites, singing songs of monsters, blood and death. Their lyrics only intensified his already insatiable lust for bloodletting in such games as Vampire: The Masquerade. The Misfits were a band out of New Jersey whose heyday was from 1977 to 1983. Dressing in ghoulish costumes and elaborate face paint, they had a driving, frenzied, almost hypnotic, sound. In the song "All Hell Breaks Loose," they sang of evil twins, broken bodies in a death rock dance hall and sending out a murdergram. The murdergram in the song was signed by the blood of parents.

In the song "Bloodfeast," they sang of pulling out someone's tongue and severing heads. In one particularly graphic line, from "Skulls," they sang of headless corpses with blood draining down like devil's rain. Fry enjoyed the imagery of bloodletting and death. He tried to convince his friends that he was just as "bad" as anyone sung about in the Misfits songs.

At some point during the party, Fry got it into his mind that a prostitute would liven things up. Pollock was not enthused about driving Bobby Fry around town on his quest, but he went along. Pollock knew how irritated Fry could get when he didn't get his way.

In the long run it was unfortunate they didn't find a hooker on the cold streets of Farmington that night. Once Bobby Fry chose The Eclectic as his pit stop, it began a lethal series of events that would destroy all of them.

The knife display case was like a magnet for Bobby Fry. He had absolutely obsessed about knives over the years. In his stories to his friends at the coffee shops and bars, he told of getting into knife fights and slaughtering his opponents. He had supposedly learned to fight well in the navy and even claimed to have taken Navy SEAL training. Once again, these were taken as flights of fantasy on Fry's part, as far as his friends were concerned. But good friend Larry Hudson also knew that Fry had a collection of at least a dozen exotic knives, everything from jackknives with inlaid turquoise to huge bowie-type knives. Hudson said Fry had even named some of them. "One of them he called Baby Bubba.'"

Once Joseph Fleming had returned to his computer game at The Eclectic, the allure of the unlocked knives was just too much for Fry. According to Pollock, Fry stole a handful of them. Pollock also mentioned later that Fry stole a sword as well, but Pollock's stories of the theft varied in their details. The rest was almost a blur to Pollock; the trip to Chokecherry Canyon to bury the stolen loot, waves of nausea and fear, and Fry's insistence on returning to The Eclectic after burying the knives. Fry never did explain to Pollock his reason for going back there, other than to say that he had to go to the bathroom again, but Pollock did not wholly believe this. If Fry had pulled over and used a gas station rest room or even the side of a building, it wouldn't have been the first time. Perhaps Bobby Fry had already decided what had to be done at The Eclectic.

Whatever the circumstances, the second version of Pollock's account at The Eclectic delved into more details than the first. He said that when he stumbled out of the bathroom at The Eclectic, things were already out of control. Pollock later said in one police report, "I saw Bobby on top of Joe wrestling with him. Bobby had his hands around Joe's throat. Then he stood up and stepped on Joe's throat. He was wearing work boots. He was acting scared. Joe had a lot of blood around him and wasn't moving. I saw Bobby wiping blood from his hands and arms."

In this report Pollock did not implicate himself. He said, "I don't think I had anything to do with the murders, but I don't remember. When we were leaving, I noticed that Matt had his throat cut. There was a lot of blood around him."

It would be years later when Pollock finally would admit to what really happened after Joe Fleming already was dead.

He said that Matthew Trecker came into the showroom from where he had been sleeping in the back of the store. He was startled by seeing Joseph on the floor, after Robert Fry had sucker punched him. According to Pollock, Trecker was knocked out. Then, according to this second version of the story, Fry moved back to Fleming and slit his throat. Pollock said that he was afraid of Fry and wanted to run away. But he thought if he did, Fry would kill him. At this point, Pollock said, Fry pulled Trecker's shirt up and stabbed him in the chest. Then Fry handed his knife to him and implored him to do the same. "We can do this!" Fry was supposed to have said. "We can be each other's alibi."

According to Pollock, he didn't want to stab Matt, but he was so afraid of Fry that he did. He plunged Fry's knife into Matt three or four times.

Robert Fry was only getting started with the bloodletting at The Eclectic. According to Pollock, Fry lurched over to a display case and grabbed two swords. One had a long, wavy blade and the other one was a samurai sword. Fry handed the samurai sword to him and said, "Let's cut his head off."

Then Fry started chopping on Trecker's neck

with his sword. Browbeaten by Fry to do the same, Pollock began hacking at Trecker's neck with his samurai sword. He would later recall, "It was like chopping wood."

But for some reason, the swords would not chop through Matt's neck. Pollock later surmised the swords were just too dull for such work. He was freaking out by now. If Bobby Fry looked energized by the murders, Pollock was aghast. He was no stone-cold killer. He could barely believe he had been involved in the bloodbath. He said, "We decided to cover up our being there. Bobby went back to the showroom, but I'm not sure what he did there." Pollock later was under the impression that Fry stole some more knives and possibly swords from the showroom. The plan was scatterbrained at best. In their rush to leave the store, Fry broke the key off in the door lock. Both he and Pollock knew that the other door to the store was electronically set to an alarm, and they didn't know the code. They were now locked inside.

Fry and Pollock discussed what to do, and Pollock was nearly paralyzed from fear. Fry finally decided to throw a computer monitor through one of the windows. It would allow them an avenue of escape and he hoped that it would make the authorities believe that a burglary had taken place by unknown assailants, who had no access to the store by other means.

Fry threw the monitor through the window and the glass shattered outward onto the sidewalk. He and Pollock were extremely lucky. No one had heard the shattering glass sometime between 3:00 A.M. and 4:00 A.M., November 29, on the deserted city streets. Fry and Pollock managed to crawl out through the window and make their escape, but their hellish night was far from over. By this time Bobby Fry had cold feet about the new batch of items he had stolen. According to Pollock, they then went out to Farmington Lake to throw the stolen items into the lake. The same lake where Matt Trecker had rescued the Indian boy and girl from a beating. Pollock said they threw six weapons into the lake and then Bobby Fry threw his bloody boots into the lake as well. Fry had another pair of boots in his car. The exact amount of the stolen loot was never fully tabulated, but manager Alex Seifert later estimated the value to be around $3,000.

After leaving Farmington Lake, Fry and Pollock drove to a convenience store and Fry went inside to buy something. As he stood in the lights of the store, he apparently saw the blood of Fleming and Trecker on his face. He laughed and told Pollock, "Look, I'm wearing war paint."

Fry soon came back out to the vehicle, however, panic-stricken. He didn't have his wallet and was sure he'd lost it during the scuffle in The Eclectic. They drove back to The Eclectic and once more both of them climbed through the broken window to try and retrieve Fry's missing wallet. Incredibly, no one as yet had discovered the broken glass or computer monitor on the sidewalk and called police.

While Pollock was a lookout, Fry searched through the bloody store, to no avail. Fry's wallet couldn't be found anywhere. Fry came outside and stood guard while Pollock went inside and looked for the wallet. Realizing that it would be light soon, and that their chances of getting caught were growing every moment, Pollock finally exited the store the way he had come in and convinced Fry they needed to leave the area.

After a harrowing and bloody night, Fry and Pollock returned to the apartment where their journey had begun the night before. The sun was just coming up from the direction of Gobernador Canyon to the east.

According to Pollock, Robert Fry told him that if he ever spoke to anyone about the incident, he would kill him. After seeing the butchery Fry had performed on Joseph Fleming, Pollock didn't have any doubts that Fry would back up his threat.

Chapter 3

The Bitter Wind

A Farmington police officer drove by The Eclectic around 5:00 A.M. on Friday, November 29, but incredibly, he saw nothing amiss, even though there was a computer monitor lying on the sidewalk amidst broken glass. Fry and Pollock had made their escape only a short time before. It was cold that morning, about 20 degrees, with snow showers predicted for later in the day. Finally, at 7:58 A.M., a business owner going to his store in the downtown area noticed the front window of The Eclectic was broken and what he thought was a televison set lying on the sidewalk. He phoned the Farmington Police Department and a squad car was dispatched to the location on a routine burglary call.

FPD officer Ed Aber drove up to the scene a little after 8:00 A.M. and found the shattered glass on the sidewalk. Aber, too, mistook the computer monitor for a television set. He entered the store through the broken window and discovered an incredibly bloody crime scene inside. There were two white male bodies lying in pools of blood, about twelve feet apart.

Officer Aber bent down to see if either man was still alive. He felt for a pulse and looked to see if they were breathing. Neither one had a pulse nor did they exhale. To Aber's eyes, both men appeared to have suffered severe lacerations to their necks and throats. He called in a double homicide, and soon The Eclectic became a beehive of police activity. This was the first Farmington double homicide in eight years. In 1988, Robert Martinez and Patrick Garcia had slain Sherwin Martinez and Edison Morgan.

Among the officers who arrived was Farmington police detective Pat Cordell. Cordell was a seasoned detective who had seen his share of homicides in the city, but nothing quite matched the heinous brutality he witnessed at The Eclectic. It appeared that the victims hadn't just been murdered, they'd been butchered.

It was still too early to tell exactly what had happened in The Eclectic or when it had occurred, though the indications were that it had happened in the not-too-distant past. Lieutenant David Gardner told reporters later that day that Joseph Fleming and Matthew Trecker had been slashed to death by a sharp object. Gardner added, "It's not known if a knife was involved, or if a weapon from the store was used. The store was in a certain disarray because of the struggle. It didn't look like it was organized in the first place."

Friends of the victims, as well as the merely curious, began to gather at The Eclectic as the news spread around town. When word reached the coffee shops where Trecker's and Fleming's friends hung out, they were stunned. One by one, and in groups, they made their way downtown and gazed upon all the police activity and the cordon of yellow police-tape around the building. One of those who showed up was co-owner of the store, Debbie Seifert, wife of Alex Seifert. She was soon questioned by Detective Leroy Miller.

Another person in the crowd that day was Les Ligon, a friend of a store owner. Ligon talked to a reporter and said that some threats had recently been made against one of the store owners by gang members. Since Ligon used the word "she" in his comments, the use of the feminine term indicated that it had to be Debbie Seifert who, he believed, was the target of the threat. Ligon said he was worried that the killings might have been in connection with a gang contract. Just what the gang contract was about, he did not elaborate on the nature of his allegations.

Asked about this by the reporter, Lieutenant David Gardner downplayed this aspect of the crime. He said, "The indications are it was something other than gang related."

Despite Gardner's statement, fears of gang activity persisted. It was already known that there were at least thirty street gangs operating in San Juan County. And Farmington police sergeant Dan Darnell would later admit, "Gangs used to be an inner-city issue, but not anymore. There is no community free of gangs." Even such tiny nearby towns as Blanco with a population of a few hundred was said to have two active gangs present.

It was estimated that there were over four hundred members of gangs in Farmington alone. Some of the gangs were third and fourth generations. Darnell told a *Farmington Daily Times* reporter, "These kids are missing something in life. Left untouched, this thing can grow rampant."

Among the crowd on the outside of the police

tape at The Eclectic on November 29 was Renota Mikel, who had been dating Joe Fleming. She was especially distraught. As she was standing outside the store, a man walked up to give her comfort. The man was none other than Bobby Fry. He put his arms around her and said, "Come here, baby girl," and gave her a hug. According to some reports, Fry would later date Mikel. She wouldn't learn for a very long time what Bobby Fry had done to her old boyfriend, Joseph Fleming.

Robert Fry looked upon the scene of police activity with rapt attention. As time wore on, he exhaled with growing relief. It was apparent that his missing wallet had not been discovered by the police, nor any other items leading directly to him. In fact, the wallet may not have fallen there at all. Fry was joined later in the day by Harold Pollock and another friend, Les Engh.

Perhaps the most distraught person that day was Christina Trecker, Matt's mom. When she got the news of her son's death, she wandered around in a daze for the rest of the day. None of it seemed real. She wanted to believe it was all a horrible joke, perpetrated by some prankster teenagers, and that Matt would come walking out of the store with a sheepish grin on his face.

Reality finally struck home when Christina went to look at crime scene photographs. She was thumbing through the photos when she nearly collapsed. She flipped over a photograph set amongst all the others, and it depicted in vivid colors Matt with his throat slashed and his head nearly decapitated.

"I wasn't ready for that," she said later. "I'm not sure what I expected, but not that. It was the most horrible thing I've seen in my life! I discovered that he had a busted nose, temple wound, was stabbed in the chest, a lung was punctured, and, of course, the gaping wound in his neck. He was butchered!"

One thing Christina did recall later in a day of horrors was that she clearly remembered seeing both Bobby Fry and Harold Pollock standing in the crowd of onlookers. She said later, "They were there with all the rest. Very intent on what was going on. He (Fry) was watching the police very carefully. He seemed to be studying them."

Lieutenant Gardner may have thought the murders were not gang related, but others in the community were less sure. Joseph Fleming had been a security guard at the Animas Mall, and Debbie Seifert was a part-time security guard herself. There were persistent rumors about Debbie Seifert and gangs. In fact, even the local newspaper reported about these rumors. Whether they had any basis in fact was immaterial, damage was being done and various security guards were afraid. The Animas Mall sent a press release out that touched on the murders of Fleming and Trecker. It read in part, "Fleming had a good record of service and he will be missed." Even then, the press release did nothing to allay the anxiety among other security guards who worked there about possible gang ties to not only the murder, but Debbie Seifert as well. Within days, three of the Animas Mall security guards resigned. This was a bad time of year for this to be happening, since the Christmas shopping season was coming up. In response, off-duty Farmington police officers were assigned to do security work at the mall.

Joseph Fleming and Matt Trecker's bodies were sent to Albuquerque, nearly two hundred miles away, for autopsies at the office of the medical investigator. It was deemed that the office there could do a much more thorough autopsy on the two victims than any facility in Farmington.

In the days after the murders, the Farmington Police Department kept tabs on The Eclectic, watching for suspicious activity. A rotating set of police officers were stationed across the street to keep an eye on the place, as well as a sensor light that would go on whenever any vehicle drove past the store.

Daily Times reporter Jennifer Duke wrote, "Up until Friday the store that sold crystals and various other items was a bustling area. There would be activity in the store even in the later hours of the night. There were many nights when *Daily Times* employees (the building being only a half block away), leaving work at 2 or 3 AM, would see numerous cars around the building."

This was not the case after November 30. The area on Allen Street remained deserted except for the lone police officer and the sensor light. A compact automobile that had been parked in front of The Eclectic all day long on November 30 was towed away and examined by police. It was later determined that the vehicle had nothing to do with the crime.

The police tape was eventually removed from outside The Eclectic, replaced by teddy bears and flowers. One white teddy bear held a card that read, "We miss you."

Jennifer Duke wrote in the *Daily Times,* "A candle with the image of the Virgin Mary tries to stay glowing in the bitter wind. It's surrounded by flowers and tiny white roses."

Duke talked to policemen and they said the investigation was still ongoing. Lieutenant Gardner told her that Detective Miller had several people to interview and some leads to follow.

The office of the medical investigator in Albuquerque told her that the cause of deaths was still unknown, but the investigation was continuing. As a sort of postscript, Duke added, "[Fleming] died on a street that bore his mother's maiden name."

It was obvious that Matt Trecker was not going to be a pretty sight at the funeral home once his body was returned. Nonetheless, Christina Trecker was determined to go there and dress her own boy for the funeral. She said later, "This was my last chance to say good-bye. I didn't care how tough it was, I insisted on dressing him nicely. I'd already seen the police photos of him at The Eclectic. Nothing was going to be worse than that."

The burial of Matt Trecker took place at Greenlaw Cemetery in Farmington on a cool and windy day. His family was there, along with many friends and even a few police officers. The officers were not only there out of respect, they were there to look for any suspicious characters in the crowd—someone who might reveal himself as the killer. Robert Fry did attend the funeral, but he did not give himself away. He hugged others and looked to be genuinely moved by the proceedings. After all, Joseph Fleming, in particular, had been his friend. He did not look out of place at all.

Autopsy reports were finally released to the press, and it was noted by one doctor that in the case of Matthew Trecker, he had two stab wounds that could have been fatal. One had punctured the heart, and there were severe lacerations to his throat. The cause of death for Joseph Fleming was deemed to be from multiple stab wounds. Both men had numerous other stab wounds and abrasions, in addition to the fatal wounds.

Even by mid-December, the rumors of gang murder would not go away, and now a new set of rumors started making the rounds as well. These rumors blamed the murders on adherents to the occult. The Eclectic had always been known for such activities and now the rumors evolved to include a coven of blood-crazed killers on the loose in the Farmington area. Stories began to circulate about what had occurred at Vampire: The Masquerade games that Trecker and Fleming had attended. These tales became more gruesome and outlandish with each retelling.

To stem the tide of stories, Lieutenant Gardner told the *Daily Times,* "We've been hearing for years of occult activities, and it's all unsubstantiated. I think it's more people blowing things out of proportion." He did admit that The Eclectic sold occult-related objects. Then he added, "We've got no indication that the killings are related to any occult activity, and no indication the killings are related to any gang activity."

Among the numerous people brought in for questioning about The Eclectic were Robert Fry and Harold Pollock. They were "persons of interest" to the police, because they were supposedly the last ones to see Fleming and Trecker alive. Fry was already known by the police to be a trouble-maker. They even described him that way in one report. Fry had several minor scrapes with them, mostly alcohol related.

Robert Fry was asked to take a polygraph test about the murder. Even though the tests have a fair degree of accuracy, they are not foolproof, especially with people who have little concept of what the truth really is. Fry passed the polygraph test, but still remained under suspicion. However, the fact of the matter remained, he was not the only one under suspicion. There were several other candidates who were even more suspicious to the Farmington Police Department at the time. They seemed to have had a stronger motive and were antagonistic either to Joseph Fleming or Matthew Trecker. And it was known that Fry had been friends with Fleming and Trecker. What motive he might have had for killing them was not readily apparent.

In time, the police began looking into the angle that someone had really been out to get either one of the Seiferts. It was posited that a killer or killers had gone to The Eclectic with the intention of harming the Seiferts and had found Joseph Fleming and Matt Trecker there instead. For some reason, things had gotten out of control and Fleming and Trecker had ended up dead. It might have come down to the matter of being in the wrong place at the wrong time.

In time, the unsolved murders became known in Farmington as "The Eclectic Murders." The fates of Joseph Fleming and Matthew Trecker became forever intertwined with that store. The New Mexico Survivors of Homicide Inc. had an interesting thing to say about the murder scene: "The Eclectic enjoyed a unique place in the Farmington business scene. The store was not considered successful as a business venture, and its real purpose seemed to be a place where disaffected youth could congregate. These teenagers and young adults would be present during business hours and after those hours for various activities."

The implication echoed what many in the area already thought about The Eclectic in general—a perception that drug use and underage drinking was going on there and had somehow contributed to the murders. Drugs began to be suspected as a prime reason the murders had occurred. In fact, many who hung out there would later say that they used drugs outside the premises, but all of them added that Alex Seifert would not allow any type of drug use within the store.

This supposed use of illegal drugs in the environs of The Eclectic only added fuel to the rumors of gang-related murder, once again. It was whispered that Fleming and Trecker somehow had become caught up in this and had been killed. But no evidence had ever surfaced that Fleming took drugs, and it was known that Trecker was totally against them.

One person who eventually discarded the drug and gang angle was Christina Trecker, but she did feel that the occult angle played a part in the murders. And this theory of hers began to lead more and more in her mind toward Robert Fry.

In the days after the funeral, Christina lived her life in a daze of grief and pain. She wandered through the apartment she shared with her husband, barely knowing what she was doing. She couldn't stand the presence of anyone—even her husband, Jeff, who was always supportive. Jeff had always loved Matt as if he were his own son. Jeff knew when to back off and give Christina space. He said later, "I realized she had to come to terms with this in her own way. It was very hard for the both of us."

Racked with pain, unable to sleep, Christina rambled through her own house like a zombie. She blamed the police for not working harder to catch the killer; she blamed Jeff for not putting his foot down to keep Matt away from The Eclectic; she blamed herself for the argument before Thanksgiving that had sent him there. She played the unwinnable game that all survivors of murdered children play with themselves: "What if I had done this differently? What if I hadn't done that?"

"I wanted to die," she said. "There seemed to be no purpose in life anymore. I was filled with anger, pain and agitation. I just wanted it all to go away. But, of course, it wouldn't go away. I kept expecting him to walk through the door as if none of this had ever happened."

As time went on, Christina slowly began to put her life back together, bit by agonizing bit. She wanted to get justice for Matt. The official investigation seemed to be stalled, so Christina and Jeff Trecker began their own unofficial investigation. Most of this focused on Matt's old friends and those who hung out around The Eclectic. Very few in The Eclectic crowd would talk to them. Christina sensed a wall of fear surrounding the case.

She related, "They were scared. I got the feeling that they knew more than they were telling. All of those people had been so close. They knew each other inside and out. They liked to brag about different things. Bobby Fry was the biggest braggart of all. Now everybody was being quiet as mice. I wasn't quite sure what they were afraid of. One thing I did know. Whenever anybody in that bunch got into trouble, they called on Bobby Fry. They called him 'The Enforcer.' There was one kid who always used to hang around with Fry. I noticed right after Matt's death he left the area." She may have been referring to Harold Pollock, though she didn't know his name at the time. Pollock did leave the Farmington area soon after the murders.

Christina began to wonder just what Robert Fry was "enforcing" now. Was it a code of silence? In a roundabout way she began asking about him. All the answers were vague and contradictory, but one story piqued her interest. An individual told her that on the day of Matt's funeral, Bobby Fry stayed behind after most of the other people had left. Then, according to the informant, Fry went up to the open hole all alone and dropped something in. This person had no idea what it was.

According to Christina, she went to the Farmington Police Department and wanted them to open the grave to find out about this. "I wanted to know what he dropped in there. It could have been a note, saying, 'I'm sorry Matt.' It could have been a confession. It could have been a bit of evidence. Something important."

According to Christina, the police dismissed her request saying that it would take a court order, and it would also be too expensive. Besides, they had their own main suspect by this time, and he was not Robert Fry. The suspect was someone connected to the Seiferts.

Sometime after this strange episode, Christina heard another story that was even more intriguing. It concerned Robert Fry at The Top Deck Lounge. The informant said that Fry was out on the dance floor with a woman. The informant related that Fry had said to the woman, "How does it feel dancing with a killer?"

According to Christina, several people overheard this remark. When she told Jeff about it, he contacted the police and related this comment to them. Jeff said later, "The response I got was 'Bobby Fry should learn to keep his mouth shut.' This was a direct quote to me. It was like they had already made up their minds who the suspect ought to be, and that it wasn't Fry."

This response from the police was viewed by Jeff in a couple of different ways. One was that Bobby Fry was perceived to be bragging again about some killing he was not involved in, something he did quite often in the past. And the second was that Fry had indeed committed the murders and was his own worst enemy. Jeff Trecker always wondered how much Gloria Fry's influence colored things with the Farmington Police Department. Even now, no collusion has ever been found, but it didn't stop the Treckers from wondering. By this point they were trying to follow every possible lead they could get, and the leads, in their minds, kept pointing toward Robert Fry. The only problem was, there just didn't seem to be a motive why he would kill both Fleming and Trecker. He was known to be violent at times, but that anger was generally directed out toward his perceived enemies, not his friends.

One person who did believe the Treckers about Robert Fry, at least in part, was Detective Bob Melton of the San Juan County Sheriff's Office. Even though The Eclectic was not on his turf, it was in the city of Farmington rather than in county jurisdiction. He was asked to join the investigation because of his extensive experience in homicide cases. In fact, during Melton's tenure as a detective, he had the remarkable record of solving every homicide case that came across his desk. Sometimes it took him years to do it, but eventually he got the culprit.

Detective Melton knew Bobby Fry well. Over the years Fry had become involved in several DUI incidents in the county. Melton knew Fry was a troublemaker who did not like the police and had disdain for authority in general. He was a loudmouth around town, always bragging about how tough he was. He drank to excess and caused disturbances in restaurants and elsewhere.

Detective Melton also knew Gloria Fry because of his contact with the probation department. As far as he was concerned, Gloria seemed to be a real contradiction. On the one hand, she had created the domestic violence shelter almost single-handedly. She was an outspoken advocate of women's rights. On the other hand, she backed up her son, Robert, on almost every occasion when he had scrapes with the law, even if he was abusive toward women. "She tended to look the other way when Bobby became involved in something bad," Melton said later. Detective Melton stopped just short of saying that she covered up for him, but he and the district attorney's office would even look in later years at that possibility. In fact, their search would not just be in the realm of speculation, it would be written down in police and court records with the possibility of a criminal arrest warrant.

After a few months the official report on The Eclectic read, "The double homicide of Joseph Fleming and Matthew Trecker was investigated by the Farmington Police Department . . . but the crimes remained uncharged."

In the San Juan County Sheriff's Office, there was a similar document, but it had one more critical line: "The last persons known to have seen the victims alive were Robert Fry and Harold Pollock."

Detective Melton may have been involved as an investigator in The Eclectic case, but he certainly was not the main one. It was more of a courtesy call for him to be involved at all, in recognition of the fact that he was considered to be such a good detective. Whatever Melton may have thought up to that point about Bobby Fry's involvement, there was no direct evidence leading from him to the deaths of Fleming and Trecker. All of this was circumstantial at best. Worst of all from a judicial standpoint, there didn't seem to be any motive. Fleming and Trecker, after all, had been his friends. None of it added up.

As 1996 slipped into 1997, there was a diaspora of those who used to hang out at The Eclectic. Many moved out of the area and Harold Pollock moved clear out of state to the Phoenix area in Arizona. One person did remain in Farmington, however—Robert Fry. For the time being, he had gotten away with murder, but it wasn't long before he had other serious trouble on his hands. As Harold Pollock knew about Fry, his trouble often involved prostitutes, and Fry would engage in activities from which even his mother would have trouble extricating him.

Chapter 4

Savior with a .357 Magnum

Robert Fry's life often paralleled Navajo legends. In Fry's twenties he had a yen for prostitutes in the Farmington area, and he might have been surprised to learn that the Navajo Prostitution Way Chant had literally started in his own backyard along the Animas River. The story began with a boy who had been abandoned by his parents. Though the Holy People tried to help the boy, they had no milk to nourish him, so for years he wandered with his grandmother all over the land. By the time he was twenty, he came into the area near Wide House (Aztec Pueblo), not far from where Robert Fry would live in centuries to come.

This young man turned into someone Fry always wanted to be—quite the ladies' man. He made his bed of luxuriant, downy bird feathers by the river and became known as Downy Home Man. He took many young women in the region to bed, and as the storyteller related, "He went around to all the pueblos gathering girls. That's all he was doing."

According to the story, Downy Home Man went to Wide House and had every young woman there except two maidens who lived down in the darkest depths of the pueblo. He learned of these two young women when he overheard the Holy People talking about them near Chaco Canyon. Many had tried to get the girls to come out of the darkness of the pueblo, but all had failed. Even the Stone People, Sunbeam People and Rainbow People were unsuccessful.

When Downy Home Man went by Wide House, he turned himself into various kinds of birds—a bird called "Red Under the Wing," a bird known as "White Head" and one named "Running on the Log." By these means he was able to sneak past the people of the pueblo without causing suspicion.

When he came to the ladder leading down into the lowest depths of the pueblo, he turned himself into a beautiful butterfly. He fluttered all the way down to the lowest depths of Wide House and discovered two beautiful maidens making intricate weavings. Boldly he fluttered down and lit on the right knee of the elder sister.

She said to the younger sister, "It's very pretty. Let's catch this butterfly."

The butterfly slowly flew up the ladder and the girls followed. Once they all reached the outside and daylight, the butterfly turned back into Downy Home Man. He asked why they had left the pueblo. They answered that they were following him and now enjoyed the sunlight. They said they did not want to return to the darkness.

Downy Home Man put one maiden on a rainbow and one on a sunbeam and they all traveled in the sky past where the Hero Twins had been born. The story would have had a happy ending there, but it soon transformed itself into a tale that closely resembled the bloodletting at The Eclectic.

Downy Home Man took the two girls as his

wives, but one day while he was gone hunting, they followed a white butterfly to its home, thinking that it was their husband. In fact, it was the warrior White Butterfly. White Butterfly had many wives whom he had stolen and kept in a cave far away.

After many adventures Downy Home Man was able to track down his wives and he sought to win them back in contests of daring against White Butterfly. If he failed, he would become White Butterfly's slave. There were four contests: throwing a ball through a hole, rolling a hoop, pulling out a strong post from the ground and racing around a hill. Downy Home Man had allies in the contest, unbeknownst to White Butterfly. A mouse helped him with the ball game, a serpent with the hoop, a woodworm with the post and the Wind People with the race. He won all four contests easily.

White Butterfly pretended to be downcast by the outcome and said to Downy Home Man, "Why don't you just kill me. You can use my ax."

It was a trick, however. The ax was called "Reversing Ax," and it killed whoever swung it. As White Butterfly lowered his head, Downy Home Man figured out the trick. He picked up his own ax and cut off White Butterfly's head.

With his two wives restored to him, Downy Home Man took them home to an area in what would later be San Juan County, but the women were afraid to live now in the sunlight. In response, he took them back to Wide House and told them to return to the dark amongst their people. He said that no one would harm them from now on.

In September 1997 Robert Fry also sought to be the protector of a young woman in San Juan County. He was ready to use whatever means to accomplish his mission. If he'd known the rest of the Prostitution

Way Chant, however, he might have thought twice about his course of action. The storyteller ended the tale by saying, "If a man who knows the whole Prostitution Way uses it against women, he'll get it himself and become dry (impotent)."

It was alcohol and an alleged prostitute that got Robert Fry into trouble in the late-night hours of September 2, 1997. Fry was roaming around Farmington in his car, intoxicated. By now, he worked for Elkhorn Construction Company of Bloomfield. Fry knew a pretty young woman named Rhonda Knott, who worked at The Top Deck Lounge in Farmington. He had been employed there for a while as a bouncer, and he and Rhonda often talked, but it went no further than that. Fry asked her out on dates, but she refused. Unfortunately for her, Fry was not one who liked to be given no for an answer.

Author Ann Cummins wrote of The Top Deck Lounge in her award-winning book, *Red Ant House*. In her short story "Starburst," she had a Farmington policeman named Barry Deemer describe the interior of The Top Deck. Deemer said, "There is a distinctive odor to this place, a metallic smell of liquor gone stale and of cigarettes—like poor quality aluminum that you can tear with your fingers."

He went on to say that he had smelled that odor before on winos, a strange odor of a human being at its most human. He described it as "that almost clean smell of cheap metal."

The Top Deck was one of Robert Fry's favorite places to party, dance, check out women and tell his outlandish stories of violence and bloodshed. He was always in search of a good time. He was also often in search of trouble.

In the summer of 1997, Fry noticed a small item

in the local newspaper that changed everything about his perception of Rhonda Knott. He had always seen her as some unobtainable "nice girl," but the article mentioned that Rhonda Knott had been arrested on charges of prostitution.

About 10:00 P.M. on September 2, 1997, Rhonda Knott was walking along a roadway in Farmington when Robert Fry spotted her near the Animas River, not far from the area in which Downy Home Man had seduced so many Indian maidens. Fry offered Knott a ride and she accepted. It was probably obvious to her that Fry had consumed alcohol, but she didn't know that his alcohol blood level was nearly twice the legal limit. Just what happened next depends upon the version of the story told by Rhonda Knott or Robert Fry. There were points, however, where their stories intersected. What is known with certainty is that they parked in a field to talk near the corner of Cochran and Miller Streets. Before long, the situation got completely out of hand. Fry pulled a .357 handgun from underneath the seat and, for the next fifteen minutes, completely terrorized Rhonda Knott. He was drunk, rambling and apparently at some point started to undress. Knott only managed to escape because the passenger door was broken and could not be automatically latched from Fry's side of the car. She tumbled out of the vehicle and began running for her life, and Bobby Fry took off after her with a loaded gun.

Someone in the vicinity saw this incident and phoned it in to the police. Before long, Farmington police officers were on the scene, and Detective Larry Miller's report attempted to unravel just what had occurred. Miller began: "10:36 PM. September 2, 1997. I responded to Orchard Street and Elm Street to assist Officer Jason Small as he made a traffic stop on a 1995 Blue Ford two-door vehicle bearing New Mexico plate 917GRM. This vehicle fit the description given by the communication center where a male subject was chasing a female with a firearm. The driver, later identified as Robert Fry and known to be hostile towards police, advised officer Small, he was in possession of a gun."

Detective Miller and Officer Small had Fry exit his vehicle and step to the back, where he was patted down for weapons, handcuffed and placed in the back of a police car. Detective Miller then spoke with Rhonda Knott, who had returned to the scene. He noted that she was extremely upset, shaking and crying. She told him, "That motherfucker put a gun under my chin and against my head." She added that the gun was big and that it was loaded.

Rhonda identified a Ruger .357 revolver that was found in the front seat of Fry's vehicle. She said it was the firearm with which he had assaulted her. She noticed that it was now unloaded and told the officers that it had been loaded at the time she was assaulted.

Rhonda Knott told the officers that she had known Robert Fry from the days he used to work at The Top Deck Lounge. She said she had been walking home from that establishment and was near the UBC Construction Store on San Juan Boulevard when Robert Fry offered her a ride. She accepted and they drove to a field near the corner of Cochran and Miller Streets, where he parked the car and they talked for a while. Then, according to Knott, Fry had become very upset because he had seen an article about her in the newspaper and he wanted to pimp for her. When she told him no, he brandished a large pistol and placed it under her chin.

Then he put it against several other parts of her body and told her he was going to kill her.

Knott said this went on for at least fifteen minutes, even though she asked to be released on numerous occasions. She also advised the officers that at one point Robert Fry had leaned forward and bitten her on the neck. When Detective Miller looked at her neck, he didn't notice any bite marks or abrasions.

Knott told the officers she was so terrorized by Fry's behavior that she had urinated in her clothes. Detective Miller said that she had been arrested for prostitution on a previous occasion and asked her if that had been the situation with her and Fry in his car. She told him that she hadn't had sex with Fry, oral or otherwise. She said that after fifteen minutes of pure terror, she was able to open the passenger-side door, which was broken, and run away. She added that she was now menstruating heavily and wanted to leave. Detective Miller allowed her to go, with the promise that she could be contacted later at her residence.

At that point Officer Small Mirandized Robert Fry in Miller's presence. Detective Miller asked him if he understood his rights. He said that he did and Officer Small told him that he was under arrest for aggravated assault upon Rhonda Knott. Detective Miller then drove Fry to the Farmington Police Station and interviewed him there.

When Detective Miller asked Fry what had happened, he explained that he was Jesus Christ and that he had wanted to save Knott. Miller asked him if he was under the influence of narcotics and Fry said no, but he admitted that he had been drinking beer. He explained that he had known Rhonda Knott for several years and had worked with her at

The Top Deck Lounge. He said he was very fond of her, but she would never date him. Then he had read an article in the newspaper that she'd been arrested for prostitution. When he saw her walking alone down the street, he said he became worried for her safety and offered her a ride. She had accepted.

Fry said that as they drove along he told her he was going to kill her pimp or anyone else that would harm her. He told her he had a gun and that he was going to use it to save all prostitutes. Detective Miller asked him if he was in possession of a firearm while he was in contact with Knott. Fry answered that he had been. When asked if he had threatened Knott with a .357 handgun, he denied that he had. He said he had merely taken it from beneath the driver's seat and showed her that it was loaded.

Detective Miller asked Fry if at any time Knott had asked to leave his vehicle and he said that she had, but he didn't want her to go because he was going to protect her. Fry said he had given her $35, but not for sex. He later said that he had given her $50.

Miller had noticed that when Robert Fry had first been contacted, he wasn't wearing any shoes and that his shirt was unbuttoned and his belt was undone. He was asked again if he had engaged in sexual activity with Rhonda Knott. He denied that he had, but he couldn't explain why his clothes were in disarray.

At that point Detective Miller contacted District Attorney (DA) Sandra Price and explained the situation. She recommended that Fry be charged with kidnapping, aggravated assault and negligent use of a firearm.

Robert Fry agreed to take a breath alcohol test, which was performed by Officer Victor Mangiacapra. The result was 1.8.

Incredibly, Robert Fry knew just about how drunk he was. He told Detective Miller that he was probably a 1.7 on the scale. He was only off by one tenth of a point.

A short time after the interview, Detective Miller phoned Rhonda Knott at her motel room. She was very upset and stated that she didn't want him to come and see her. She also said that she just wanted to go somewhere with her boyfriend.

She then asked Miller, "Did Fry have any blood on his hands?"

Miller said, "No." Then he asked, "Why would you say that?"

She answered that Fry had sexually assaulted her with a metal bar. He had inserted it into her vagina and that was why she was bleeding. She wasn't menstruating at all.

Detective Miller asked her why she had made up the story about menstruation when he'd first contacted her.

"I just wanted it to go away," she answered.

Asked once again by Miller if she was bleeding now because of menstruation, Knott replied no, she was bleeding because she'd been cut by the metal bar that Robert Fry had forcibly raped her with. She stated, however, that it was a small cut and had now stopped bleeding.

Detective Miller told her, small cut or not, she should seek medical attention and that he could transport her to the hospital. Knott adamantly refused. She said she had already washed herself and would not be subjected to that kind of examination.

Detective Miller told her several more times the importance of seeking medical help, but Rhonda Knott became angry and hung up the phone.

Detective Miller once again contacted DA Sandra Price and explained about the new development. She advised him to place a police hold on Robert Fry's vehicle. This was done, and Fry's car was towed to the Municipal Operation Center Police Compound.

Detective Miller wrote later in his report, "As Ms. Knott was being uncooperative in the investigation, the possible criminal sexual penetration was not pursued any further at the direction of District Attorney Sandra Price. Officer Small attempted to find the metal instrument used in the assault but was unsuccessful."

Two firearms, however, were retrieved from Robert Fry's car and placed into evidence. One was a Ruger .357 and the other was a H&R .32-caliber handgun. Also placed into evidence were .357-caliber rounds that were taken from within the pistol and a belt with holster containing eleven .357 magnum rounds.

The officers took various photos of Robert Fry's vehicle. Little did they know at the time, one of the photos would become very significant in years to come. It depicted the rear storage area of his blue Ford Aspire. In this area was a shovel with spade-type blade and a three- to four-foot wooden handle.

DA Sandra Price may not have received cooperation from Rhonda Knott about the sexual assault, or recovered the metal bar used in the attack, but she persuaded a grand jury to list it among charges leveled against Robert Fry. The charges read:

Count 1
Robert James Fry did unlawfully assault or strike

Rhonda Knott, with a deadly weapon, to wit: a Ruger .357 Revolver, contrary to Section 30-03-2.
Count 2
Robert James Fry did unlawfully take, restrain, transport or confine Rhonda Knott, by force, intimidation or deception, with the intent that Rhonda Knott be held to service, against her will or to inflict physical injury or sexual offenses on her, contrary to Section 30-4-1.
Count 3
Robert James Fry did endanger the safety of another by handling or using a firearm or other deadly weapon in a negligent manner or in the alternative did carry a firearm while under the influence of an intoxicant or narcotic, contrary to Section 30-07-04.
Count 4
Robert James Fry did unlawfully and intentionally cause penetration by insertion, to any extent, of a foreign object, to wit: a metal pipe into the genital or anal openings of Rhonda Knott, and did so by use of force or coercion and did result in great bodily or great mental anguish, contrary to Section 30-9-11.
Count 5
Robert James Fry did drive a vehicle while having sixteen one-hundreths or more by weight of alcohol in his blood contrary to Section 66-8-102.

There was also a list of potential penalties included if he was found guilty:

- Count 1—eighteen months and $10,000 fine
- Count 2—eighteen years and $100,000 fine
- Count 3—six months and $500 fine
- Count 4—eighteen years and $100,000 fine
- Count 5—six months and $500 fine

From the time of arrest to his trial date, Fry was allowed to be out on bail, which was insured by a bond of $60,000. He was not to leave San Juan County and was to be in touch with his defense attorney, Randall Roberts, at least once a week.

Justice was not swift, however, and the case tap-danced through the court system for nearly a year and a half. On March 23, 1998, Fry's attorney asked for and received an extension for the trial date. It was granted and the trial date was moved to July 6, 1998. Before this date arrived, he asked for another extension and it was granted as well. The new trial was scheduled for February 7, 1999.

During this period Robert Fry apparently did something that was against the rules of the court order. On September 18, 1998, the district attorney's office contacted the presiding judge for a motion to revoke Fry's current status. It read in part: "Motion to revoke defendant's conditions of release." This led to a hearing on September 25 and another in November. This, too, was continued until December.

Robert Fry's attorney wrote a motion to the court. He asked for "a revelation of the following evidence to the defendant prior to trial . . . requiring the state to disclose all criminal investigations, arrests or criminal charges against the alleged victim, Rhonda Knott."

Clearly, Fry and his attorney were going to try and bring into play Knott's alleged past activities as a prostitute and whatever other illegal activity they could dig up on her.

The jury trial finally got under way in March 1999. Key witnesses for the state were Detective Miller and Rhonda Knott. The deputy district attorney (DDA), June Stein, also brought into evidence several photos. These included photos of the .357 Ruger handgun, holster with eleven rounds, four bullets from the gun, a breath card and map. Defense attorney Randall Roberts only had one exhibit to show the jury, a piece of rebar (a metal rod used in construction).

The trial was not going particularly well for the prosecution. Rhonda Knott was troublesome once more and uncooperative at times. And the jurors, who normally are a passive and attentive bunch, were full of questions in this trial. One question from a juror was: "Did Detective Miller smell urine odor on the evidence collected in the vehicle where the supposed assault occurred?" Another was: "As I recall, yesterday Officer Miller stated that the call to 911 was from a pay phone, but Ms. Knott says it was made from a cell phone." And a third question was: "Why was not [*sic*] the physical evidence examined or secured from the plaintiff at the state laboratory?"

There were a lot of problems with this case for the prosecution and the biggest one was Rhonda Knott herself. She was very evasive about the sexual contact between herself and Robert Fry. Her answers and demeanor brought into question all of the evidence. On March 19, 1999, the jury reached its decision on all five charges against Robert Fry. He was found not guilty on the most serious charges: Count 1, use of a deadly firearm; Count 2, kidnaping; Count 4, sexual penetration. He was only found guilty of Count 3, the illegal use of a firearm, and Count 5, intoxicated while operating a vehicle.

Robert Fry received his sentence from Judge William Birdsall. Judge Birdsall said, "It is the judgment sentence of this court that as to Count 3, that the defendant be committed to the custody of the

San Juan County Detention Center to be confined for a term of 179 days. It is also the judgment and sentence of this court that as to Count 5, that the defendant be committed to the custody of the San Juan County Detention Center to be confined for the term of 364 days."

These sentences were to run consecutively, and when Fry was released, he was to be placed on unsupervised probation for one year and seventy-nine days. He was to pay $65 for an Intoximeter fee, $10 corrections fee, $3 traffic safety fee and $75 comprehensive community program fee. He was also to pay $5 to something called the brain-injury fee. No explanation was given as to what that fee concerned.

Interestingly enough, Robert Fry was "ordered to a condition of probation, that the defendant shall comply with the Farmington Municipal Court Probation Office." His mother, Gloria, was a probation officer, and she had many ties to this very office, although she mainly dealt with misdemeanors.

As Robert Fry passed into the detention center, his physical characteristics were noted and recorded. He was six feet tall at this time and weighed 245 pounds. He had a couple of tattoos on his arms—a lion head on his right bicep, and a wolf with a mountain scene on his left bicep.

The authorities may have jotted down various statistics and information on Robert Fry, but there was one very important thing he knew that they didn't know. Between the time he was arrested for assaulting Rhonda Knott and released on bail, and the time he was sentenced for the crime, he had murdered once again. He'd done it right under the noses of everyone in their own backyard of San Juan County. Robert Fry was so audacious that he shrugged off his possible conviction in the Rhonda Knott case and murdered a man in a heinous act of incredible rage and bloodletting that would have mirrored a Misfits song at its most violent.

Chapter 5

Point of the Scorpion

By ethnicity and religion, modern-day Navajo Donald Tsosie knew from a very early age the legends of the Hero Twins. Born in 1957 on the Navajo Reservation, Donald was only a year old when his drunken stepfather had a violent argument with his mother. The stepfather chased his mother behind a shed and clubbed her to death. Along with his older sisters, Linda and Nora, Donald was sent to live with his maternal grandparents west of Gallup, New Mexico. Raised in a very traditional way, young Donald inhabited a world of hogans and sheep pens. He was taught about the exploits of the Hero Twins and the Holy People. Each morning he greeted Dawn Boy with prayer:

In the house made of dawn,
In the story made of dawn,
On the trail of dawn,
O, Talking God!

His feet, my feet restore.
His limbs, my limbs restore.
His mind, my mind restore.

Then there were verses of beauty all around, above and below, ending with:

It is finished in beauty.
It is finished in beauty
In the house of evening light.

Years later, Donald's sister Linda told a reporter for the *Gallup Independent,* "We didn't have toys like kids do now. We played games we made up. And herded sheep." In fact, Donald and his sisters became the caretakers of their grandparents' flock that would sometimes number more than two hundred sheep. They herded them over the arid landscape west of Gallup, always in search of the scant vegetation to keep them alive. The grandparents were so old-fashioned that they and the children rode into town in a wagon drawn by horses. By the time Donald was seven years old, the wagon became his summer bedroom.

On one occasion his sisters played a prank on Donald and his cousin, who were sleeping in the wagon. While they were asleep, the sisters sneaked up on them and pushed the wagon down a small hill. The sisters giggled as the wagon rolled away. Linda said later, "When Donald woke up, he didn't know where he was. There were many times of jokes and fun."

Nora added, "Our grandma didn't want us to go to school because they needed our help with chores and sheep." Even at an early age, the Tsosie children were proficient in herding and even butchering the sheep. Their loss from the hogan would be a real hardship to the grandparents, who would have to do all the tasks when the children were gone.

Nonetheless, the authorities made the children go to school. Donald was sent off to boarding school at Toyei, a very small village in eastern Arizona, nestled below the cliffs near the Hopi Reservation. It was even more isolated than the area where he had grown up. Donald's beloved sisters were sent even farther away to boarding school in Utah. This dispersion of children was not unusual for Navajo children on the Big Rez in the 1960s.

The Tsosie children were lucky in at least one regard—before 1960, the United States government had run the schools, and life was much more harsh for Native American children. In that era, even up through the 1950s, the main concern of the schools was to turn Indian children into assimilated adults with the emphasis on being Anglo. A student could be forced to eat lye soap for talking in his native tongue. Traditional long hair was cut short for boys and girls to match the prevailing style of the era. They were often punished for acting "too Indian."

Robin Tsosie, who went to boarding school before 1960, later told a *Christian Science Monitor* reporter, "It was scary. It was heartbreaking. It brings back bad memories. It's sad that we were forced to change our identities when all we wanted to do was be ourselves."

Peterson Zah, who eventually became president of the Navajo Nation, told a reporter for a Canadian news service about his boarding school experience: "My father and mother explained to me that I was going to a strange world. They prepared me very well for the occasion with religion. As I left home, my mother gave me a pinch of corn pollen. She said, 'Keep this. This is like your Bible.' "

Most likely, Donald Tsosie's traditional grand-parents also fortified him with their religion be-fore he was sent away to Toyei. And he was lucky in the fact that by the time he went to school, the Navajo religion and language were no longer being banned there. In fact, Navajo culture started being emphasized. English was taught as a second lan-guage. The "Indianness" that had been punished in the previous years was now actively being pro-moted. Many boys let their hair grow long, as in the old ways, and adorned themselves with turquoise and silver. Slowly but surely, traditional ways were creeping back into the collective psyche.

Donald Tsosie's life after attending boarding school at Toyei took its ups and downs. He only at-tended school through seventh grade and then quit school for good. Tsosie did, however, become proficient as a carpenter, and this gave him an oc-cupation. Moving around throughout the Southwest, he plied his trade in construction work in the Phoenix, Arizona, area.

When a sawmill opened on the Navajo Reservation closer to the area where he'd grown up, Tsosie got a job there and moved back home. Now he was back in the heartland of Dinétah, around his own kind. These may have been some of the most satis-fying times in Donald's life.

The mill only operated for six years, though, and when it shut down, Donald fell back on car-pentry and odd roofing jobs around the village of Ganado in western Arizona. Situated in a rolling countryside of pinyons, juniper and nearby pon-derosa pines, Ganado was more forested than some of the more desert area surrounding it. There was wild game in the countryside, including deer.

Near Ganado was the Hubbell Trading Post, one of the most famous and historic on the Navajo Nation. Donald went to the Hubbell Trading Post on occasion and the people there knew him by sight. Within its dark, cool corridors behind thick stone walls, he occasionally shopped for household groceries and goods.

The area around Ganado had always been a major meeting and trading place for Native Americans, first with the Anasazi and then the Navajo. In 1878, John L. Hubbell bought the trading post and named the surrounding settlement for his Navajo friend Ganado Mucho. The trading post has been in business ever since, making it the oldest continuously run post on the Navajo Nation. It garnered such a good reputation for fair trade that Navajo, Zuni, Hopi and other tribes came there to sell or trade rugs, jewelry, baskets and pottery.

Hubbell originally traded mostly cotton goods, farm implements and canned peaches for sacks of wool. His son later wrote of him, "He became everything from merchant to father confessor, justice of the peace, judge, jury, court of appeals, chief medicine man and de facto czar of the domain." Later, artist Maynard Dixon would agree: "J. L. Hubbell lived like a Spanish hidalgo of old at his trading post."

By the 1890s, the Navajo discovered they could make a lot more profit by keeping their wool and making it into blankets. Traders formed a loose association with them, supplying new aniline dyes. The introduction of the dyes almost ruined what had once been true works of art. The Navajo flooded the eastern markets with cheap, gaudy rugs, and their wares became a byword for cheap goods.

In part, J. L. Hubbard helped save the old-style Navajo rugs. He had artist E. A. Burbank make watercolor portraits of every old rug design that he could discover in the region. It helped preserve the old ways of soft native colors and design. By the 1920s many Navajos reverted to the ancient designs and colors that Hubbell had helped preserve.

By Donald Tsosie's time, the latest in a long line of managers who ran the post recalled Tsosie coming into his trading post to do business. "He was a quiet man who brought his pawn in once in a while. I would say he was polite. There were quite a few of the Tsosies from around this area. I never had any trouble with him or them. They were all good folk."

A couple of the Tsosie relations were his sisters, Nora and Linda, and his niece Regina Dennison. Regina loved her uncle and spoke of what a valuable person he was in her life. Maternal uncles in some respects are the most important person in a young Navajo's life, someone they can talk to when things aren't going well with their parents.

Regina later told the *Gallup Independent,* "He always had a smile to give out. He had lots of friends and everyone liked my uncle."

She said that he loved children and liked to play basketball with the kids. Donald's sister Linda said that he always liked playing games and having a good time. He fixed things up around the relatives' homes and was an all-around handyman.

Linda added that he was a great cook. "He could make tasty Navajo tacos filled with peppers and chunks of lamb, lamb stew and fry bread. His specialty was something called 'Crazy bread.'"

Donald Tsosie was associated with the Ganado Chapter House. Chapter houses on the Navajo Reservation are part town hall, part recreation center and part spiritual center for the people in that region.

One of the men who worked at the Ganado Chapter House stated that "Donald was a quiet man, but he had lots of friends around here. He never caused any trouble. If you needed something, he was always ready to help someone. He was a good carpenter and mechanic. Didn't have a lot of schooling, but he knew a lot of things. Do-it-yourself kind of things."

Yet for all his friends and handyman qualities, Donald had one all-too-common affliction, he had become addicted to alcohol.

Like many Native Americans who were only part-time laborers, Donald Tsosie was afflicted with alcoholism when he wasn't engaged in work. Even though alcohol is not sold on the Navajo Reservation, there are plenty of stores selling beer and stronger spirits right on the borderline. Since alcohol could be confiscated if carried back to the reservation, many Navajos stayed at bars or bought their liquor at convenience stores off the Rez and consumed it there. It was not uncommon to find Native American alcoholics who had passed out in the parking lots or alleyways near a bar or place that sold liquor.

There were several bars and saloons in Farmington that catered to a Native American clientele. Donald Tsosie's saloon of choice was the Turn Around Bar. At least he was lucky in one respect—he found a good woman, Genevieve Chee, who loved Donald despite his occasional drinking binges. Genevieve, who was from Crownpoint, was in her forties when they met, just about Donald's age. They became friends in 1997 and enjoyed each other's company. Then she said, "We became girlfriend and boyfriend on February 14, 1998—Valentine's Day."

They were good for each other. She brought out the best in him once again—his kindness and helpfulness to others.

"He was a good man," Chee said. "He wouldn't hurt anybody."

Donald Tsosie moved in with Genevieve Chee in Crownpoint right around this time. He still did have a problem with drinking, but at least he kept it out of their home, only going to drink in Farmington with his friends. He and Chee developed a routine where she would take him into Farmington to sell his blood for plasma at BCI Biological Laboratories in exchange for cash.

Tsosie became quite a regular at BCI Biological Laboratories in Farmington, located on the west side of town, not far from where Jeff and Christina Trecker lived. It was a low, flat building on Main Street that had many Navajos as its clients, giving blood in return for cash. The director there kept a record of Donald Tsosie's visits and noted that he came in three times in January 1998 and seven times in February 1998. Tsosie always had to give proof of identity and pass a general-health exam. He also had to be free of drugs and not intoxicated. In some ways BCI Biological was good for Donald. He could not be on a drinking binge before going in there; so in essence, his drinking was confined to only certain days of the week.

The routine that Donald Tsosie and Genevieve Chee worked out was that she would drive him eighty miles from Crownpoint up to Farmington along the Bisti Highway to BCI Biological Labs and let him off there. He would give blood and visit friends around town, and then she would take him home. At other times he might spend a couple of days in

Farmington visiting friends. On these occasions Chee would always pick him up at the local Safeway store.

Their drive up through the Bisti Badlands took them through a region of an incredible jumble of multicolored rocks shaped into fantastic forms by wind and erosion. Just before they dropped off the plateau toward the San Juan River, the road descended a cliff area, "the Bluffs." On the very tip of the Bluffs was an eminence known locally as "Scorpion Point." To some young couples it was a make-out spot. To others it was a place to drink or get stoned. It was fairly isolated, could only be reached by a small dirt road and was rugged in places, with cliffs and a steep drop-off.

On the afternoon of March 31, 1998, Donald had a problem at BCI Biological labs. He couldn't give blood because his blood pressure was too high, and so was his protein count. Chee wanted Donald to come back home with her to Crownpoint, but he said no. He would stick around town, visit friends and try again at BCI on the next day.

Donald walked into town and may have even talked to his half brother Paul James, near the Safeway store. James would later tell police of this encounter with Tsosie. But James had a drinking problem even worse than Tsosie's and was apt to get dates and times mixed up. James would admit later that he had drunk a liter of vodka on the day he supposedly talked to Donald and his recollection was hazy at best.

Whether Donald Tsosie ran into his half brother on the streets of Farmington or not, he did, in fact, visit with others there and eventually wound up at the Turn Around Bar on the evening of March 31, 1998. There were two other men out drinking that night in Farmington as well—Bobby Fry and his buddy Leslie Engh.

It could be a dangerous proposition to be a friend of Bobby Fry's. Harold Pollock had learned that the hard way, and Les Engh was just about to get a very tough lesson as well. Engh, not unlike Pollock, had his own scrapes with the law around Farmington.

Like many of Bobby Fry's friends, Les Engh was much shorter and weighed a lot less than Fry. Physically and emotionally, Fry was the dominant character in their relationship. In 1998, Engh was five feet eleven inches and weighed 146 pounds, almost one hundred pounds less than Fry. He had longish brown hair and blue eyes.

Engh and Fry had both worked at Calco, a gas-and-oil-field-related company. Engh's job was to do pressure testing in the oil fields. This mainly meant he had to record pressure readings and check the valves for any leaks. This job took Engh out into the countryside around San Juan County, mainly on night work. It was often lonely, tiring and boring out in the hinterlands. Engh looked forward to nights he could spend drinking with his buddies, especially Bobby Fry. Fry was always good for a rowdy time at either one of the local bars or all-night coffee shops around town.

One thing Engh knew about was Fry's disdain for the local Native Americans. Engh said later, "Robert called them 'trogs,' which was short for troglodytes. He said they were dirty and a bunch of drunks. He pretty much hated them."

This was a far cry from the portrait that Fry's sister Jeanne had portrayed of him as a child who was enamored of his Mohawk ancestry. Perhaps to

Bobby Fry's mind, Mohawks were equated with "good Indians," while the local Navajos, Utes, Apaches and Pueblo Indians were equated with "bad Indians." Robert Fry could romanticize about his Mohawk predecessors, but he despised the Native Americans he saw on the streets of Farmington, all too many of them who had come into town for the express purpose of drinking.

Interestingly enough, Bobby Fry hated Native Americans for the one thing he could be accused of himself—overindulging in the consumption of alcohol. By this time Fry was often a mean and vicious drunk, always itching for a fight. Les Engh said, "Robert often talked of going out and rolling an Injun." This meant finding some drunken Native American outside a bar, beating him up and stealing his money.

This practice was not reserved to Bobby Fry alone. In fact, during the 1960s and early 1970s, it had been a real problem in the Farmington area and victims were easy to find. Behind bars or in alleyways, local teenage boys would seek out the drunks and kick them, stomp them, beat them and rob them. In a book by author Rodney Barker, a local teenager admitted, "They (the Native Americans) had no self-respect and we had no respect for them either. . . . Goddamn, you'd say, let's kick some Indian ass!"

One teenager told Barker they called Indians "subs," as in subhuman. They weren't really human at all to the boys, just targets to be beaten and robbed. It became a rite of passage for some boys in the area. They weren't really a man until they had "rolled an Injun."

Susan Rickman, Farmington High School class of 1974, later told reporter Laura Banish, "Trust me, it (rolling Indians) happened. It was a Friday-

and Saturday-night thing that boys got involved in. It didn't happen every night. But it happened."

Many would blame this problem on the huge in-flux of gas- and oil-working roughnecks from Oklahoma and Texas. Marlo Webb, who was mayor of Farmington in 1974, later told a *Farmington Daily Times* reporter, "The oil and gas industry, their values were different than ours (the pre-1950s citizens of Farmington). They were not used to living with someone of a different culture."

Stella Webster, a Native American, found out just how dangerous it could be to be a person of a different culture from the Anglo boys who cruised up and down Farmington's streets in the early 1970s. While she and her husband were walking home from a movie theater in downtown Farmington, a carload of Anglo boys attempted to run them down. They barely escaped with their lives.

By 1974, it was getting way out of control, a bru-tal scenario of one-upmanship. Instead of fists and boots, the boys began to use sticks, bats, pipes and rocks to beat up Indians. It reached its climax of ferocity when three teenage boys murdered three Native Americans in Chokecherry Canyon that year. One of the boys admitted later to pulling the clothes off one intoxicated Native American and setting his hair and pubic hair on fire. They took branches off a tree and beat him. They put a plastic cup in his mouth and set it on fire. Then they rolled him down a hill to his death.

The boys killed two other men in a similar, bru-tal manner. When they were finally caught and ar-rested, the boys were hardly remorseful. Indians, after all, were just subs. Young ADA Thomas Hynes commented later, "It was just so brutal, humanity at its worst. We'll never know what was on those kids' minds. You could just see there was a lot of anger."

Unfortunately for delivering appropriate justice, the prosecution and judge's hands were tied by New Mexico law. Because of the boys' ages, the most they could be sentenced to was the maximum in a juvenile-detention center. To the outraged Native Americans of the area, it was as if no justice had occurred at all. The region was rocked with a Native American revolt. There were meetings and protest marches. Many Anglos and Hispanics of Farmington were also revolted by the savagery of the attacks. They joined the marches and protests. Rolling Indians was no longer an accepted practice. It brought shame to the area.

But by 1998, Robert Fry was about to bring it back full force, in an outburst of savagery that would match the Chokecherry Massacre. All he needed was a victim.

Fry was always talking about getting into fights and Les Engh even witnessed the weapons he carried around. Of course, Fry always had his knives, Bubba and Baby Bubba, but he also had a stash of more unconventional weapons in his Ford Aspire. Sometime in late March 1998, Fry and Engh stopped at a tennis court in a local park. Fry scrounged through a garbage can and found a heavy industrial-style broomstick. He took it out of the trash can and placed it in the rear compartment of his Ford Aspire. The rear compartment was an open trunk-like area, easily reached from the backseat of the vehicle.

"Why do you want that?" Engh asked him.

"I like to tape 'em up and use them as weapons," Fry answered. "They're good in fights."

Engh knew all about Fry's method of fighting.

For him there was no such thing as "fighting clean."
Like Michelle Hearn, Engh knew that Fry had said,
"I always get in the first punch. A sucker punch."

On Tuesday, March 31, 1998, Engh and Fry went
to Chelseas Bar on San Juan Boulevard. It was a
popular local hangout that served food and drinks.
They always tried to go there on Tuesday nights
because it was karaoke night. The place was usually rocking with a late-night crowd, people going
up to the microphone and either belting out good
renditions of their favorite songs, or making fools
of themselves with off-key singing. It was a fun and
rowdy atmosphere, and both Engh and Fry enjoyed the company of their friends at Chelseas.
Engh said later, "We went there to drink, dance
with some women we'd meet and tell stories."

Fry's stories usually depicted his wild escapades,
which included fighting. And on March 31, as he
began drinking to excess once again, his stories
became more belligerent and violent. It was a scene
that had occurred there several times before and
at some point it was obvious to the bartender that
Fry was drunk. The bartender cut him off from
further alcohol consumption. In a disgruntled mood
Fry and Engh made their way across town to another bar called Gators, where Fry continued to
drink. While there, Engh noticed that Bobby Fry
had four more beers. By closing time Fry was definitely inebriated and itching for a fight.

Engh recalled later, "Bobby got more aggressive
at Gators. He kept wanting to get into a fight. Like
he was a tough guy. When we left, he was pretty intoxicated and so was I."

After leaving Gators, they drove around Farmington for a short while until Fry turned to Engh and
said, "We can roll a drunk Injun."

Engh said later, "I didn't really want to, but I said okay."

Engh knew what a bad mood Bobby Fry was in and ready for a fight. He didn't want to cross Fry on this issue and incur his wrath, so he reluctantly went along with Fry's suggestion.

They cruised around town some more and drove by the front entrance of the Turn Around Bar at about 2:30 A.M., April 1, 1998. Engh recalled, "We looked at the Indians outside the bar. We noticed one guy, he seemed cleaner than the rest. He had on a white cowboy hat, jeans, Western shirt, rodeo jacket and short haircut. He was a little more clean-cut than the rest. Like he had money."

The man Engh and Fry spotted was Donald Tsosie, and rather than being rich, he had exactly fifteen cents in his pockets.

Bobby Fry pulled up alongside the clean-cut man and acted friendly. He asked Donald if he needed a ride.

Tsosie said that he did, but it was clear out to Crownpoint.

Fry lied and said they were headed that way and could give him a ride. Leslie Engh crawled out of the front passenger seat and climbed in back, while Tsosie took his place up front.

As they drove through Farmington, Fry asked Tsosie his name. He answered, "Donald."

Engh remembered that Fry made up a couple of names, one for himself and one for Engh. He couldn't remember what they were later, just that the names weren't Robert and Leslie.

Fry drove his Ford Aspire westward through town, across the San Juan River Bridge, and up Highway 371, the Bisti Highway. The road led upward, ascending a steep rise known officially as Shannon Bluffs, but everyone locally just called them the Bluffs. As they drove along, Engh said later, "I knew they (Fry and Tsosie) were going to get into a fight. But I didn't expect it in the car. As soon as we got to the top of the Bluffs, Fry hit him. He hit him in the face with his elbow. It was a sucker punch. They began pushing back and forth while driving. Swerving all over the place."

Right near the top, Fry suddenly swerved off onto a small dirt road that ran along the steep escarpment. Even though the road was bumpy, narrow and dangerous, Fry wouldn't slow down as he and Tsosie continued to fight. Les Engh was terrified. He said, "I was watching the edge. I was scared. I knew about the drop-off."

To help Fry in his struggle, Engh grabbed a belt, which was in the back compartment where Fry stored many items. Les threw the belt around Tsosie's neck in an attempt to choke him into submission, but Tsosie kept on struggling.

Engh said, "I did this on my own. It was to make him stop fighting. I reached over the top of the seat and pulled back on the belt. He kept lunging forward, trying to get it off. I did this for maybe half a minute."

It was a ride of sheer terror for Engh in the backseat, since he had no control of the car as it barreled down the road along the edge of the Bluffs, which dropped steeply off into Head Canyon. Engh said, "Robert was yelling at that point, driving pretty fast. The road was really bumpy. He suddenly pulled off and stopped the car. He swerved right to a stop."

The car was about five feet from where the land dropped away from the ridgetop. Fry pulled into an area of soft dirt alongside the road. Donald Tsosie managed to extricate himself from the belt and tumbled out the passenger door. Fry jumped out the driver's-side door and went around the car to fight Tsosie. Both men had more room to maneuver in the open air, and Fry got a lot more than he bargained for. Even though he was six feet tall and weighed about 250 pounds, Tsosie was no pushover. Donald was six feet tall, too, and lifted weights. Tsosie gave Fry as good as he got, and then some. In fact, he soon got the upper hand and beat Fry down to the ground.

Engh recalled, "The fight was going on right outside the passenger door. Robert was down on his knees. The Indian was punching him from above. I wasn't sure what I was supposed to do. Robert yelled at me, 'Grab the shovel!'

"I reached in back and got the shovel. I did it partially to help Robert. Partially because of what he would do to me if I didn't. Donald was a little above him, fighting. Robert was yelling angry words at the world. I swung the shovel and hit Donald twice in the back. He stumbled forward and lost his balance.

"Robert got up and started hitting and kicking him as he was down. Then Robert grabbed the shovel and started using it. He kept yelling, 'Die Injun!' He was yelling at Donald and the world.

"There were lots and lots of hits, mostly on the body area. But he also hit him in the head and everywhere. By now, Donald was on the ground, rolling from side to side.

"Fry kicked him, too. Then he dropped the shovel and grabbed the broomstick. He started hitting him with it, but it kept breaking. He thought this was funny. He laughed.

"Robert took one of the broken pieces and stabbed him with the sharpened point, in the face, the eyes and the genitals. He seemed to be poking hard and Donald was still rolling a little bit."

While Fry was doing this, Engh said later, it was as if he were possessed. Fry kept yelling and cursing into the night sky.

Engh continued, "Donald didn't get up or say anything. But I could hear him breathing. Robert began to kick him down toward the edge. He moved him about five feet toward a little drop-off. Then Robert said, 'Let's check his pockets.' "

Both Fry and Engh rifled through Donald Tsosie's jacket and pants pockets and came up empty, even though he still did have fifteen cents on him. Engh continued, "Robert said, 'Let's check his boots. Indians sometimes hide their money there.' Robert took off one boot and didn't find anything. I had to struggle to take off his other boot. I didn't find anything. I could still hear him breathing.

"Robert kicked him off a ledge. Then he threw his boots down at him."

Fry apparently hit Tsosie in the head with one of the boots. He laughed and made a comment about it.

Engh said, "He also threw his cowboy hat over the edge. I couldn't tell if Donald was still moving. After that we tried picking up all the broken sticks. But it was pretty dark and I don't know if we got them all."

Les Engh had been terrified through most of the ordeal, but he said of Robert Fry, "He was hyped up and excited. A lot of energy."

They left Donald Tsosie lying below the cliff's edge, without any socks or boots, on a night when the temperature would drop down below freezing. They both knew that Tsosie was in bad shape, if he was still alive at all. Fry, for one, didn't care. He and Engh hopped back into his car and Fry started the vehicle, still pumped up about "rollin' the

Injun." He talked about it all the way down the Bluffs.

Donald Tsosie may have survived the push over the cliff, but he didn't survive for long. Sometime in the early-morning hours of April 1, 1998, he succumbed to his numerous wounds and died alone out on the Bluffs.

When they reached the San Juan River again, Fry stopped the car and threw the bloody sticks into the water. Engh thought they got rid of the shovel there as well, but he may have been mistaken about this. Fry would claim to have the shovel later on—a shovel that would eventually have its handle replaced.

Engh said, "We went to the river and threw the stuff in. I slipped and fell down a small bank into the river and got wet. I started climbing back up and Robert helped me up the bank."

Cold, wet and dispirited, Les Engh was in a dreadful mood by the time Fry drove them to an all-night restaurant after their murderous struggle out on the Bluffs. Engh wandered away from Fry to get some coffee and sit with friends. He not only wanted the warmth of the coffee, he wanted to get away from Fry as much as possible. Engh didn't tell his friends anything about what had just happened.

Bobby Fry, on the other hand, couldn't wait to tell someone. He sat down in a booth right across from his friend Darrell Hare, who was sitting alone. Hare noticed that when Fry walked up, he seemed very agitated and excited. Hare said later, "He was all hyped up. He began right away talking about how he and Engh had just rolled an Indian. He said, 'I pulled him out of my car and hit him. I told Les to grab the shovel. Les hit the guy in the neck with the blade. I think we killed him. Then we searched for money but didn't find any. Finally we pushed him over the cliff.' "

Fry was very animated during the whole telling of the story, but Hare thought it was just one more of Fry's bullshit tales. Fry had told so many stories of beating up people and killing them that Darrell Hare no longer gave them any credence.

In the days after the murder, both Les Engh and Robert Fry looked in the newspapers and listened to the radio for reports about a dead Native American up on the Bluffs. Engh said he even listened to the police scanner. Neither man heard a thing about any one being dead up there, and with good reason—once Fry had pushed Tsosie over a thirty-foot cliff, his body was hard to spot. Even if vultures came out to the spot, they were always to be seen circling around some dead animal out in the wilderness. The presence of vultures in the sky was nothing new in that area.

Engh said later, "Since I didn't hear anything, I thought Donald was still alive. That maybe he got up later and got a ride to the hospital. I was in denial. I never went back up there to check."

Engh was even more in denial about Tsosie's fate when he met Robert Fry a couple of nights later at Gators Bar. Engh related, "Robert said he went back up there and didn't see anything. I felt relieved. I never told any of my friends about the incident. I just wanted to forget it."

Fry may have told Les Engh that he went back to check on Donald Tsosie and the man's body wasn't there, but he told some of his other friends a very different story. Fry waited awhile to tell them this story, but he clearly indicated that he had gone back to check and found a dead body over the cliff. He later told Larry Hudson that he'd been in a fight on the Bluffs and killed an Indian. Then he said, "I went back a few days later and looked at the body. It had been eaten by coyotes. It was a real mess."

Hudson didn't believe the story about the murder or the body.

Genevieve Chee was worried when Donald Tsosie did not show up at the Safeway store, where he'd promised to meet her. He had always been punctual before and it was not like him. She went around Farmington and talked to a couple of his friends, but didn't know where he was. She even went to talk with the bartender at the Turn Around Bar, but he didn't have any information as well. She said later, "I looked all day. I looked all week. I couldn't find him. I was worried."

Between a week and two weeks after Robert Fry pushed Donald Tsosie over the cliff, a Navajo named Kenneth Jose was walking in the area. Jose had relatives who lived in the region. As he walked near the edge of the Bluffs, he spotted what he thought was someone lying in the dirt between some bushes, down the side of the cliff. He recalled, "At first I yelled down at him. I thought he was drunk or passed out. I went down a ways and saw blood. I got scared because he had blood on his head. I was pretty sure he was dead when I saw that."

Jose also saw some bloody sticks on the ground where he was standing. He didn't touch the sticks, but he did pick up a wristwatch that was nearby. Even though the wristwatch might have contained "ghost sickness," apparently Jose kept it for a while. It wasn't long, though, before he had second thoughts about keeping it.

Jose took the wristwatch and walked to a relative's house. He told the relatives there about the dead man. It's not clear if he said they shouldn't report it, but he did not want to become involved at this point. Jose had a warrant out for his arrest because he had failed to complete a DUI treatment course. And while he was there, Jose apparently thought more about the wristwatch. He gave it to a cousin, who soon passed it on to someone else.

During this period a couple of children may have also spotted the body as well, since police reports would later indicate that they did. The children, however, did not report it to the police. Unfortunately, on parts of the reservation near towns that sold liquor, like Farmington, the sight of a dead Native American out in the bushes or alongside a road was not a totally uncommon sight. Some died where they fell during inclement weather; others were hit by a vehicle as they stumbled down the road. Too many of them had been drinking. Too many of them died.

Donald Tsosie's sisters, Nora and Linda, were worried about him because so much time had gone by since they'd heard from him. He had not been seen by anyone since Genevieve Chee had let him off in Farmington on March 31. The sisters contacted the Navajo Tribal Police, but the officers could not find Tsosie, either. He was not in one of the jails or a detox center, and it was a large reservation. Men such as Tsosie often left from one region to another without telling anyone beforehand.

Weeks went by, and Kenneth Jose's conscience finally got the better of him. He walked all the way to the sheriff's office in Aztec, not an insubstantial feat, and reported a dead body up on the Bluffs. He said later, "I knew I might get arrested when I told the police about the body. I did it anyway."

This event occurred on April 29, 1998, almost a month after Fry and Engh murdered Donald Tsosie. Jose talked to Detective Tim Black and was indeed arrested for his outstanding warrant, but not before he told Detective Black about all that he'd seen. Jose told Detective Black that he'd discovered the body the day after Christmas. Being somewhat unfamiliar with Christian holidays, Jose had mistaken Easter for Christmas. He and Black finally realized that he was talking about Easter, which had taken place on April 12. This would have put him on the Bluffs almost two weeks after Donald Tsosie was murdered.

Detective Black, realizing there might be important shoe impressions up at the area near the body, asked for Kenneth Jose's shoes, and received them without an argument. With Jose's declaration about the body, a host of law enforcement officers began to congregate up on the Bluffs. Two of the first officers on the scene were San Juan County sheriff's deputy John Sampson and sheriff's sergeant Mike Marshall.

At 6:20 P.M. on April 29, Deputy Sampson contacted a woman who said she knew where the body was. Whether she was a relative of Kenneth Jose or not is not clear. The officers were directed to Milepost 102 on the Bisti Highway and then down a dirt road for about a quarter mile. While Sampson talked to the woman, Marshall climbed down the slope and determined that the body was that of a deceased male.

Detective Black arrived on the scene at 6:45 P.M. to find that the area was by now swarming with law enforcement officers. Besides the San Juan County deputies, there were also law enforcement agents of the Bureau of Land Management (BLM). Black worried about contamination of the site by so many officers walking around with no police tape cordoning off the area. He said later, "Guys were walking all over the place."

Detective Black had been with the force since 1992 and had received four hundred hours of police academy training, five hundred hours of advanced training and many hours of concentrating on homicide cases. He was a skilled crime technician as well as detective, but he had his work cut out for him on the Bluffs with a body that had been there for nearly a month.

Detective Black noted that the body was lying facedown, dressed in new blue jeans, blue-and-white-striped shirt and turquoise jacket. Detective Black also noted there were lots of shoe prints up near the roadway, but none leading down to the body, which lay on a ledge just before a steep drop-off of about 150 feet into the canyon below. He saw a couple of cowboy boots; one near the body and another slightly past it near the ledge. He also discovered a cowboy hat with the name Donald Tsosie stenciled inside. At this point he didn't know if it belonged to the dead man or was dropped by someone else who had been in the vicinity. With winds always blowing in the area, it even could have drifted there from a long way away.

It was starting to get dark at that time of year up on the Bluffs, and Detective Black made a quick videotape of the area, took some crime scene photos with a regular camera and put up yellow police-tape around the perimeter. He and the others also determined one other piece of very key evidence—the body lay about fifteen hundred feet outside of the Navajo Reservation. This meant that it would be a San Juan County Sheriff's Officer case. Had it been on reservation land, it would have been a case for the FBI.

The next morning Detective Black and Detective Eric Johnson went back to the scene of the body and began to photograph the area and items they thought might be related to it. They were already treating the area as if a homicide had occurred there rather than a natural death. One of the first photos was of tire impressions in the soft sand on the roadway above the body. The impressions seemed to be made by a vehicle that had suddenly swerved off the road into the sand. It left a deep impression where its front passenger tire had been. The tire impression also appeared to have been there for some time, perhaps a month, which would be consistent with a body in the area showing this many signs of decomposition.

Up in the locale by the tire impression, Detective Black said, "It looked like something had happened there. Like some kind of altercation. Everything happened in about a ten- to twenty-foot area." Unofficially, this was called the "scuffle zone."

Detective Black also noticed a lens that had popped out of a pair of sunglasses. He didn't know if it belonged to the crime, but he photographed and collected it. Even more important, he observed several broken sticks lying on the ground. They appeared to have dried blood on them. He photographed and collected them as evidence as well.

The detectives made plaster casts of the tire impressions and shoe impressions in the immediate scuffle zone. It was hard making impressions in the soft sand, and many didn't work at all for shoe prints. Their best means of preserving them as evidence was by photography.

The detectives worked all around the immediate area, the primary scene, which contained some Budweiser beer cans, which had been ripped apart after the contents had been consumed. It was not known if these cans had any relation to the crime scene, but they were noted anyway. As the officers worked their way up the road, they came to a place termed the secondary scene. It was about three hundred feet from the primary scene, but like the first area it contained some Budweiser cans that appeared to have been ripped open in the same way. This secondary scene was located at the end of the Bluffs in an area known locally as Scorpion Point. From above, it did look like the tail of a scorpion at the end of a long ridge. There didn't seem to have been as much activity up here, and the officers weren't sure if it was connected to the primary scene, or not, but they weren't ruling it out.

Another San Juan County sheriff's officer arrived on the scene that day as well. He was Detective Terry Eagle. He had already been involved in sixteen homicide cases and was a fingerprint analysis expert. Even though that was his area of expertise, for some reason he was put in charge of taking photographs that day. Eagle didn't have as much training in this area, and he forgot to bring along one important piece of equipment, a tripod. Without it, he couldn't get the clarity in some shots that he needed, nor could he get the right angle. The best angle for taking a crime scene photo is directly from above and a tripod is essential. A photo from directly above gives the truest image without any distortion.

As Detective Greg Fallis pointed out in his book *A Murder,* "Detectives don't always know what information is going to be important in solving the crime and getting the perpetrator convicted. It's better to waste film on photographs that may not be needed than a photograph not taken. Film is cheap." With this in mind, nearly two hundred evidence photographs were taken at the crime scene on the Bluffs.

As Detective Eagle walked through the area, photographing items with yellow numbered plastic cones set up next to them, some of the first key items he shot were three bloody sticks. He recalled later, "They were like a broom handle. Not a pool cue." The bloodstains were mainly around the sharpened ends.

There was also a patch of blood-soaked soil and a hank of blood-soaked hair. To Eagle's eyes, it appeared that the hair might have been ripped off someone's head during a fight. This bit of bloody hair was later matched to Donald Tsosie.

A Budweiser can was collected near the primary scene, as well as a sock. Since the body of the man down the cliff had no socks, it was assumed that the sock probably was his. The detectives also found a broken tooth lying on the ground and surmised someone had lost it during a fight.

Detective Black was still worried about all the activity in the area. Sheriff's officers and Bureau of Land Management officers had tromped all over the top of the Bluffs. The area certainly did not fit into the hypothetical guidelines laid down by the Sichie Finger Print Laboratories Evidence Collection manual. The manual stated, "Clear all except essential and authorized persons from the crime scene area. This includes all officers who are not needed for specific functions. The more people present, the more chance for damage and loss of evidence."

Of course, crime scenes rarely match up to ideal guidelines. Former major-crime investigator and Ph.D. Anne Wingate commented in her writer's guide, *Scene of the Crime*, "The ideal situation is what you never have. The least competent person in the police department [for these types of crimes] is always the first on the scene."

Unfortunately for the crime scene on the Bluffs, someone had even made a swipe mark on one of the boot prints. The swipe appeared to have come from someone rubbing their fingers over the print. Whether this had been intentional or an accident, it was impossible to say except by the person who had done it. Detective Black said later, "The crime scene was already contaminated." But then he added, "At least the area where the 'scuffle' had taken place was not contaminated. Everyone had stayed out of there."

Detective Black noted that the decomposition of the body indicated that the crime had taken place some weeks in the past. He knew that in the interval it had rained on the Bluffs and the wind had blown every day as it does in spring in the desert. At times the wind had blown with strong gusts, which tended to obscure footprints and tire tread marks even more.

Finally it was time to remove Donald Tsosie's body from the scene. Since it was down about thirty feet from the roadway, and right on the edge of a 150-foot drop, the county's search-and-rescue crew was called in to extricate it. Ironically, this was the same search-and-rescue team that Matt Trecker wanted to join someday. The crew finally got Tsosie's body up to the roadway and into an ambulance by midafternoon. The body was shipped off to the medical examiner's office in Albuquerque, to the same ME office where Fleming and Trecker's bodies had been taken in 1996.

* * *

Dr. Marcus Majowsky was the forensic pathologist and ME investigator in Albuquerque by May 1998. On May 1, 1998, he examined the body of Donald Tsosie and noted that decomposition was consistent with someone who had died a month earlier. Dr. Majowsky examined the body both externally and internally. Even though the injuries were altered or obscured by decomposition, he was still able to make several findings.

Majowsky decided that Tsosie could not have moved very far once he had been tossed down the cliff due to injuries to his head, eyes and neck. Majowsky could see bone in some areas on the head through lacerations. Internally the neck was severely injured, with fractured cartilage. There were also four teeth missing and he surmised they had come out around the time of the death, and not before.

There were fractures to the ribs, three on the left side and two on the right. There were also injuries to the arms, hands and over the knuckles on the right hand. These were tearing or cutting injuries consistent with defensive wounds. Two crescent-shaped wounds on the back were consistent with wounds that could have been made by a shovel blade.

Dr. Majowsky's initial cause of death for the body was listed as an injury to the neck. He later amended this conclusion by saying that the victim could have died from hypothermia. If this was the case, then Donald Tsosie was not dead when Robert Fry pushed him over the cliff. Instead, he may have lingered on for a while, unable to move, and eventually died in the bitter cold of an April night.

Meanwhile, a couple of detectives ran tests for

latent fingerprints on the items seized near the body. One of the detectives was Terry Eagle, who tried to lift prints from the broken bloody sticks, but was unable to do so. He also tried lifting prints from beer cans taken from the primary scene and at the secondary scene at Scorpion Point, but these had been exposed to the elements for too long. Lifting prints from slick items like beer cans is difficult under the best of circumstances. On metal surfaces particle reagent fingerprinting may work. The small particle reagent adheres to the fatty constituents of latent fingerprints to form a gray deposit. But enameled surfaces, such as those on beer cans, disrupt the process and make it less viable.

Detective Thomas Brown from the Farmington Police Department had better luck on some items. He'd been a crime scene analyst since 1982, completing two FBI courses on fingerprint examination. He'd also taken 240 hours of training with the New Jersey police. By 1998, he'd done literally thousands of fingerprint collections. Like Detective Eagle, he got no prints from the beer cans, and Detective Brown determined that the sunglasses' lens were not part of the crime scene. But he did receive a copy of Donald Tsosie's fingerprints from the Gallup detoxification center. These fingerprints matched prints found on several items, as well as those of the victim. Now the police could say for sure that the body belonged to Donald Tsosie. The cowboy hat with his name in it definitely was connected to the victim, and not from a perpetrator or simply in the area by accident.

Prints belonging to Tsosie were found on several items picked up at the Bluffs, but there was not one print linked to either Robert Fry or Les Engh. In all the fighting and bloodletting, they had been incredibly lucky not to have left a single fingerprint on any item.

The prints may have proved that the victim was Donald Tsosie, but they did not tell where he came from or what he was doing up there on the Bluffs. An inquiry went out through the Navajo Tribal Police and Investigator Ernie Yazzie ran across information that two Navajo women were asking about their missing brother, Donald Tsosie. He had been missing for over a month by May 1998. Yazzie contacted the San Juan County Sheriff's Department, and Detective Black went to visit Donald's sisters. Linda told him the last time they had seen Donald was when he came by her residence on March 29, 1998, in the company of his girlfriend, Genevieve Chee.

There was one more law enforcement officer who joined the case by May 1998—Detective Bob Melton. On May 21, he spoke with Genevieve Chee about Donald, and he wrote in his report, "Ms. Chee stated that she was the girlfriend of Donald Tsosie and the two had been living together since the 14th of February 1998. Ms. Chee went on to say that the last time she saw Donald was on the 31st of March 1998, when she dropped him off at BCI Biological where he would go every week [sic] to sell his plasma. When she returned to pick him up, he was not there. When he returned, he told her that they would not take his blood because his blood pressure was too high. As a result, he made an appointment for the next morning to try again to sell his plasma. Although Ms. Chee tried to convince him to return home with her, he stated he wanted to stay in Farmington to make his appointment in the morning. When she returned a few days later at their prearranged meeting place, Donald was not there, and she was unable to locate him."

Detective Black did some asking around with people who lived up on the Bluffs near Scorpion Point. He discovered that a couple of kids had seen Donald Tsosie's body weeks before the police were there, but they had not reported it to the authorities. Black interviewed these two for several hours, with the initial thought that they might be suspects. As time went on, however, he dismissed them as being involved with the crime. Whoever had done the murder used a vehicle, and the kids didn't have access to one. They also had an alibi as to where they were at that time, and it seemed to hold water. The two had no fingerprints that were lifted from any of the items at the scuffle zone, nor did their shoe sizes fit any of the imprints left in the sandy soil.

For a while, Kenneth Jose was looked upon as a potential suspect in the case as well. After all, he was the one who reported the body to police, weeks after he said he'd seen it in the first place, and often the first person who reports a murder is the one who perpetrated the crime. But after a while, Jose's alibi checked out and he was dismissed as a suspect.

Two short articles came out about Donald Tsosie's death in the *Farmington Daily Times*. They were just brief descriptions of who he was and how his body had been found up at the Bluffs. The police withheld one vital piece of information—that his boots had been found near his body. If anyone in the future ever mentioned this fact, then the police knew the person had to have been out at the crime scene or at least heard of it from someone who had been there at the time of the murder.

As time went by, a couple of strange incidents helped divert attention away from what had really occurred to Donald Tsosie and when it had taken place. Detective Black recovered a letter from a black duffel bag that had belonged to Donald Tsosie. Tsosie had stored it at one of his sister's homes. The letter mentioned a white woman who lived in the Farmington area. It was not apparent that Tsosie was romantically involved with her, but it did portray her as a friend. It was posited that he had gone to see her in Farmington around March 31 and she was somehow connected to his murder or at least had seen him on that date.

This idea was given added credence when Paul James, Donald Tsosie's half brother, gave a very rambling, but intriguing, story to the investigators. Detective Melton went out to find James on the very extensive Navajo Reservation, which was akin to finding a needle in a haystack. James lived near Sheep Springs out on Highway 666, which was in some parlance known as "the Devil's Highway," for its symbolic numbering. To certain people, 666 meant "the Mark of the Beast." James was not there, but Melton had a hunch. He knew about James's proclivity for alcohol. Melton drove down to Gallup and found James in the detoxification center there. In fact, by 1998, James had been in that center or the one in Farmington nearly two hundred times.

James was brought back to Farmington and began telling a circuitous tale to officers about the last time he saw Donald Tsosie alive. He said it had occurred around Easter, because he remembered children hunting Easter eggs. But James had a habit of mixing up dates, and the date was only approximate. Nonetheless, the Easter eggs anecdote gave a clue as to the time frame.

James told the detective that he had seen Donald Tsosie in the Safeway parking lot with a white woman. She was driving a purple Neon. She and Donald were together, and three white men were giving them a bad time. They didn't seem to like the fact that Tsosie was with a white woman. James supposedly said to Tsosie that they ought to leave the area, but according to James, Tsosie said leave him alone. Then Tsosie and the white woman left in her car. The three white men also left. According to James, the white men were driving a white pickup with a horse on the license plates. The image was not unlike the symbol of a bucking horse displayed on Wyoming license plates.

Paul James's story muddied the waters as far as the investigation of Donald Tsosie's death went. The officers didn't know how much of it to believe, since James was a chronic alcoholic and inebriated on the day he told his story. Nonetheless, his mention of the Safeway store jibed with Genevieve Chee's admission that it was the spot where she and Tsosie always met when she picked him up in Farmington. And James's mention of the white woman might have corresponded to Tsosie's letter found in his duffel bag. The detectives could not rule out three white men giving Tsosie a bad time, nor the item about the Wyoming plates.

None of the items found at the murder scene gave any clues as to who his murderer was. Detective Melton said, "During the next several months, numerous interviews were conducted and leads were followed, but no additional information was obtained to allow officers to identify a suspect in the case."

Genevieve Chee and Donald Tsosie's relatives were heartbroken. Chee cried later, "I kept expecting him to come home. He never did."

Regina, Donald's niece, said, "I couldn't believe he was gone. I keep thinking he's just out of town having a good time."

Regina went on to say that she was about to

graduate from high school at the time when the news about her uncle arrived. All of the graduation plans had to be put on hold and the family had to deal with Donald's death. Everyone was devastated. "It was terrible," she said, and even worse, she didn't have a photograph of her uncle to remember him by.

One person not devastated by Donald Tsosie's loss was Robert Fry. He had other things to deal with in 1998 and 1999. Incredibly, he had taken time out during his whole ordeal of the Rhonda Knott rape and kidnapping case to murder Donald Tsosie up on the Bluffs. He had done the crime as if he had not a care in the world, as far as other serious legal matters went.

However, once the jury decided Fry was guilty of reckless use of a firearm and drunk driving in the Knott case, he was sent to the San Juan County Detention Center in 1999. He apparently never talked about the murder of Tsosie while he was incarcerated. But that was certainly not the case once he was released in spring 2000.

When Fry got back on the streets of Farmington, he began bragging about what he and Les Engh had done to an Injun back in March 1998. And all of these stories came in slightly different versions.

Around May 1, 2000, Robert Fry was playing a computer game with his friend Larry Hudson. While playing the game, Fry suddenly said, "Me and Les picked up a guy at the Copper Penny (a restaurant connected to the Turn Around Bar). An Indian. He was dressed nicely. Had a nice hat. Nice shirt. We figured he had money. He asked for a ride. We said we were going to Grants (a town down the Bisti Highway past Crownpoint). We started on the road that way and I heard a choking sound. I saw Les choking the guy with a belt. I got up to the top of the hill and pulled off. Then I pulled the guy out and started to beat him."

Hudson knew this area on the Bluffs well, having been there in the past. Fry continued, "At some point I got a stick and was hitting him with it. I was laughing because the stick kept breaking. Then I started stabbing him with the sharp end. I stabbed him in the eyes."

Fry then spoke of using a shovel on the Indian. He said, "I told Engh to get the shovel out of the back of the car. He hit him with it and then I did."

For some reason Fry decided to embellish his tale, which was mostly true, with a falsehood. He said, "I finished the guy off with a hammer blow to the head."

Hudson had heard so many of these violent stories from Fry that he blew this one off as just one more "bullshit tale."

Fry kept on with his story, however. He said, "We (he and Engh) went home and watched the news and read the newspapers. For weeks there wasn't anything about it. So I went back out to the Bluffs. The coyotes had eaten the body. It was a real mess."

Hudson particularly dismissed this part of the story. He said later, "Generally, coyotes will eat part of a body, but not all of it. Bobby's story sounded like a pack of lies."

Hudson and Fry decided about a week later to go fishing and do some camping at Navajo Lake, about thirty miles northeast of Farmington. It was May 6, 2000, and Fry stopped at the local Kmart and bought a fishing license. The two men took along camping gear, sleeping bags and food. They stopped at a convenience store near the lake and bought some beer. Bobby Fry was soon in his drinking mode, once they got to the lake, and he had eleven beers for every one Hudson drank.

Once Fry started drinking, he began to tell his story again about "rollin' an Indian up at the Bluffs." Hudson was tired of it, and said, "I'd rather go watch my fishing pole than listen to this!"

Not long after the fishing trip, Robert Fry took a drive up to Alexis Diego's residence near Durango, Colorado. She had moved up there but still remained in touch with him, even though she alleged that he had raped her when she was only sixteen years old. She also would say later that although he had raped her, she had forgiven him. Whatever the reason, Diego was still in touch with Fry and had some very interesting things to say about Fry's trips up to the Durango area.

According to Alexis Diego, Fry had several homosexual "boyfriends" in the Durango area. She also surmised that he might have been a "switch-hitter," someone who liked sex with men or women. After all, according to her, he had raped her while she was passed out when she was sixteen years old and was known to have other girlfriends around the Farmington area over the years, but he seemed to like boys as well. She even wondered if his confusion about his preferred sexual partners helped fuel his rage.

Diego said, "When Bobby came up to Durango, he painted his fingernails, put on mascara and acted real swishy. It was very odd, since he always tried acting tough down in Farmington. It was like he was leading two different lives. I think he only acted that way up here (in Durango) so he could have that other image back in Farmington. He didn't want people there to find out about it."

Only one other person ever alluded to this side of Robert Fry. Larry Hudson said that back in his teenage years, Fry had put on a miniskirt as a joke.

On this particular occasion of Robert Fry being

in Durango in May 2000, Darrell Hare was also on hand with Alexis Diego. All three of them were sitting around watching *America's Funniest Home Videos* on television and in one of the videos a person threw a shoe and hit someone in the head. Bobby Fry laughed and told Hare and Diego, "That's what I did. I threw a boot down and hit an Indian in the head. It was so funny." Then he proceeded to tell them about the murder scene up at the Bluffs, where he had killed Tsosie. He even mentioned Scorpion Point.

Diego said later, "The whole time he told the story, he was laughing and excited. I never believed these stories before. But this time I began to wonder."

Part of the reason Diego believed him was his inclusion of the shovel in the tale. She knew he always kept a small shovel in his car. She said, "I don't think there was a time it wasn't there."

Robert Fry may have been emboldened to tell his story of murdering Donald Tsosie to friends exactly because he had told so many stories like this before. It was hard for anyone to tell what was true and what was pure fantasy. Besides, he had gotten away with three murders so far, and law enforcement seemed further away than ever in tracking them back to him. But most of all, Bobby Fry needed an audience for the stories of his murders. He just couldn't keep the truth hidden for long. Both Hare and Diego told later of how animated he was while telling the story about killing an Indian. Hare said, "He was very excited about it." And Diego added, "His eyes—they'd light up when he talked about it."

Curiously enough, the one detail in his story to Larry Hudson about using a hammer blow "to finish off the guy" was one thing Fry had never done, but it must have been an image that he savored. Perhaps Fry remembered such references from the days when he used to listen to the Misfits. In their song "American Nightmare," the lyrics spoke of putting an ax in a girl's head. Strangely enough, the song also spoke of going down a highway with three inverted 9s on a road sign, in other words, 666—just like the highway near Shiprock. Within a month this flight of fantasy would become all too real for Robert Fry and his next victim. He would deliver a hammer blow to the head of a woman near Highway 666.

Chapter 6

Sledgehammer Blows

Betty Lee, a Navajo, had several brothers and sisters. One sister, Margaret, later said, "Betty and I were daddy's girls. Father believed in the traditional ways and had a sense of humor. So did Betty. She used to tease him a lot, and he liked it."

Her brother Phillip said that when their father died, Betty took it very hard.

Another relative, Dorothy, would recall growing up in Shiprock, saying that Betty's mother was very traditional and spoke very little English. She was very wise, however, and insisted on a good education for all her children. Unlike Donald Tsosie and his sisters, Betty could go to school in her own home-town of Shiprock, with friends, right up through high school.

Betty's mother stressed to the children that they should live both in the traditional world and the modern Anglo society. Her sister Evelyn added that Betty learned the most Navajo of arts, weaving, by watching her mother. She had a real talent in that area and a respect for the old ways. She could make rugs of intricate design and beauty.

She strove to attain *hozro,* a Navajo concept akin to the Anglo concept of harmony—harmony with all things around her, both animate and inanimate. Even rocks and trees around Shiprock were imbued with spirit. Betty Lee was cognizant of her clan and its interconnection with all the other clans of the Navajo people. She was a daughter of Dinétah.

From a very early age, Betty Lee had an appreciation for the landscape of her youth. She noticed the changing of the seasons and commented to her sisters about the return of life each spring. On a very personal level, she lived in the way Dawn Boy had admonished, "Go with beauty all around you." Betty did appreciate the beauty of her homeland and often spoke to others about it.

She was a girl who lived in two worlds—that of the Anglos in the region, whose stores, gas stations and fast-food marts were in the town of Shiprock. In fact, she enjoyed the McDonalds and Kentucky Fried Chicken outlets there, but the legends of her people were never forgotten or ignored. These were not half-remembered legends, but rather a living link to the past.

With most Navajos, the world of stories and the world of reality are one. The Holy People live in the surrounding area—in fact, they are right outside the doors of the Kentucky Fried Chicken and Taco Bell outlets. There is no contradiction in a Texaco station being next to a rock where one of the Hero Twins once took his rest. It may be hard, sometimes, to live in both worlds, but it is not impossible.

Betty Lee knew this. She knew the sacred chants that connected her people to the Holy Ones, the Yeibachai, in the Night Way. For Betty Lee, like others, the Night Way was the introduction into the Navajo ceremonial life.

The Night Way is very important to the Navajo and can only take place between the first frost and the first thunderstorm, when the snakes are in hibernation and there is no danger from lightning. The Night Way goes on for nine nights, and on the last night, boys and girls between the ages of seven and thirteen may be brought in for initiation to the ceremonial life of an adult. Two masked figures appear before the youths—Grandfather of the Monsters and Female Divinity. Each of the boys is led out into the firelight and one of the masked figures places sacred corn pollen on his naked shoulder. Another masked impersonator strikes the boy with a handful of reeds. Then the girls are marked with sacred corn pollen.

After the corn pollen is dispersed, the impersonators remove their fearsome masks and reveal to the children that they are not really gods, but people that they know. Then the children have masks placed on their heads so they may see out through the eye slots. It is so they can see the world the way a god does.

Finally at the end of the ceremony, with the coming of dawn, everyone faces to the east and says the Dawn Prayer, followed by the Bluebird Song:

> *The Bluebird has a voice.*
> *His voice is melodious and flows with gladness,*
> *Bluebird calls, bluebird calls.*

By the summer of 2000, Betty Lee of Shiprock, New Mexico, was thirty-six years old and had five children. She was taking business courses at the local campus of Diné College to get a good-paying job. Sitting atop a rise near town, the college looked out over the vast plain of the San Juan River. To the west, Rock with Wings was plainly visible like a sentinel to the memory of Monster Slayer.

Betty Lee had led a fairly conventional life within her community and her clan, but that had not been the case for one of her brothers and one of her sisters. Her brother Norman Lee was an officer with the Navajo police force. He served in the nearby region around Shiprock, the same area where Jim Chee, Tony Hillerman's fictional hero, was an officer.

Betty Lee's sister Dorothy Fulton had an even more incredible tale despite humble beginnings. In 2000, Fulton was the chief criminal investigator for the entire Navajo Nation. She oversaw an area that covered twenty-five thousand square miles and included a quarter million of her fellow tribe members. In 1998, she gave a very insightful interview on the radio program *Native America Calling*. The subject was about Native American peace officers.

By that year, Fulton had been in law enforcement for fourteen years and was the mother of three children. Asked how she had become interested in law enforcement, she said that originally she hadn't been interested in it at all. She had wanted to go to Georgetown Law School and become a lawyer. But while interning for a local lawyer in the Navajo region, she took a leave of absence one summer to work with an officer of the Navajo police on crime investigation. Fulton said she became immediately hooked. The following winter, she dropped all plans of becoming a lawyer and went to the Navajo Police Academy in Window Rock, Arizona.

Asked by the radio host what she found fascinating about criminal investigations, Fulton answered, "A sergeant took me on a case that was a homicide.

I was fascinated by the fact that a life could be taken just like that. The spirit of a person."

Fulton was always interested in the medical aspects of a crime scene. She did many drug and narcotics investigations with surrounding state agencies and the United States Drug Enforcement Agency (DEA). She also worked on some cases with the neighboring Jicarilla Apache police force. All of these cases exposed her to different managerial practices than were used within the Navajo Tribal Police.

When Fulton got back to her own reservation, she wasn't always satisfied with the way things were done, and there were other investigators who thought the same way she did. One day a fellow investigator told her that instead of complaining about things, they should do something about it. Fulton agreed and made a pact with the others to change things. She was then a sergeant, but before long became a lieutenant. When time came for applications for the top post, she scored highest among the contenders and was named chief investigator.

During the radio interview the host pointed out that Navajos traditionally do not like dealing with the dead, especially if they have been murdered. He asked how she personally dealt with that aspect of Navajo life.

Fulton answered that her department dealt with over three hundred death cases annually. Then she said, "From my personal perspective, I come from a very traditional background. My mother is not English speaking. She prepared me from the very beginning. She told me never to be afraid. She would say, 'That person, whose spirit has been taken, still needs your care.' "

Fulton admitted that even in the present day,

Navajo emergency medical technicians were still apprehensive about approaching a corpse. She said often her own investigators had to cover a body with a blanket or tarp before the EMTs would place it in an ambulance for transportation to a medical examiner.

Asked how good the training was for a Navajo police officer just joining the force, Fulton said that the new recruit received two or three times the amount of training a policeman might get at a nearby city or county off the reservation. Part of the reason was that they had to know so many regulations. The recruits not only had to deal with Navajo law, but they also had to deal with New Mexico, Arizona and Utah state laws. It all came with the territory out on the Big Rez.

Asked what were her greatest challenges, Fulton answered that the pay needed to be higher for investigators and they needed more sophisticated equipment. And there was always the need for more officers for such a large jurisdiction. As an example, she pointed out a recent murder on the Navajo Reservation that included four victims. The nearest tribal police station had been in Crownpoint, about a two-hour drive over bad roads from the murder scene. A lot of terrible things could happen out there on the reservation she said. Little did she know at the time of the interview, one of those "terrible things" was about to happen to Betty Lee.

One hundred fifty miles northeast of where Dorothy Fulton sat in her office at Window Rock, Arizona, Betty lived along the margin of the San Juan River. As June 2000 came on, she commented to a friend that she was glad to see spring finally arriving on the high desert. Betty always had an eye for the beauty around her—taking notice of the changing seasons as the Holy People had instructed. Betty had recently given a heart-shaped clock to her sister Evelyn for her birthday. She told Evelyn that whenever she looked at the clock, she would be reminded of her.

On June 8, 2000, Betty Lee looked forward to a field trip from Diné College, scheduled for the next day. On the night before the trip, however, she took a ride into Farmington with two individuals, Gloria Charley and a woman named Tina. They decided to have a few drinks in town before heading home to Shiprock.

Two other people were drinking in Farmington that night—Leslie Engh and Robert Fry. Engh had apparently learned nothing about how dangerous it was to hang around Fry, especially when he'd been drinking to excess. And that's exactly what Fry did at The Top Deck Lounge that night. Once he'd had a few too many, he became belligerent and loudmouthed, as usual.

After The Top Deck closed at 2:00 A.M., Fry and Engh went to one of their all-night hangouts, The Kettle restaurant. Fry was still in an antagonistic mood. It wasn't long before he got into a heated argument with another customer, "CC" inside the restaurant. Several of Fry's friends witnessed this altercation and recalled it later.

Steve Lavery noted that Fry looked over at CC and became very agitated. After a while Lavery noticed Fry go out to his car and come back into the restaurant wearing his jacket. Lavery thought that Fry might have a pistol in the pocket.

Telani Sokolowski, another friend of Fry's, noted

the argument between Fry and CC. Fry went out to his car and came back wearing the jacket; she thought he might have a knife underneath it.

When he sat down next to her, she asked him, "What's going on, Bobby?"

He muttered, "Someone's going to die!"

Robert Fry then got up and spoke for a while with his friend David Johnson. He told Johnson that he had a bowie knife and that he was going to stick someone. He seemed to indicate that CC was his intended victim.

Les Engh was getting very nervous about the whole affair. He was worried that Fry might jump up with his knife and attack CC at any time. Engh recalled later, "Robert was very intoxicated and speaking out obnoxiously. He was wanting to kick CC's ass. I tried to keep them apart. Robert went outside and came back in with a jacket on and was a little perturbed. He was acting antsy and didn't want to settle down."

In an attempt to get Fry out of there before things escalated, Engh said that he wanted to leave and go get some cigarettes. This comment had the desired effect and Fry left the restaurant with Engh after giving CC a few more insults. Unluckily for Engh, his action to avoid trouble was just about to take them out of the frying pan and into the fire.

Angry, and perhaps embarrassed that he had backed down from a fight in front of Les Engh and his friends—after telling them repeated stories of what a tough fighter he was—Robert Fry once again muttered, "Someone's gonna die tonight."

Fry began to cruise around Farmington, and Engh had the feeling that he was looking for someone to get into a fight with. Engh felt that Fry was in the same frame of mind as he had been when they'd picked up Donald Tsosie at the Turn Around Bar two years before. In fact, it was almost the same time of night when they stopped at the Apache Y convenience store so that Engh could buy some cigarettes. Fry did not follow him into the store.

When Engh came outside, he found Robert Fry talking to a woman who was standing at a phone booth and crying. Engh thought that she was either Native American or Hispanic. Engh distinctly heard Fry say to the woman, "I hate to see a woman cry. So I'll take you at least as far as Kirtland."

Kirtland was a small town between Farmington and Shiprock. As in the case with Donald Tsosie, Les Engh climbed into the backseat of Fry's Ford Aspire and the woman hopped into the front passenger seat next to Fry. As they began to drive west on Highway 64/550, toward U.S. 666, Engh discovered that the woman had been crying because two of her girlfriends had left her in Farmington without a ride back to Shiprock, where she lived. The woman had medium-length brown hair and appeared to be in her thirties.

As they were driving toward Kirtland in the dark, early-morning hours of June 9, Fry suddenly turned off onto a dirt road called County Road 6480, more commonly called CR 6480. He kept driving up the narrow road until they were out of sight of all habitation. Then he pulled to a stop. By this point the woman was getting very nervous. Robert Fry tried to calm her down by saying, "I've just got to take a piss."

She didn't buy it. The woman jumped out of the car and started to run up the dirt roadway, back toward Highway 64. Fry ran around to the back of the car and yelled for her to come back. She didn't comply.

Fry cursed and jumped back into the driver's seat. He turned the vehicle around, drove back on the dirt road and pulled up alongside the woman. He said he was sorry for scaring her, and that he'd give her a ride back home. She still seemed edgy about him, but decided that she was too far from home at this time of morning to be wandering around alone. She got back into the car with Fry and Engh.

Once the woman was back in the car, Fry drove as if he was going toward the highway. Before he'd gone very far, however, he suddenly stopped, and once again Les Engh watched with mounting horror as things spun out of control, knowing he was about to be pulled into one more of Bobby Fry's murderous schemes.

Fry got out and moved around to the front passenger door and pulled the woman out of the car by her hair. The woman screamed, "Why are you doing this to me?"

"Grab her legs!" Fry yelled at Engh.

Engh got out of the car and did as Fry instructed. He wasn't sure if Fry wanted to rape her or not. It certainly looked that way. But the woman kept struggling and yelling and in response Fry grabbed her top and pulled it up over her breasts. She struggled and Fry yelled for Les Engh to help him subdue her.

The woman kept wiggling and fighting back. Fry angrily reached around from behind her and pulled out his knife. He stabbed her in the chest. It was such a savage blow that the knife became stuck in her chest wall only a fraction of an inch above her heart.

Incredibly, the woman was able to pull the knife out, break free from Fry and run away. As she did, she threw the knife down into a small ravine by the side of the road.

The woman staggered naked and bleeding down the dirt roadway, back toward the highway. Fry yelled at Engh to grab a flashlight and go look for the knife. Then Fry grabbed a very deadly instrument and ran after her—a small sledgehammer that he carried around in his car. It was the same kind of hammer he had lied to Larry Hudson about, claiming that he had used it to kill an Indian up on the Bluffs. Now he was in deadly earnest to do just that.

The woman could only stagger ahead as her wound continued to bleed. Fry came up from behind and tripped her. She tumbled into the dirt. As Robert Fry restrained her, Les Engh happened to look in his direction. The woman was still screaming. Engh caught his breath. Fry lifted the sledgehammer and brought it downward to where the woman lay. She screamed one more time. Fry lifted the sledgehammer and swung it again and again. It wasn't long before all of the woman's screams had ceased. Les Engh had no doubt in his mind that she was dead.

Engh couldn't find the knife, but rather than giving up in that quest, Fry ordered him to keep searching for it. Engh did this until the batteries of the flashlight started to fail. At that point Fry had Engh help him pull the woman's body off the road. They dragged her facedown in the dirt for 120 feet and dropped her body behind some bushes. Then they both kicked her clothing into a small ravine.

During this whole episode Engh noticed that once again Fry seemed very "energized" by a killing. "He was all hyped-up," Engh later said.

Robert Fry had just become energized by the murder of thirty-six-year-old Betty Lee.

As in the murders at The Eclectic and the killing of Donald Tsosie, no one had seen the crime except for the person Fry was with at the time. And he had Engh so afraid of him, he was sure that Les would never tell. His luck seemed to be holding.

But luck has a funny way of disappearing. In Navajo legend, Coyote is the trickster who leads humans down a trail of deceit to their own destruction, and Coyote was just about to pull one of his tricks on Robert Fry.

Fry drove his Ford Aspire back toward the blacktop highway when suddenly, a little over a mile from the crime scene, he became stuck in soft sand. The harder he tried to pull the vehicle out of the sand, the worse it became stuck. No amount of pushing or pulling could get it unstuck.

Fry did not panic yet, but he was becoming worried. Just like at The Eclectic, it would be light in a few hours, and they had to get as far away from the murder scene as possible. Fry used a cell phone that his mother had let him borrow. In fact, the cell phone was from the probation department. He called his parents at their home, even though it was around 4:00 A.M., to come out and help them be extricated from the sand. Gloria woke her husband, James, they got dressed and drove out to the isolated area.

Gloria and James finally found where Robert's car was bogged down, and gave Les Engh a ride home. Then the two of them took Robert back to their house to change clothes before returning to try and get Robert's car out of the sand. Robert and his dad went in James's pickup truck and Gloria went in another vehicle. When Gloria finally got out to the area, she drove around a bend and discovered that not only was Robert's Ford

Aspire stuck, but that her husband's pickup truck was stuck as well.

Now began a scenario of rescuers and rescued, which would have been comic, had a murder not just occurred. The Frys called a tow truck service and the tow vehicle arrived, driven by a man named Floyd Robinson. He tried to extricate the passenger car and pickup truck, but became stuck himself. Now there were three marooned vehicles out on CR 6480. Robinson had to call for assistance from another tow truck company named Bloomfield Towing.

Charley Bergin, of Bloomfield Towing, arrived with his large rig, and he was finally able to pull everyone out of the quagmire. But even he was having unexpected problems—not with his tow truck, but with an older cell phone that had terrible reception. In anger and in frustration, Bergin threw the cell phone into the dirt. It was dark at the time and Robert Fry and the others did not see him do it. The cell phone lay hidden from view as the morning light began to rise to the east of Angel's Peak.

At around 7:00 A.M., Frank Johnson, of the service company PNM, bounced down route CR 6480, checking transmission lines. Just north of the intersection of CR 6200, he spotted a large amount of blood in the roadway. His first thought was that someone had killed a deer out of season and field dressed it on the road. Stepping out to investigate, he noticed a blood trail leading off into the bushes. Johnson followed the trail until he saw a human foot sticking out behind a bush. Not wanting to look any farther, he hurried back to his vehicle and called 911.

The 911 operator contacted the San Juan County

Sheriff's Office and at 7:03 A.M. Deputy Sheriff Carrie Livingston was dispatched to the scene, where she met up with Frank Johnson. Deputy Livingston walked with Johnson up the bloody trail to where a body lay, and Livingston discovered that it was the body of a nude female, lying facedown behind some bushes. She immediately called for assistance.

Among those who responded to the call for assistance were Detective Bob Melton and his partner, Tyler Truby. Detective Truby had been in law enforcement for five years. He had received special training for investigations in felony crimes, including classroom and field experience. In fact, he and Detective Melton had just come off a bizarre homicide case when they got the call about a woman's body found on CR 6480. When Melton heard about this latest homicide, he said to Truby, "You've got to be kidding. Another one?"

The previous homicide had occurred in Bloomfield, a town about five miles east of Farmington. Judy Gomez, thirty-two, had called 911 saying she had gone to the store and when she returned home, she found her husband, Ray, twenty-six, dead in bed, victim of a gunshot wound. She said he had been despondent and apparently killed himself. When Detective Melton arrived, he said she was an "emotional mess."

Melton continued, "She was crying and very upset. I told her I was sorry for her loss. It really did look like a homicide. She claimed she hadn't touched anything at the scene. I was about to leave the bedroom when a lightbulb went off in my head. It was something so obvious, I almost missed it. I turned to her and said, 'Uh, ma'am—where is the pistol he supposedly used on himself?'

"You should have seen the look on her face,"

Melton said. "Suddenly she realized that Ray couldn't have killed himself, got up and hidden the gun. What at first looked like a suicide suddenly became a homicide case, with Ms. Gomez as the chief suspect in the murder of her husband."

Now, barely two days later, Melton and Truby were out on CR 6480, staring down at the nude body of a Native American woman lying in the dirt. She was about twenty feet from the dirt roadway. About five feet from her body, they discovered a brassiere and underpants. Thirty feet away were a pair of sandals that appeared to belong to the dead woman.

Detective Truby began his report: "Upon examining the body, I observed obvious head trauma with brain matter exposed. On turning over the body, a wound was observed in the victim's chest which looked to have been made by a sharp instrument.

"In analyzing the crime scene, we observed large amounts of blood and drag marks on the dirt road, indicating that the body had been dragged down the middle of the dirt roadway for approximately one hundred feet before being taken off the roadway. I also observed tire tracks that had two rear tires with treads and front tires with treads that were different from each other as well as from the rear tires. The tire tracks indicated that the vehicle had been stopped and been backed up and turned around twice on the dirt roadway.

"A preliminary assessment of the scene appeared to indicate that the sandal-footed prints left the vehicle running and were then followed by the vehicle. At one point along the roadway, the vehicle and sandal prints were side by side. The vehicle appeared to have cut off the victim's path as she was trying to run away. Near this area were found a sledgehammer on one side of the roadway and her clothing on the other side.

"The scene also showed drag marks and pools of blood. Additionally, there were sets of shoe prints in the form of approximately size eleven male shoes as well as shoe prints that matched the sandals believed to be from the victim. Also, two earrings for a pierced ear were found near the body. These earrings were a copper-colored ball and a silver-colored dangle.

"Further examination of the scene revealed a sledgehammer that appeared to have been used in bludgeoning the victim. In particular there was blood on the hammer end of the tool as well as splattered on the handle from the head down to approximately thirteen and a half inches. Additionally, a knife with a ten inch long blade was located next to the body. The knife appeared to have blood on it."

As Detectives Melton and Truby moved around the crime scene, they happened to look up the roadway and spotted a very unusual sight. They saw Gloria Fry talking with police officers.

Melton, who knew Gloria Fry very well from his forays at court, asked Truby, "What's she doing here?"

Truby shook his head. Her presence was just as much a mystery to him as it was to Melton.

The detectives went up the road to investigate, and Truby wrote down in his report, "While officers were investigating the scene, Gloria Fry appeared. Ms. Fry spoke with officers and stated that she had seen all the activity and come to check out what was happening."

She may have been curious about all the police activity, but that still didn't answer in the detec-

tives' minds what she was doing there on that isolated dirt road, so early in the morning. Had she
heard about it on a police scanner? Or been in the
neighborhood on some unrelated matter? After
all, she was a probation officer for the county and
drove around its environs all the time. The detectives put the matter behind them for the moment,
to concentrate on the evidence they were finding,
but they did not forget it.

None of the law enforcement officers knew who
the female victim was until one of them searched
her pants and found a small purse. Inside the
purse was an identification card. She was Betty
Lee, thirty-six, of Shiprock, New Mexico. It didn't
answer, however, what she was doing here on this
out-of-the-way dirt road so many miles from home.

As the evidence was collected by others, Detectives
Melton and Truby began an odyssey to trace Betty
Lee's last movements. They drove around the Kirtland and Farmington area, asking about Betty Lee.
They discovered she was supposed to have been
on a college field trip this very day, but she had
never shown up at the college.

More questioning of individuals revealed the
fact that Betty Lee had been partying with two
women in Farmington on the previous night. One
woman was named Gloria Charley. The other only
had the first name of Tina. Then a very curious
thing turned up. It appeared that Gloria was now
missing as well. Melton and Truby wondered, was
she dead as well or was she connected to the murder somehow? Each question only seemed to lead
to several others.

Further investigation led to a man who had seen
a red Toyota pickup in the general area of the murder scene, early on the morning of June 9. This
man was pretty sure that the driver of the pickup

was a Navajo and lived down around Sanostee, fifty miles to the southwest. The man even remembered a couple of numbers from the license plate.

With this clue in mind, the detectives started out for Sanostee and headed through Shiprock. It was around there that they learned a few more important facts about Betty Lee. One of her brothers worked for the Navajo Tribal Police, and Dorothy Fulton was the chief investigator for the entire Navajo Nation.

Sanostee is a small Navajo village that lies along Pena Blanca Creek. It is nestled below nine-thousand-foot Beautiful Mountain, one of the tallest in the Chuska Range. Strangely enough, the mountains behind Sanostee are the epicenter of tales concerning a creature that is the equivalent to a Navajo Bigfoot, or Sasquatch. Both sheepherders and cattlemen claimed over the years to have caught glimpses of it in the forest. It was large, with a hairy bearlike body and fearsome characteristics.

When the detectives arrived at Sanostee, they eventually found the red Toyota pickup in question. The owner of the pickup, however, was able to prove that he had been nowhere near the crime scene within the previous few days. Since the blood on CR 6480 had been so fresh, this murder could have only occurred a short time before the PNM lineman had discovered the body.

Just as Detectives Melton and Truby were about to leave Sanostee, they received a call that a red Toyota pickup matching the description of the vehicle they were looking for had been seen by Colorado police up in Durango, nearly one hundred miles to the northeast over mountainous roads. It not only matched the description of the pickup, it had one more interesting item about it—there was blood on one of the doors.

"Keep an eye on it," Detective Melton said. "We'll be there as soon as we can."

There was no freeway from Sanostee, New Mexico, to Durango, Colorado. The two-lane road wound along the La Plata River, up through the small towns and fields. It crossed into Colorado through the southern Ute Reservation and the villages of Red Mesa and Marvel. Off to their left as they drove were the enchanted ruins of Mesa Verde, high atop a cliff, just as Willa Cather had described it on another night nearly a century before.

She wrote, "I saw a little city of stone. It was as still as sculpture. . . . A fringe of cedars grew along the edge of the cavern, like a garden. They were the only living things. Such silence and stillness and repose—immortal with the calmness of eternity."

It was nearly midnight when Detectives Melton and Truby arrived in Durango. As Detective Melton drove up to the red Toyota in question, he whistled. This seemed like a sure collar. There was indeed blood on one of the doors, and when the owner came outside, the man had a large bloodstain on his shirt.

After intense questioning, however, the pickup owner with the bloody shirt was able to prove the blood came from a bar fight he had been involved in at Durango. He hadn't been anywhere near the crime scene down in New Mexico on CR 6480.

The detectives now had more miles of driving, back through La Posta, Twin Crossings and Flora Vista, and it was nearly 5:00 A.M. when Melton and Truby got back to the Farmington area. They had been up nearly twenty-four hours straight now, without any sleep, but they weren't giving up. Not by a long shot. They knew that the first seventy-two hours of a crime are the "golden hours," when most crimes are solved. After that, the odds grew much worse.

"Go take a shower," Melton told Truby, "and I'll pick you up at eight A.M." Then he poured himself some coffee and got ready for the long day ahead.

Across town, near the now-empty Eclectic store, reporters for the *Daily Times* were putting together a story about the dead woman's discovery on CR 6480. The newspaper had sent a reporter to the scene on the previous day and he wrote, "Splatter patterns and a large prominent blood stain were visible on the rock which rests near the edge of a dry arroyo nearly lined with cut branches, a few animal skeletal remains and scattered garbage."

Of particular interest to the reporter was a decaying carcass of a dog. Its hind legs had been tied together and it had been dragged to death. The reporter wondered if the person who had done this terrible deed had also murdered the woman.

Detective Melton had spoken briefly to the reporter on the previous day and his quote was in the June 10 issue of the *Daily Times.* "We're investigating potential leads," Melton said. "We have no suspects arrested at this point."

In fact, they had no viable suspect period, as Detectives Melton and Truby took off again at 8:00 A.M., June 10, in pursuit not only of the killer, but an understanding of Betty Lee's last movements around the area.

The detectives eventually found Gloria Charley safe and sound, back in Shiprock. As they interviewed her, she poured out her story of what she and Betty Lee and Tina had been doing on the night of June 8 and the early-morning hours of June 9. Charley said they had all gone into Farmington and had a few drinks. Then she and Tina hooked up with two Navajo men. Betty Lee became like a fifth wheel to Charley and Tina. One of the Navajo men was named Johnny Miller and the other one—Charley couldn't remember exactly what his name was, except it sounded like "Pretty Boy." She didn't know if that was a nickname or his real name.

Since Charley didn't want to drive Betty Lee all the way back to Shiprock, she left her off by a phone booth in Farmington. This was sometime after 2:00 A.M. It was understood that Betty Lee would call for a ride from there. Charley, Tina and the two men took off, and she hadn't seen Betty Lee since.

Gloria gave the detectives one more interesting bit of information. Johnny Miller lived in Red Rock, and he owned a red Toyota pickup truck.

Before leaving Shiprock, the detectives discovered one more interesting fact. Betty Lee had once dated a man who had a violent reputation. This man was now dating Tina. This individual had become so violent with Betty Lee that at one point he put her in the hospital. She stopped seeing him after that.

Since this man lived nearby, Melton and Truby decided to contact him before going to Red Rock. Even though the man seemed a likely candidate on the surface, his alibi checked out and he was ruled out as the killer.

It was late afternoon before the detectives could make their way to the small village of Red Rock near the Chuska Mountains. The road took them directly south of the Rock with Wings and through the spiny rock outcrops known as "the Dragon's Teeth." This definitely was a terrain for Navajo werewolves and skinwalkers, for those who believed in such things. If the detectives were readers of Tony Hillerman mysteries, they would have known this was also the locale where Jim Chee had discovered the murder of Officer Delbert Nez. It was a wilderness of huge rocks, such as Mitten Rock and "the Thumb," and volcanic necks that looked "like great black cathedrals." As Hillerman had pointed out, "This part of the Reservation was notorious for witches."

In *Coyote Waits*, Chee had also gone to talk with a pretty teenager of the Towering House Clan at a gas station/convenience store in Red Rock. Melton and Truby's quest was of a different nature, however, and they wound their way through the back-roads to find Johnny Miller and his red Toyota pickup truck. Such locations are not always easy to find on the Navajo Reservation. It is often a matter of asking at the local gas station or chapter house where an individual might live. The directions may consist of such advice as, "Go 4.2 miles down the highway, turn right, follow the dirt track for .3 of a mile, turn left at the old boot on a fence post."

Melton and Truby eventually did find a John Miller in the Red Rock area, but he was not their Johnny Miller. Out of sheer frustration Detective Melton smashed his fist down on the dashboard. He told his partner, "I feel like we're on a roller-coaster ride and this case will never end. It's like a nightmare you can't wake up from."

Detective Truby nodded his head in agreement. Fatigue and frustration were taking their toll. Truby said later, "I was worried that this case was going into cold-case territory. The first seventy-two hours of an investigation are critical. Every hour that goes by after that lets the perp tamper with ev-idence, witnesses begin to forget key details, and time and weather degrade evidence."

Bob Melton knew all about cold-case territory from the Donald Tsosie murder. There had been

Rock with Wings, known as Tsi Bit Ai to the Navajos, is the site
where legendary Monster Slayer killed Cliff Monster.
Victim Betty Lee lived nearby. *(Author's photo)*

A Native American dancer recounts the stories of Monster Slayer
and the Enemy Way during a ceremony in New Mexico.
(Author's photo)

Robert (Bobby) Fry played violent fantasy games and invented bloody tales. *(Photo courtesy of San Juan County Justice Center)*

Bobby Fry and his friends hung out in this coffee shop in Farmington, New Mexico. *(Author's photo)*

Fry and his friends played vampire games in this park along the Animas (Spirit) River. *(Author's photo)*

A tiny drop of blood on Fry's Misfits tee shirt would help prosecutors convict him of murder. *(Photo courtesy of San Juan County Justice Center)*

On Thanksgiving 1996, Robert Fry and Harold Pollock murdered Joseph Fleming and Matt Trecker at The Eclectic. *(Author's photo)*

Donald Tsosie traded at the Hubbell Trading Post, one of the most historic on the Navajo Reservation. *(Author's photo)*

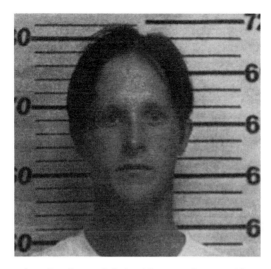

Fry's friend Leslie Engh helped him murder Donald Tsosie.
(Photo courtesy of San Juan County Justice Center)

Sheriff's officers and an ambulance crew pulled Donald Tsosie's
body up from a canyon at The Bluffs nearly a month after he was
murdered. *(Photo courtesy of San Juan County Justice Center)*

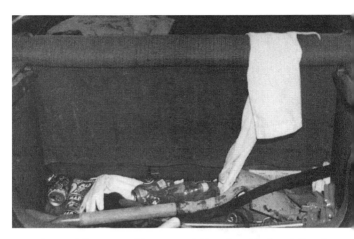

Robert Fry beat Donald Tsosie with this shovel before killing him.
(Photo courtesy of San Juan County Justice Center)

Fry broke a broom handle while beating Tsosie with it. He used the sharpened points to stab him in the body, face, and eyes.
(Photo courtesy of San Juan County Justice Center)

Donald Tsosie's boots were found at the murder scene by investigators. They later became a key piece of evidence against Fry. *(Photo courtesy of San Juan County Justice Center)*

Betty Lee was phoning for a ride home from this phone booth when Fry and Engh picked her up.
(Photo courtesy of San Juan County Justice Center)

Fry and Engh disrobed Betty Lee out on a deserted road and
allegedly attempted to rape her. Her bra and other clothes
were later discovered by investigators.
(Photo courtesy of San Juan County Justice Center)

Both Robert Fry and Les Engh pulled off Betty Lee's
jeans and threw them in the dirt.
(Photo courtesy of San Juan County Justice Center)

Robert Fry used this sledgehammer to kill Betty Lee.
(Photo courtesy of San Juan County Justice Center)

Blood stains from Betty Lee were discovered by investigators on a
dirt road. *(Photo courtesy of San Juan County Justice Center)*

Robert Fry gave both Donald Tsosie and Betty Lee rides in his Ford Aspire before killing them.
(Photo courtesy of San Juan County Justice Center)

A small amount of Betty Lee's blood was discovered on the floor mat of Fry's car. *(Photo courtesy of San Juan County Justice Center)*

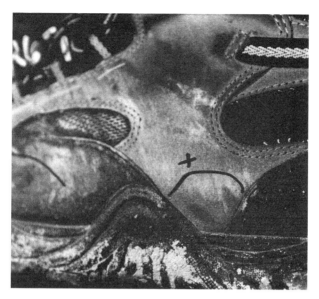

A small amount of Betty Lee's blood was also discovered on
Robert Fry's boots. *(Photo courtesy of San Juan County Justice Center)*

Fry's boots left prints on the road where Betty Lee was murdered.
(Photo courtesy of San Juan County Justice Center)

After Robert Fry's car became stuck on a sandy road a few miles away from the murder scene, a tow truck had to pull him out of the sand. *(Aerial photo courtesy of San Juan County Justice Center)*

Expert trackers followed unusual tire tread marks for over a mile to a spot where Robert Fry's car had become stuck in soft sand. *(Photo courtesy of San Juan County Justice Center)*

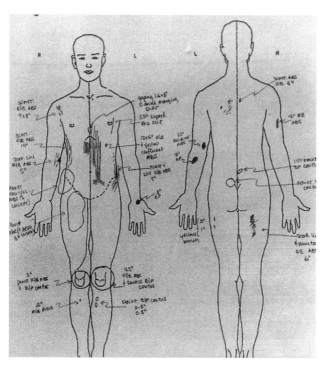

A diagram of the wounds Robert Fry inflicted upon Betty Lee.
(Photo courtesy of San Juan County Justice Center)

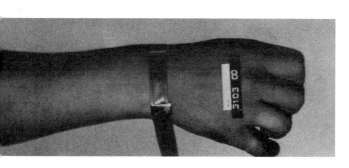

The arm of Betty Lee, who fought back against her attackers,
clawing and scratching them.
(Photo courtesy of San Juan County Justice Center)

Detective Bob Melton began tying the murders of Joseph Fleming, Matt Trecker, Donald Tsosie, and Betty Lee to Robert Fry.
(Photo courtesy of Bob Melton)

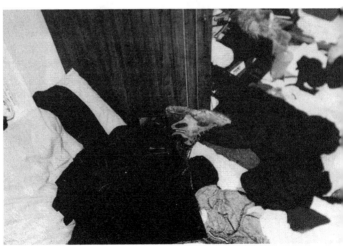

Detective Tyler Truby dug through a pile of clothes in Robert Fry's bedroom and found a tee shirt that had blood on it.
(Photo courtesy of San Juan County Justice Center)

Robert Fry was arrested for the murders of Joseph Fleming, Matthew Trecker, Donald Tsosie, and Betty Lee. *(Photo courtesy of San Juan County Justice Center)*

Les Engh had much shorter hair by the time he was arrested for the murders of Tsosie and Lee. *(Photo courtesy of San Juan County Justice Center)*

Judge William Birdsall presided over the Betty Lee murder trial. He eventually sentenced Robert Fry to death. *(Photo courtesy of Brett Butterstein)*

Thomas Hynes was the presiding judge in Fry's trial for the Donald Tsosie murder. *(Photo courtesy Brett Butterstein)*

Matthew Trecker is buried a few blocks from where he lived and where he died at the Eclectic store. *(Photo courtesy Brett Butterstein)*

initial months of investigation that led nowhere, always coming back in an incomplete circle to Scorpion Point. Now the Betty Lee case seemed to be going in its own set of circles that emanated from the scene of the crime, like a stone thrown into water, until the waves finally dissipated into nothing.

"We're running out of luck," Truby told Melton.

But luck has a tricky way of turning when you least expect it. Navajo traditionalists believed in such matters, fate turned upside down by the trickster Coyote. And Coyote's trick on Robert Fry was about to come to fruition.

In the crime scene area on June 10, Navajo trackers and sheriff's officers followed the mismatched tire tread marks from where the body lay, to see where they might lead. It was not always easy to follow them, and in some places they disappeared over slick rock. In other places they were in a web of other tire patterns. Over some locales, the wind had erased the tracks completely, but the trackers were able to follow their irregular path for over a mile back toward the main highway, and it led them to an incredible discovery. Deputy Matt Wilcox found a cell phone on the ground near the roadway. It was in an area of a mass of tire tread marks, as if many vehicles had been there about the same time.

Once the cell phone was in the officers' possession, Detective Jason Waybourn served a search warrant for the ownership information regarding the cell phone with All-Tel Cellular. From this warrant Detective Waybourn learned that the cell phone belonged to Charley Bergin at Bloomfield Towing.

Waybourn contacted Bergin and discovered that he apparently had thrown the cell phone to the ground while helping pull another tow truck out of the sand on CR 6480. This tow truck was driven by Floyd Robinson. Robinson had been trying to extricate two passenger vehicles, one of them being a sedan and the other a pickup truck, which had become mired in the sand. In the process Robinson had become stuck as well. When Bergin arrived on the scene, he pulled Robinson's tow truck out of the sand, as well as the two other vehicles. Bergin related that the pickup truck was owned by James Fry and the sedan was owned by his son Robert Fry.

When Detective Waybourn relayed this news to Detectives Melton and Truby in Red Rock, it was like a thunderbolt out of a blue sky. Things began to fall into place as to the reason why Gloria Fry had been on that road the previous day. Melton and Truby forgot all about Johnny Miller and red Toyota pickup trucks. They were now certain that the mystery of Betty Lee's death ran in a very different direction than the one they had been pursuing, and now all leads led right back to the Fry family.

"Let's hope this pans out," Melton said, realizing that they'd already been on numerous false leads. Time and fatigue were wearing them both down.

With a growing sense of anticipation, the detectives drove back through Shiprock, around the Hogback, through Waterflow and up CR 6480. When they finally talked to the trackers and officers there, the news couldn't have been better. The trackers had traced a direct line of strange tire tread marks from the murder scene to the dropped cell phone. In their opinion, the vehicle that had been in a chase with the sandal wearer, had been at the murder location, had been pulled out by a tow truck a mile down the road, were all the same vehicle. Now all Melton and Truby had to do was see if one of the Frys' vehicles had tires that matched.

Detective Melton said later about the trackers, "These tracks could have never been followed by the untrained eye. Wind and dust devils blew away some of the tracks. Other times they were crossed over by the tread marks of other vehicles or completely lost over rocky areas. It was a great piece of police work."

After 2½ sleepless, nerve-racking days, Detectives Melton and Truby pulled up in front of the Fry residence and spotted Gloria, James and Robert Fry all standing in the front yard next to Robert's blue sedan. To Detective Melton's eyes they all seemed uneasy at the detectives' approach. Then Melton took one look at the tires on Robert Fry's blue Ford Aspire and yelled to Truby, "Look at that! Those are our tires!"

Even from a distance the tires looked exactly like the ones the Navajo trackers had been following on CR 6480. In Detective Truby's report, he wrote, "I and Detective Melton observed that the pattern on the tires on this vehicle matched those found at the crime scene. Additionally, Detective Melton measured the proportions of the tires with those of the patterns at the scene, and they matched well."

What happened next has to be viewed through what Gloria and Jim Fry knew at this point concerning Robert Fry's activities of the past two days and nights. There are various speculations among law enforcement officers about what Gloria and Jim did know and when they knew it, and these were broken down into three categories. One of law enforcement's suppositions was that Gloria and James Fry at this point only knew what Robert Fry had told them about why he had been out on

CR 6480 in the early-morning hours of June 9. This supposition posited that James and Gloria Fry knew nothing about a murder until they witnessed all the police officers out there after 7:00 A.M., June 10, 2000, and that even then they did not draw any connection between the murder and their son, since he had lied to them so convincingly.

The second speculation was that Robert Fry did not tell them the truth of why he was on CR 6480, but once Gloria and James Fry saw all the police activity and learned about the murder, they did draw the conclusion that Robert was involved. What their actions were from that point on could only be speculated.

The third theory was that when Detectives Melton and Truby showed up at the Fry residence, Gloria and James knew very well what Robert Fry had done, and they helped him in trying to destroy evidence. In time the district attorney's office would look very carefully at this possibility and they considered filing charges against James and Gloria Fry. They even wrote up their suspicions in a brief document. To James and Gloria's benefit, charges against them were never filed, which seems to point to the fact they may have been innocent of any collusion or conspiracy to hide or destroy evidence. To some in the law enforcement and judiciary community, they were also victims of Robert Fry's murderous habits. To others in that same community, at least in the Betty Lee murder, they seemed to be accomplices. All discussions of arresting either Gloria or James Fry went on behind closed doors, and only minimal documentation has seen the light of day. Perhaps some of the discussions were not even recorded.

Whatever the circumstances, what Gloria and James Fry did next had very important consequences as far as Robert was concerned. Detectives Melton and Truby asked permission to search Robert Fry's vehicle and the home. Without the issuance of a search warrant, permission was granted by all of the Frys, including Robert.

How much Gloria Fry knew about her son's activities at this point, only she knows for sure. She definitely had knowledge about law enforcement and court proceedings, being a probation officer herself and having been a police officer in Albuquerque in her younger years. If she believed Robert Fry's story that he was out on CR 6480, only to take a "piss" and didn't know anything about a murder, then she obviously believed the detectives wouldn't find any incriminating evidence in Robert's vehicle or in the house. If on the other hand, she well knew what Robert had done, as some officers suspected, and helped him try to destroy evidence, then she might have believed all that evidence was now beyond the detectives' ability of finding it. Once again, no evidence of this collusion was ever brought forward in court, but for months to come this possibility was given credence at the San Juan County Justice Center, and an investigation moved forward in that regard. Gloria Fry was indeed looked at as a suspect by some in San Juan County law enforcement and judicial circles.

Whatever Gloria Fry's reasons, Detective Truby wrote, "Officers received permission to search the vehicle from the Fry's [*sic*] and observed what appeared to be blood inside the vehicle under the dash as well as on the hood release under the dash."

Detective Truby went into the Fry home and searched the bedroom that Robert Fry was staying in. The bedroom was a complete mess with clothes scattered everywhere. On the bedroom door there was a poster of slain singing-idol Selena. At first

Truby couldn't find any evidence in the jumbled piles of clothing. Then near the bottom of the pile, he spotted a black T-shirt with a white skull on the front—a Misfits T-shirt. Way down on the lower portion of the skull was a tiny droplet of blood. Truby took the shirt as evidence and the tiny droplet would later prove to be Betty Lee's blood.

Digging around through the jumbled mass of clothing and shoes, Truby seized a pair of shoes that appeared to match the shoe size of prints discovered at the murder scene. The shoes had several stains that appeared to be bloodstains. The patterns on the soles of the shoes also seemed to match patterns that Truby had seen in the dirt out on CR 6480.

Detective Truby continued with his report, "While at the Fry residence, I and Detective Melton spoke with Gloria Fry, who stated that Robert had called her on his cell phone and tried to give her directions to where he had gotten his vehicle stuck in the sand. However, she was unable to find him immediately, but she was eventually able to locate him near CR's 6400 and 6480. Gloria Fry said that she and her husband went there together and found her son with Leslie Engh, a friend of his. She said that they took Engh to his house, and then she took her son back to their residence where he cleaned up and changed clothing. She said that the vehicle she drove out there to pick up her son was a Chevrolet Malibu. She picked up Fry in the Chevrolet and brought him home.

"After Robert Fry changed his clothing, she took him back to where the vehicle was stuck in an S10 pickup truck that they owned so they could attempt to pull Robert Fry's vehicle out. They were unable to pull the vehicle out and in fact the S10 got stuck as well. As a result, the second tow truck they called had to extricate both of the Fry's [*sic*] vehicles and the other tow truck.

"At this same time, Sergeant Melton spoke with Robert Fry. Fry indicated that he and Les Engh had been at the Top Deck Lounge until closing time, which is between 2 and 2:30 AM. They then went to The Kettle. After leaving the restaurant they drove down Broadway where they picked up an individual named Ryan, whose last name Fry said he did not know. Fry also stated that he, Engh and Ryan went past Kirtland. Fry went on to say that they drove to Kirtland because that is where he was going to drop off Engh at his home in Kirtland. Fry admitted that he was in the area of the homicide but that he only drove through without stopping until he had traveled several minutes down the road where he only stopped to relieve himself. However, the tire tracks that match his vehicle indicate several places where the vehicle was stopped, turned, and redirected in contrast to the story told by Fry."

While Detective Truby continued to search the Fry residence, Detective Melton went back to the justice complex in Aztec. The name Les Engh rang a bell with Melton, and he discovered that Engh was currently in the San Juan County Detention Center for an unrelated crime. After being deposited at his home by Gloria Fry on June 10, Engh had been arrested on an outstanding warrant for a matter that had nothing to do with Betty Lee's murder.

In the spring of 2000, Les Engh had been arrested for the possession of a stolen firearm. Instead of serving jail time, he was deemed fit to be admitted into the Pre-Prosecution Diversion Program. By being in this program, Engh would not have to go behind bars, but would serve eighty hours of community service.

Engh did not want to do any extra work on community service, however. Instead, he forged a signature on a work sheet twelve times, stating that he had completed eighty hours of community service. The signature that he forged was that of Pastor James Fleming, head of Christ the Rock Lutheran Church. (It is unknown if Pastor Fleming was related to Joseph Fleming, a victim at The Eclectic.)

When Sonya Duke from the DA's office checked up on this, she discovered from Pastor Fleming that he had never signed any work sheet, nor had Les Engh done any community service. When the police finally caught up with Engh on this after the murder of Betty Lee, they put him in jail on a third-degree felony charge for forgery.

At 2:00 A.M. on June 11, 2000, Detective Melton went into an interview room with Les Engh to see if his story jibed with the one Robert Fry had told as to why they were out near Kirtland on June 9. Melton had been up for nearly three days straight now, without any sleep, but he felt that he was getting close to a big break in the homicide of Betty Lee.

Les Engh told Detective Melton that he and Fry had been at The Kettle at approximately 2:20 A.M. on June 9, 2000. They then drove in Fry's Ford Aspire to the Apache Y gas and convenience store, where Fry stayed outside and Engh bought some cigarettes. Now Engh's story differed dramatically from the tale that Fry had told the detectives. Engh didn't mention anybody named Ryan, but he said that when he came out of the store, Fry was speaking with a Native American or Hispanic woman at a phone booth. At this point, however, Engh lied. He said that they did not pick her up. He said he overheard Fry say to the woman that he would get in touch with her later, and then Fry drove him home to his residence in Farmington. This last part about the residence also differed from Fry's story. Robert Fry had said that he left Engh off at his residence in Kirtland. Engh said he lived in Farmington.

Detective Melton asked Engh what types of tools Fry kept in his car. Engh told him that he had various types in there, and then he mentioned one item that made Melton's ears perk up. Les Engh said there had been a small sledgehammer in Fry's vehicle.

Once again, the sledgehammer was looked at as evidence. It clearly seemed to contain bloodstains, not only on the hammer, but several inches down the handle as well.

Detective Truby went to interview Les Engh and he told Engh what they already knew. Realizing that he was in jeopardy of being tied very directly to the murder of Betty Lee, Les Engh decided to quit telling lies and cut his losses. He began to tell Detective Truby the truth of what had happened in the late-night hours of June 8 and early-morning hours of June 9, 2000.

Engh was Mirandized and Truby wrote down in his report, "Engh recanted the story he had originally given and instead gave a detailed account of the murder of Betty Lee. Specifically, Engh stated that he and Fry went as he had previously said to the store at the Apache Y where he went inside to buy cigarettes. When he came out, Fry was speaking with a Native American or Hispanic female who was crying. Fry said, 'I hate to see a woman cry. So I'll take you at least as far as Kirtland.'

"Fry told Engh to sit in the back and the female sat in the front passenger seat. As they were driving toward Kirtland, Fry turned off onto a dirt road

and drove a distance until coming to a point in the
roadway where Fry pulled over and stopped the vehicle. Fry explained that he had to relieve himself
at which point the female got out of the car and
started to run back toward the highway. Fry ran to
the back of the car, yelling for her to come. When
she did not return, Fry got back into the car and
drove up beside her. He induced her to get back
into the vehicle with the promise of a ride.

"Once she was inside, he continued to drive up
the road, stopping suddenly. At that point Fry got
out again, went around to the passenger side, and
pulled the female out of the car by her hair. At this
point, the female started to yell, 'Why are you
doing this to me?' Fry struggled with her, manag-
ing to pull her clothing up from her chest. Fry
then reached around the female from behind and
stabbed her in the chest with a knife. The female
then struggled free and managed to pull the knife
from her chest, throwing it in the direction of the
ravine. At some point during this struggle, Fry told
Engh to grab her legs, at which time Engh did as
instructed. It was during this time that the remain-
der of her clothing was removed.

"The female again got away from the pair and
ran naked toward the highway. Fry went to the rear
of the car, extricated a sledgehammer and chased
after her. Catching up with her and tripping her
from behind, Fry ordered Engh to look for the
knife. As Engh was looking for the knife, he heard
the female scream. He then saw Fry swinging the
sledgehammer downward in the direction toward
where the female was lying. Soon the woman
stopped screaming."

Truby's report went on to tell of Engh searching
unsuccessfully with the flashlight for the knife,
and then helping Fry drag Betty Lee's body into a

small ravine and kicking her clothing off the road. The report did not get into the part where Fry's car was stuck in the sand, or the extrication process. In order to obtain an arrest warrant, the report was basically laid out in a manner to prove that Robert Fry had murdered Betty Lee.

Detective Truby filled in the affidavit-for-arrest warrant with the story that Engh had just told him, and he signed his own name to the bottom. The warrant stated in part: "Wherefore your affiant respectfully requests that an arrest be issued for the above named defendant, Robert Fry, for the crimes of murder in the first degree, attempted criminal sexual penetration, and tampering with evidence."

The affidavit was signed by a judge and filed with the district attorney's office at 5:03 A.M. on June 11, 2000.

Less than an hour later, Robert James Fry was arrested at his parents' home. Detective Melton and Truby's marathon journey without any sleep through the Four Corners Region had paid off.

Chapter 7

Connecting the Dots

Detective Tyler Truby wrote on June 11, 2000, on his report of Robert Fry's arrest, "I transported Robert Fry to the San Juan County Medical Center for evidence collection. The evidence collection was performed by Phyllis Walden, a nurse at the hospital. During her examination, she observed what is in her opinion to be scratch marks on Robert Fry's stomach. She noted this observation in her emergency room treatment record. 'I observed the marks and photographed the marks. Robert Fry stated that the marks were stretch marks, not scratch marks.' "

Detective Truby requested that a physician be consulted to determine whether the marks were scratch marks or stretch marks. When one talked to Truby, he said that the easiest way to determine the difference was to wait awhile. He said that scratch marks would heal and that stretch marks would not. If the marks were still present at a later date, they were stretch marks. If the marks were not there, then they were scratch marks.

In addition to this medical examination, Detective

Truby collected and studied clothing obtained from Robert Fry and Les Engh. He noted that both individuals had blood spattered on their clothes, which had become transferred to the inside of the vehicle. Engh told Truby that once he got home, he laundered his clothing and cleaned himself off. He also stated that he couldn't remember if the shoes he was wearing at the crime scene were at his residence of if he had been wearing them at the time of his arrest and were in the property room at the San Juan County Detention Center.

Later, the detectives interviewed Robert Fry's mother, Gloria. According to their report, she stated in part, "I am a probation officer for six years. Robert lives in our home. After work that evening (June 8th), he came home for dinner. He was wearing jeans and a black tee shirt with a skull on the front when he left. I don't remember what shoes he was wearing that night. When he left he was driving his Ford Aspire and he was alone.

"It was late, sometime between 2 and 3 AM when I called him to see if he was okay. He was at the Kettle Restaurant. He called later to tell us he was stuck sometime around 4 AM. I woke my husband and we went to get him unstuck. When we met him he was with Les Engh. Les Engh was wrapped up in a sleeping bag. I was upset because my son had a drinking problem and he smelled of alcohol.

"I took them home. When we got home Robert changed to sweats. We went back and tried to find the area the car was stuck in. Then Robert went with his father to find the car and I tried to find another route in. (Robert and his father apparently got stuck around this time in the pickup truck.) I finally found a road, but it was getting late so I went home to change for work. I got my cell phone and I went back to find them. After I found them (stuck in the sand), I gave them rugs for traction and then went to work. Before I gave them rugs, I went to the crime scene. I saw people and patrol cars, so I went to see what was going on."

Farther down in the report it was noted by Detective Truby, "She never asked her son why he was out there?" It was more in the form of a question than a statement. The next phrase was a direct statement: "She never told the police that her son had been out there."

Robert Fry faced several charges put together by the San Juan County District Attorney's Office:

Count 1
Did kill Betty Lee, a human being without lawful justification or excuse—a capital felony.
Count 2
Did unlawfully, take, restrain, transport Betty Lee, by force, intimidation or deception, against Betty Lee's will with the intent to inflict death, physical injury or sexual offense on Betty Lee—first-degree felony.
Count 3
Did attempt to unlawfully and intentionally cause Betty Lee to engage in sexual intercourse, cunnilingus, fellatio or anal intercourse or caused the penetration of the genital or anal openings of Betty Lee while in the commission of another felony, to wit: kidnapping—second-degree felony.
Count 4
Did destroy, change, hide, place or fabricate physical evidence, to wit: a body, blood, and or clothing with the intent to prevent apprehension, prosecution or conviction—fourth-degree felony.

The arrest of Robert Fry for the murder of Betty Lee hit the front page of the *Daily Times* the next day. Now, at last, Fry's friends knew that not all of his stories about killing were "bullshit." There it was in bold print that he had actually killed someone. One of the people stunned by this revelation was Larry Hudson. As little as a few weeks before, Hudson had blown off Robert Fry's story about killing an Indian up on the Bluffs. Hudson had been so tired of this story he'd walked away from Fry to check on his fishing pole at Navajo Lake. Now in the newspaper was an allegation that Fry really was a murderer.

Hudson said later, "It was hard to believe. But there it was in the *Times*. He'd really done it."

The fact that Fry had murdered Betty Lee in such a vicious manner made Hudson think again about the Indian-on-the-Bluffs story. Betty Lee had been killed by a sledgehammer blow to the head, and in one of Fry's stories, he'd talked about "finishing off" the Indian on the Bluffs with a hammer blow to the head. Even more than that, Robert had been so excited about telling the story, as if it were real. When Fry was obviously lying, he didn't seem to get so worked up about something, but when he was telling the truth, especially about something of a violent nature, he was more persistent and dynamic in the telling. The fact that most of the details in the stories about the dead Native American at the Bluffs were consistent made Hudson begin to believe that the tale was more than just Robert Fry's figment of imagination. Hudson didn't want it to be true, but now he felt he had to tell someone.

Hudson agonized over the next three days about whether to go forward and tell the police about the Indian-on-the-Bluffs story. After all, Robert Fry was such a good friend of his, he considered him to be a brother. As he had said, "I cared about his mom and dad. I even called his parents Mom and Dad. I cared about him, but I knew I had to do this. It was the right thing to do."

On June 16, 2000, Hudson phoned Detective Terry Eagle at the San Juan County Sheriff's Office. He talked to Eagle for fifteen minutes about Robert Fry's robbing an Indian in 1998 and throwing him off a cliff. This was all very interesting to Eagle, but he knew that Hudson could have seen those details from reports in the *Daily Times* back in 1998. Eagle told him that Detective Bob Melton would contact him later in the day. The Donald Tsosie murder case was now Melton's case.

Detective Melton was indeed interested in Hudson's story and contacted him as planned. In fact, Hudson went to the San Juan County Sheriff's Office around 2:00 P.M. and spoke with Melton there. As he drove over, he said later, "I hoped it was just all BS at the time."

Larry Hudson began telling the story that Fry had related about "rollin' an Indian." As he did, Melton said later, "My eyes lit up." Hudson gave Melton details that exactly matched the crime scene at Donald Tsosie's murder. Hudson gave the location as being near Scorpion Point, the fact that Tsosie was wearing new clothes and a cowboy hat, the body was left there for a period of time before discovery—and he gave details about the broken sticks from a broom handle. But the clincher, as far as Detective Melton was concerned, was the detail about Robert Fry throwing boots down at the Native American. That detail had purposefully been withheld by police to weed out any false stories from true ones. Hudson obviously knew what he was talking about.

Then Larry Hudson added one more very important detail. He told Detective Melton to talk to Les Engh about the Indian at the Bluffs. According to Hudson, Engh had supposedly been there with Robert Fry on the night of the murder. Melton could hardly believe his good luck. Les Engh was in the detention center, only a short distance away from where they sat because of his ties to the Betty Lee murder.

At 2:30 P.M., June 16, 2000, Detective Melton questioned Les Engh about the murder of Donald Tsosie. Immediately Engh began to lie. He said he was passed out in the car when he, Fry and an Indian named Donald went up to the Bluffs. If Donald and Fry got into a fight up there, Engh said, he didn't know about it, and he didn't know where the Indian had gone after he had awakened.

Detective Melton didn't believe any of this and told Engh so. Melton said what Engh was saying now didn't jibe with what Fry had told Hudson about the incident. And then Melton had Les Engh escorted back to his cell.

It didn't take Les Engh long to figure out that he was in big trouble if Melton knew all about the Tsosie murder because of Robert Fry's big mouth. Engh was not about to be left holding the bag for a murder that Fry had committed. He decided that same afternoon to go back and talk with Detective Melton again and this time tell him the truth.

When the two men met for the second time, Engh asked Melton, "What's going to happen to me?"

Melton told him he would get the same sentence as Fry, first-degree murder, since he was an accessory, but if he told the truth, the death penalty against him would probably be taken off the table. That was enough incentive for Engh and he began talking.

Engh told the whole story, beginning with picking up Donald Tsosie at the Turn Around Bar because he was better dressed than the other Native Americans there and appeared to have money. Engh discussed the fight between Fry and Tsosie in the car on top of the Bluffs and the two men fighting outside the car. He told of Tsosie getting the upper hand and Fry yelling for him to get a shovel. Engh even told of hitting Tsosie twice in the back, making him lose his balance, and Fry taking the shovel and pummeling Tsosie with it. Then he spoke of Fry using a broomstick on Tsosie, but it kept breaking. Fry thought this was funny and laughed. Tsosie was barely alive when they searched his clothing and boots for money. Lastly, Engh said, Fry pushed Donald over a cliff and threw the boots down after him. What happened to Donald after that, he didn't know.

There was even one more key piece of evidence to back up the allegations in the Donald Tsosie murder. When Fry was arrested for assaulting Rhonda Knott in 1997, officers had photographed his car inside and out. Clearly shown in one of the photos was his rear compartment area, and in that area was a shovel that matched the one that was supposedly used on Donald Tsosie. As Alexis Diego would later say, "It was always there. I don't think there was a time that I didn't see it in his car."

When this new revelation hit the local newspapers that Robert Fry had murdered two Native Americans in such a vicious manner, it sent shock waves through the nearby Navajo Nation. All of this was very reminiscent of the 1970s case where three Farmington teenagers had beaten and burned three Navajo men to death. The details about using a stick to stab Tsosie in the eyes and a sledgehammer to kill Betty

Lee were particularly disturbing. People wondered once again how Farmington could have in its midst individuals with such hatred for Native Americans.

The headlines of an *Indian Country* newspaper story was RACISM A POSSIBLE ISSUE IN RESERVATION BORDERTOWN MURDERS. It reiterated all the facts about the murders of Betty Lee and Donald Tsosie that were known at the time, and said that Farmington again was a hotbed of Native American unrest and difficulty. It posited that the murders were hate crimes.

DDA June Stein told the reporter that it was a possibility. And Detective Bob Melton said they were looking into that aspect of the murders. He added, "Any time you have that kind of anger and that kind of rage, and the random nature, you have the possibility of pattern killings."

There were also messages posted on a Web site called Indigenous People's Issues that dealt with the possibility of other Native American victims in the area who might have been killed by Robert Fry. It quoted Bob Melton as saying, "There's an unsolved homicide involving a Native American from 1998, Pernell Tewagonitewa, age 21, whose body was never found but whose car was discovered empty but burned outside of Farmington is one such instance."

In fact, Pernell's sister had told police that on May 29, 1998, she had seen him driving away from Gators Bar in Farmington. The same bar where Robert Fry had been a bouncer. According to Pernell's sister, Pernell was going to drive to the Glades (Chokecherry Canyon) to party with some friends. His burned-out car was later found there, but a live Pernell or his body was never found. Now that the murders of Donald Tsosie and Betty

Lee came to light, Robert Fry became a prime suspect in the Pernell Tewagonitewa case.

Melton added that Fry was "always a braggadocious individual," and anyone who had heard his stories about killing people should come forward. One unsolved local case that Melton had in mind was the murder of Native American Thomas Juan on July 27, 1997. Juan's body was found behind a convenience store with a wire ligature around his throat. Though this didn't quite match Fry's MO, it was hard to determine at times what his standard MO was when he was enraged. So far, Fry had used a broom handle, knife, sledgehammer and shovel as murder weapons. A wire ligature was no more bizarre than any of these other weapons.

Juan's sister told a reporter that Farmington was a dangerous place for Native Americans, especially if they were street people. She said that one person she knew, named Cindy, was beaten up almost monthly. Alcohol and homelessness were always problems in the border town.

One of Robert Fry's old nemeses, Don Ogle, wondered, as the detectives did, just how many murders Fry had committed in the region. Ogle told *Albuquerque Tribune* reporter Joline Gutierrez Kruger, "He (Fry) was troubled about his violence. He didn't know how to stop it, and that's why it was frightening for him and frightening to talk to him. He was quite scared of what he was capable of."

Ogle had been concerned about Robert Fry for years. During 1999 and 2000, he had told the sheriff's office, "Fry would brag about who he had beaten up and tell about incidents until you would see people moving from their seats (at restaurants) in order to get away from him. I just took it upon myself to notify them that Fry was a potential problem."

Sheriff Michael Davison at the time acknowledged the letters that Ogle sent him and said later, "I received a letter from Mr. Ogle, answering, among other topics, Robert Fry. And to the best of our abilities we addressed his concerns and investigated every lead that Mr. Ogle gave to us."

Just what Fry was capable of, Ogle had heard rumors circulating around Farmington. He said, "I've heard eleven murders and as many as thirty-two. Those are the rumors here in Farmington."

When Detective Tyler Truby was asked about this by Kruger, he said that the numbers quoted were on the high side. He did say, however, that besides Betty Lee and Donald Tsosie, they were looking at five other murders—two of them having to do with The Eclectic case. Detective Bob Melton had never counted Robert Fry out as a suspect in that case. Truby said, "We cannot rule Fry out in these investigations."

One of the investigations concerned eighteen-year-old Travis Killen from Farmington. He was last seen on November 23, 1997. A day later, his car was found abandoned out on Navajo Route 36, near the Chaco River, but not a trace of Killen was found. Because of the suspicious nature, Killen's disappearance was thought to be a homicide by the San Juan County Sheriff's Office. And because it occurred in Robert Fry's "comfort zone," he was deemed to be a suspect.

Christina Trecker was interviewed by the *Albuquerque Journal*, even though there was still no solid evidence that Robert Fry was connected to the killings at The Eclectic. She told the reporters, "Bobby Fry had a baseball bat with a hole drilled in the end of it, and a leather lace put through and tied.

He would talk about how much fun it was to beat up Indians."

There was indeed growing anger on the Navajo Reservation about the murders of Donald Tsosie and Betty Lee and Robert Fry's apparent hatred of Native Americans. The *Gallup Independent* reported that the Coalition for Navajo Liberation, a splinter group of AIM, was organizing a protest for the date that Fry and Engh were scheduled for their preliminary hearing. In a statement they said, "The 1970s incidents against Navajo people continue to exist and even worsen. The millennium of this new generation must awaken to address these serious acts of violence against all people."

Interestingly, both the families of Betty Lee and Donald Tsosie asked that there be no protests outside the courtroom, but rather let due process run its course. They still had faith in the judicial system.

In one issue the *Gallup Independent* rhetorically asked what a hate crime was, and then answered it by citing the United States Congress on the issue: "A hate crime is one in which the defendant intentionally selects a victim . . . because of the actual or perceived race, color, national origin, ethnicity, gender or sexual orientation of any person."

New Mexico did not have a law regarding hate crimes, so it was not part of the FBI database concerning such crimes. There was an FBI file on crimes against Native Americans in general, however, and it stated, "While communities around the nation are experiencing reduced levels of crime, that is not the case for communities in Indian Country. The consensus among law enforcement officials, academicians and community groups is that hate crime problems are far more pervasive than currently recognized."

An indication of how bad things had become was a report that showed violent crime had dropped 20 percent nationwide during the 1990s, but it had increased 87 percent on Indian Reservations.

Native American Public Telecommunications backed up these statistics with one of their radio shows about hate crimes. In most cases, it cited that not only the victim had been intoxicated, but the perpetrators were as well. This definitely fell into the parameters of Donald Tsosie, Robert Fry and Les Engh. Alcohol seemed to fuel whatever prejudices the perpetrators already had against Native Americans. A case in point happened during this same period up on the Standing Rock Sioux Reservation in South Dakota. Four intoxicated white teenagers came upon twenty-two-year-old Robert Manyhorses Jr., who was also intoxicated. They beat him to death and then stuffed his body upside down in a trash can.

Back in New Mexico, DA Sandra Price submitted a letter of intent on July 12, 2000, to seek the death penalty against Robert Fry for the murder of Betty Lee. She told a reporter for the *Gallup Independent* that she and law enforcement officers were also looking into the possibility that Gloria and James Fry had helped their son in trying to destroy evidence. Price said if this was the case, the possible charges would be tampering with evidence and aiding and abetting a felon.

The people made most angry, of course, were the ones who had personally known Donald Tsosie and Betty Lee. Margaret Whalawatsie told a reporter, "Betty was a good mother. She had dreams for the kids to better themselves. She really loved her kids."

And Betty Lee's sister Dorothy Fulton, chief investigator for the Navajo Nation, said, "Until it happens to your own family. . . . It's quite painful. I've now been at both ends. It can happen to anyone."

Among traditional Navajo people, the stories about Robert Fry took on an even more sinister tone. Because of newspaper reports, it was known that Fry was fascinated with Dungeons & Dragons and Vampire: The Masquerade. From these stories it was only one more step to his possibility of being a were-animal, or skinwalker. These creatures almost always did their killing at night, as Fry had done, and were often seen wearing the skins of animals such as wolves or bears. Even Fry's friends had commented about his bearlike appearance and manners.

Anglos generally were not thought to have the power to transform themselves into these ferocious creatures, but then there was Fry's own admission that he was part Mohawk. Even though it was not known if Mohawks had this power, traditionalists had often spoken of Hopis, Zunis and Pueblo Indians having the power. If they had it, who knew what other tribes might consort with witches and wizards. After all, The Eclectic had been full of books on that very topic.

Even the description of Robert Fry's Misfits T-shirt lent credence to these tales. The T-shirt with Betty Lee's blood on it contained a white human skull with dark eye sockets and mouth. Old-timers spoke of witches that had a face that was black on the nose, blue on the mouth and white on the head, rather skull-like in appearance.

As summer 2000 moved into fall, tensions kept simmering on the Navajo Reservation about Fry and Engh's crimes against Native Americans. Detective Bob Melton was all too aware of what had happened in the 1970s when the teenage boys of the Chokecherry Massacre had been given a light sentence for their crimes. It was a perception that law enforcement and the judiciary did not care about Native American rights in San Juan County. Detective Melton wanted to show that things had changed in the intervening years for the better, and he certainly didn't want things getting out of hand once again.

Just how out of hand it had become in 1974 was undeniably demonstrated on June of that year. Members of the Coalition for Navajo Liberation disrupted the Sheriff's Posse Parade in downtown Farmington. They particularly objected to a unit from Fort Bliss, Texas, that was dressed up as nineteenth-century U.S. Cavalry. To the Navajos, this was a slap in the face and a reminder of their brutal Long Walk and captivity in the 1860s. Before long, a full-scale riot had erupted on Main Street. Police tossed tear gas; batons were swung; protestors fought back. Officer Jerry Steele was run over by a car driven by one of the protestors. Thirty people were arrested, most of them Navajos. It was a scene right out of the heyday of the Vietnam War demonstrations in Berkeley, California.

One way to diffuse the potentially dangerous situation in 2000 would be to prove that Robert Fry had been the killer at The Eclectic in 1996. Neither one of the victims in that case were Native Americans. If Fry could be proved to be the murderer, then it could be shown that his crimes were not just hate crimes—he was very capable of killing anyone— Native American, Anglo, Hispanic or African American—when enraged.

Detective Melton had always thought that Robert Fry was "the doer" in the killings at The Eclectic. The very savagery of the attacks on Betty Lee and Donald Tsosie had the same MO as in The Eclectic case. An arrest, of course, cannot be made on mere conjecture and hearsay, it needs tangible evidence, and in the Eclectic homicides there had always been a missing link between the actual killings and Robert Fry. Detective Melton knew he was going to need help in bridging that one vital gap. And in November 2000, during Thanksgiving week, four years after the murder, he got it. It came through his partner, Detective Tyler Truby.

Truby had contact with an informant who let him know that Harold Pollock was back in Farmington from Arizona, visiting his family for Thanksgiving. This informant had been told by Robert Fry years before that he and Pollock had done the killings at The Eclectic. Fry had also told the man that if he ever told authorities, he would kill him. Very afraid of Robert Fry, the man had kept his mouth shut, but now that Fry was in jail, and Pollock was back in the area, the man contacted Detective Truby and said that he should talk to Pollock about the murders at The Eclectic.

Truby contacted Pollock, who said that he would agree to a meeting with police, if he had a lawyer present. This was agreed upon, and Detective Truby, along with Farmington police detective Pat Cordell and Detective Melton, met with Pollock. Pat Cordell wrote in his report about the whole scenario, "On November 29, 2000. Lt. Bob Melton of the San Juan County Sheriff's Office interviewed Harold Pollock. In the course of the interview with Harold Pollock he indicated that he had information relevant to the murders which were committed at The Eclectic but that he wished to speak with an attorney before he divulged any information. Pollock indicated that he wished to speak with Randall Roberts. Pollock indicated that Roberts had represented him previously.

"Lt. Melton contacted Randall Roberts and informed him that Pollock would be contacting him. The District Attorney, Sandra Price, was also contacted to discuss whether Pollock could be considered for a grant of immunity from prosecution if he gave information regarding the murder if he was not physically involved in the murders. Through discussion between the District Attorney, Randall Roberts, Lt. Melton and Harold Pollock, an immunity agreement was reached, signed and an interview was scheduled for the following day. Present at the interview of Pollock on the 30th of November 2000 were this affiant, Lt. Melton with the Sheriff's Office, Detective Tyler Truby with the Sheriff's Office, Randall Roberts and Lt. Doug Kennedy with the Farmington Police Department."

During his interview Pollock stated that on the night of November 28 to 29, 1996, he was at a party with Robert Fry and several other individuals. He said that at some point he and Fry decided to leave together in Fry's vehicle. After they drove around for a while, Fry wanted to use the rest room at The Eclectic. Once inside, Pollock said he saw that Joseph Fleming and Matt Trecker were the only individuals in the store. He and Fry stayed at the store and visited awhile with Fleming, and then Fry decided to steal some merchandise. After they stole the items and went to Chokecherry Canyon, they began to discuss what had happened and became concerned that the theft would be noticed and they would be the primary suspects. They decided to bury the items in the canyon area.

Pollock then told the officers that Fry drove back to Farmington and entered The Eclectic once again. Upon entering the store, Pollock said, he used the bathroom. While he was in there, he said, he heard loud noises coming from the showroom. When he exited the rest room, he saw Fry on top of Joseph Fleming and that Fry was choking Fleming. At some point Fry stood up and placed his boot on Fleming's throat. Pollock described Fry as having a look of rage on his face. He said that he became so afraid of Fry and what was happening, he went back into the bathroom and hid.

After a period of time, Pollock said, he came out of the rest room and saw Fry standing over Fleming with blood on his face, hands and clothing. He said that Fry was now acting apprehensive and no longer in a rage. It was at this point that he noticed that Matthew Trecker was also lying on the floor and appeared to be dead. Afraid of Fry, Pollock said, he agreed to help him remove evidence that both of them had been at the crime scene. He said that he told Fry to wash blood off himself in the bathroom, and as he did so, Pollock wiped down the bathroom floor.

Pollock told the officers the nature of the wounds on both Fleming and Trecker. These wounds were consistent with what the officers knew about the victims. Pollock then stated that Fry gathered items from the crime scene to take with them. The key to the front door, however, broke off in the lock, and that made an exit from the front impossible. Since they knew the only other exit was alarmed, he and Fry decided to break the front window by throwing a computer monitor through it and escape by that route.

Pollock said they then went out to Farmington Lake and disposed of the weapons taken from the store. He also stated that Robert Fry changed his clothes and boots there. While he was doing this, he realized that his wallet was missing. Concerned that the wallet might still be at The Eclectic, they went back there. While Pollock stood guard, Fry went inside and searched for his wallet. Not finding it, he went back outside and stood guard while Pollock searched for the wallet. Unable to find the wallet, they left before it got light.

Pollock told the officers they returned to the residence from which they had left the night before. They agreed upon a story to tell the police with a specific alibi as to why they had been to The Eclectic. Pollock told the officers one more thing—he said that if he ever went forward to the police about what had really happened at The Eclectic, Fry threatened to kill him and his family.

For the most part, Harold Pollock's statement of what had occurred at The Eclectic on November 29, 1996, was true and accurate. The only part he left out was that he had actually been ordered by Robert Fry to join in the killing of Matthew Trecker, which he did. Pollock covered this up by saying he went back to the rest room after seeing Fry stomping on Fleming's throat, and when he reemerged from the bathroom, that was the first time he saw Matthew Trecker's body. What he had divulged, though, was compelling, and Sergeant Cordell wrote in his report, "Pollock's statements regarding the crime scene are consistent with evidence and facts known to law enforcement. The description of the injuries seen and described by Pollock were consistent with the actual injuries sustained by the victims. Also, the locations of specific items given in Pollock's statements are consistent with the actual locations that were discussed during the initial investigation."

After Pollock's interview, Detective Melton interviewed some other friends of Fry's to see what they had to say about The Eclectic. Three of them came forward with very telling statements about Fry, and Cordell wrote down in his report, "As part of the investigation of this homicide, Lt. Bob Melton interviewed three individuals who stated that Fry had confessed his commission of the murders which occurred at The Eclectic. In an interview with Les Engh, Engh stated that Fry had indicated that he had committed the murders at The Eclectic. Engh further stated that he was threatened with his life if he ever told anyone what Fry had done."

Detective Melton also interviewed Jae Williams, who stated that Robert Fry had told him that he committed the murders at The Eclectic and that he would do the same to him if he ever told anyone what he had done. Williams was with another individual at the time and Fry threatened that person as well.

Given all this evidence, Robert Fry was arrested on several counts on December 5, 2000:

- Murder in the first degree of Joseph Fleming
- Murder in the first degree of Matthew Trecker
- Larceny over $250—a fourth-degree felony.
- Two counts of tampering with evidence—a third-degree felony
- Three counts of intimidation of witnesses—a third-degree felony

When details of this new arrest came out in the local newspapers, it helped ease the tensions that had been simmering on the nearby Navajo Reservation. As Bob Melton had hoped, the allegations of murder at The Eclectic showed Robert Fry for who he really was—an "equal opportunity killer" who didn't care whom he murdered when he was enraged. He didn't just target Native Americans, the basis of a hate crime, he targeted anyone who got in his way when he was in a murderous mood.

In the long run Detective Melton's initial hunches

about Robert Fry's ties to The Eclectic had been correct. It had taken the fortuitous return of Harold Pollock to the area four years later to confirm them. One other person's hunches had also been vindicated—Christina Trecker, Matthew's mom. She had always surmised that there was something going on with Robert Fry's friends after the murders. She said, "They were all scared. Didn't want to talk about it. They started distancing themselves from him. After I heard about his threats, now I knew why. He would kill them if they ever told. One thing that scared me after the murders at The Eclectic—Fry and a buddy actually moved into the same apartment complex we were in. They lived just a block away. Who knows what he would have done if he had the chance. He was a very dangerous person."

At this point things were about to move from the police to the judiciary, but not before Robert Fry proved how dangerous he still could be.

Chapter 8

Trials and . . .

Even before trial proceedings were very far advanced on the Betty Lee case, both Les Engh and Robert Fry were in trouble again. Les Engh's problems started when he attempted to force another inmate into a sexual act. When the inmate resisted, Engh beat the man and threatened him if he went to the authorities. The inmate did anyway, and Engh was charged with attempted criminal sexual penetration, extortion, assault and battery.

Robert Fry was also causing a disturbance in his own cell. His jailers found an eight-inch metal shank hidden underneath his mattress. When they confronted him with this, Fry tried to blame it on his cellmate, Michael Kightlinger. Fry said that he and Kightlinger were cleaning up the cell when a piece of metal fell off the bucket. He said that Kightlinger then stashed the metal piece under Fry's mattress. The authorities did not buy this story from Fry, and they slapped him with a new charge of being in the possession of a concealed and deadly weapon. In fact, it was a very poor decision on Fry's part to be in possession of a potential weapon, and his rash act would come back to haunt him.

By the autumn of 2000, Leslie Engh's attorney, Gary Mitchell, could see the writing on the wall as far as the Betty Lee case was going, and he sought a severance of his client's trial from that of Robert Fry. Engh always contended that Fry had been the instigator and killer in both the Betty Lee and Donald Tsosie murders. Mitchell wrote a lengthy motion for severance and his most telling point was: "There has never been a case in the state of New Mexico since the current Capital Felony Sentencing Act, where two people charged with the penalty of death have been tried together due to the requirements of that act . . . and the New Mexico Constitution regarding individual judgement."

Mitchell's request was granted and he received the severance that he sought for Les Engh.

Robert Fry's main attorney, Edward Bustamante, a lawyer from Albuquerque, received a very different and intriguing offer from the San Juan County District Attorney's Office around this same time. The offer was that if Robert Fry pleaded guilty to the Betty Lee murder, as well as the killings of Donald Tsosie, Joseph Fleming and Matthew Trecker, the prosecutors would take the death penalty off the table and give him a life sentence. Fry mulled this over for a while and came back with his decision—he would go to trial and gamble that a jury would acquit him in the Betty Lee case.

Fry's defense attorney's concern about the widespread publicity of the case in San Juan County led to an appeal for change of venue by Ed Bustamante. Changes of venue are not taken lightly by any judge, since they require great shifts in resources, time and energy for a county's justice team to switch to a different county. Everyone would be unfamiliar with the new courtroom and all evidence and transcripts would have to be carefully filed, packed and transported to the new locale.

In the end, however, Judge Birdsall believed that there had been so much publicity about the Betty Lee case in San Juan County that Robert Fry could not get a fair trial there. He opted for the case taking place in Albuquerque, the largest city in the state, and Bustamante and the prosecutors agreed. The change would allow for an extensive jury pool, something crucial in a possible death penalty case. Not only would there be fewer people who had heard of Betty Lee or Robert Fry, but there would be more individuals available for the entire jury pool, many of whom were certain to be dismissed for various reasons.

Albuquerque is a cosmopolitan city, situated along the banks of the Rio Grande River, below the Sandia Mountains. The Sandia Peak Aerial Tramway is one of the world's longest, and takes visitors to an elevation of 10,300 feet above the city. Colorful hot-air balloons are often seen drifting in the sky because of the updrafts near the mountains. By 2002, the city contained nearly a half-million residents—a far cry from the original thirty families who had settled the region at Old Town in 1706, not far from the present-day federal courthouse.

Robert Fry's trial was destined for the federal courthouse in downtown Albuquerque because it was determined that this venue could best handle the logistics and complexity of what was sure to be a fairly lengthy trial, and they had a courtroom open for such contingencies. Yet even with the new venue, almost 180 miles away from Farmington, many people in Albuquerque had already heard or read about Robert Fry. There had been a lengthy article in the *Albuquerque Journal,* not only about the

Betty Lee case, but also about Fry's possible connections to the murders of Donald Tsosie, Joseph Fleming and Matt Trecker. It gave a fairly detailed account about Fry and his friends in the old Wild Bunch days and Fry's ties to The Eclectic. Ed Bustamante brought to the judge's attention that there were stories being posted on the Internet about the different cases as well. He said, "They are reporting about all three cases."

Judge Birdsall replied, "I will make sure to instruct the jury panel not to read the paper or watch the news." This included Internet stories about the news and anything else concerning Robert Fry.

To help the San Juan County District Attorney's Office with its trial, Michael Cox joined their team. Cox was assistant attorney general of New Mexico and director of the state's Prosecution/Investigations Division. One of the cases he had worked on shortly before the Fry case concerned Luis Acosta of Taos County. Acosta had kidnapped, robbed and murdered Erik Sanchez, throwing him off the towering Rio Grande Gorge Bridge into the canyon below. With Cox's help, the prosecution in that case got a plea bargain from Acosta. Instead of the death penalty, Acosta received life plus seventy-one years.

Cox also helped in the Capital Litigation Unit that provided legal and logistical support and security for the execution of Terry Clark. Clark had raped and murdered nine-year-old Dena Lynn Gore in 1986. While Robert Fry's case was making its way through the court system, Clark was executed on November 6, 2001. He was the first prisoner to be executed in New Mexico since David Cooper Nelson had been sent to the gas chamber in 1960. Clark was executed by lethal injection, the gas chamber having gone out of use since the 1960s execution. Clark's execution hung like a dark shadow over Robert Fry and his defense team. It was a clear warning that New Mexicans were willing to implement the death penalty once again after a forty-one-year hiatus.

Everyone concerned in the Betty Lee trial knew that just empaneling a jury was going to be a marathon event. This became abundantly clear right from the start as judge, prosecutors and defense team weeded out prospective jurors who leaned too far to one side or the other on the death penalty issue. Prospective juror #2 said that he had not heard anything about the Betty Lee case, but on questioning from Bustamante, he said that he agreed with the death penalty. Then the man added, "But I have a pretty open mind."

When given a rough overall idea about the murder of Betty Lee, prospective juror #2 said, "The appropriate penalty would be death."

Bustamante told Judge Birdsall, "This juror seems to be pretty wedded to the death penalty."

Prospective juror #2 was excused.

Prospective juror #3 was even more of a problem. He said, "I'm very conservative and I feel if a person is found guilty, they should do the time. I have two sons that are police officers. They protect us from what criminals do. I would probably vote for the death penalty if no other circumstances were found. Especially if this was premeditated."

Asked if he already had made up his mind, #3 said, "I wouldn't prejudge, though death would be appropriate if there was aggravated circumstances."

Prospective juror #3 was eventually excused.

Prospective juror #4 had her own set of issues. She said, "I have a problem with transportation. I would have to be brought and picked up by my friends." Then she added, "I believe the penalty should be severe."

This led to her being excused.

Prospective juror #5, on the other hand, gave answers that both sides wanted to hear. The prospective juror said, "I'm in favor of the death penalty if it fits the crime, but it depends upon the circumstances. I'd wait until the penalty phase before making a decision."

This candidate was allowed as a juror.

And so it went down the line with those admitted and those excused. Among the excused were people like prospective juror #6 who said, "I work for Las Lunas Corrections and I don't feel I'd be a good candidate for this trial. I had a brother killed in February of last year and the killer hasn't been found."

A schoolteacher was excused because she was "philosophically against the death penalty." She added, "I'm glad that New Mexico doesn't use the death penalty often."

Prospective juror #14 thought that New Mexico was spending too much money for murderers in prison by feeding and warehousing them. Then he added, "I have one sister who was raped. I also have another sister who was raped and left for dead." This candidate was immediately excused.

Interestingly enough, there were two Catholics who were excused for diametrically opposite reasons. Prospective juror #32 said, "It would be difficult for me as a Catholic to impose the death penalty." Prospective juror #80, on the other hand, said, "I am a Catholic and I believe in the death penalty."

One who had no chance of getting on the jury was prospective juror #13. She said, "If they (the murderer) kill someone in a certain way, they should be killed in the same way." Her implication was that Robert Fry should be executed with a sledgehammer blow to the head if found guilty.

Those who were eventually chosen as jurors were in the middle ground between the extremes of pro– and anti–death penalty advocacy. Prospective juror #86 felt that some, but not all, killers should be subject to the death penalty. He said he would weigh all the facts before deciding. Prospective juror #33 said, "The death penalty should be reserved for extreme cases and should depend on the circumstances."

There was a lot of give-and-take on prospective juror #10, who taught at a junior college. He said, "I'm certainly open to either life or death. You have to look at the circumstances before making a decision. Your actions have consequences. And there's the value of human life." He agreed he could change his mind during the sentencing phase. "I wouldn't make a decision without knowing all the facts. It would be hard to put myself in Mr. Fry's shoes."

The prosecutor said to the judge, "I feel that number 10 would be a good juror."

Bustamante wanted #10 to be excused, but Judge Birdsall replied, "I think he indicated he could follow the instructions. We will retain him."

Prospective juror #9 was acceptable to both for subtle reasons. She was a single mother who worked in a law office with civil work and had been a legal assistant for three years. She said, "I'd like to know more about the victim and the defendant. I'd hold the state to their burden of proof. Even though I sometimes feel that life in prison costs the taxpayers too much, I'd keep an open mind."

She seemed like an ideal candidate to both Ed Bustamante and Joe Gribble, the lead prosecutor from San Juan County.

In some regards, Robert Fry was lucky that he had committed the murder of Betty Lee in New

Mexico. New Mexicans, historically, were loath to implement the death penalty. There were only three men serving on New Mexico's death row in 2002. Timothy Allen, of Bloomfield, had raped and murdered seventeen-year-old Sandra Phillips, of Aztec, in 1995. Michael Treadway had been in the act of robbing a place called Playorama in Texico, New Mexico, when seventy-two-year-old Red Prather walked in. Treadway demanded Prather's wallet, but Prather moved toward the phone instead. Treadway shot Prather twice in the chest and once in the eye, killing him.

Perhaps the most brutal crime of the three death row inmates was perpetrated by Francisco Martinez. In 1993, he and two others kidnapped and raped twelve-year-old Crystal La Pierre, of Grants. Then to keep her quiet, Martinez beat, kicked, strangled and stabbed her. When she didn't die immediately, he drowned her in a mud puddle.

Fry was also lucky in that Albuquerque was the most cosmopolitan of all the cities in New Mexico, and a wide background of races and ethnicities was mirrored in the jury. Albuquerque was also a more liberal area, by and large than San Juan County, where an eye-for-an-eye concept was more prevalent than in the big city.

Robert Fry was lucky in another way. Judge Birdsall had determined that the jurors would not hear about the other possible murders by Robert Fry. There would be no mention of Donald Tsosie, Joseph Fleming or Matthew Trecker, and the circumstances surrounding their deaths. These other "bad acts" were seen as too prejudicial by the judge. The jurors would solely judge Robert Fry in this case on the murder of Betty Lee.

Yet in one key area, Robert Fry was very unlucky. This concerned the attempted rape and kidnapping charges that were included with the murder charge. If he was found guilty of these, and of first-degree murder as well, then because of New Mexico's law, he was eligible to receive the death penalty. Knowing this was the case, Ed Bustamante tried his hardest with the judge to have these two "extra" charges dismissed. And Bustamante did it by using Les Engh's own words. Back in early June 2000, after he was arrested, Les Engh had told police that he and Fry had picked up Betty Lee at the convenience store and driven out toward Kirtland. Engh indicated that at this point, not even he knew for sure what Robert Fry planned to do with Betty Lee. It was not a clear case of kidnapping at this point as far as Engh or Bustamante were concerned.

Engh had said, "Fry pulled off the highway onto a dirt road, saying, 'I just have to pee.' When the car stopped, the woman got out and started walking away. Bobby Fry said, 'No, don't, don't you worry. I'm just peein',' and she walked a little bit more and Bobby actually peed then, and she came back."

Bustamante summed up the prosecutors' theory of kidnapping this way:

1. By deception at the gas station when Fry first offered Betty Lee a ride.

2. By deception on the dirt road by convincing Betty Lee to get back into the car after she started to walk away.

3. By force by pulling Betty Lee from the car.

4. By force by chasing Betty Lee down and killing her with a sledgehammer.

Bustamante countered these arguments, one by one.

1. There was nothing in Engh's account to suggest that at the time of offering Betty Lee a ride, Fry had any intention other than simply giving her

a ride to Kirtland. Once she was in the car, Fry indeed began to drive in the direction of Kirtland.

2. After Fry pulled off on the dirt road to relieve himself, Betty Lee got out of the car and started to walk away. Again, there was no indication that his stated need to relieve himself was a ruse of any kind. As Engh stated, "Bobby actually peed then, and then she came back." If Fry had, at that moment, a secret intent to harm Betty Lee, it is not reasonable that he would begin to drive back out toward the main highway after she reentered the car.

3. There is no factually distinct kidnapping before the homicide, but rather a homicide that begins with being pulled from the car. Engh claimed that Fry stopped the car in the middle of the dirt road, walked around to the passenger side, and pulled Betty Lee out by her hair. Almost immediately, by Engh's account, Fry told him to come hold her legs, while Fry lifted up her shirt and stabbed her in the chest. The force used to pull Betty Lee from the car is the beginning of the force used to kill her, not a separate crime unto itself.

4. The state's assertion that chasing Betty Lee down before killing her constitutes kidnapping is unsupportable. By this logic, any homicide in which the victim does not remain cooperatively stationary throughout the assault culminating in death must also involve a kidnapping, and would thus be eligible for the death penalty.

Bustamante also argued against the state's contention that Robert Fry had attempted to rape Betty Lee. He stated, "While pulling clothes off a victim might be viewed as inherently sexual in nature, by itself, it sheds no light on the intent of the attacker. Disrobing a victim could be the first step in an attempt to commit criminal sexual penetration, or an attempt to commit sexual contact, or even some lesser degree of intrusion. Nothing in the evidence presented suggests that any sort of penetration was contemplated, much less overtly attempted."

Bustamante used Engh's words to back up this last contention, from the following exchange between Engh and detectives in a report.

Detective—Did he (Fry) say why he wanted her clothes off?
Engh—No, he never did. My presumption is he wanted to get her naked or do something.
Detective—Do you think he wanted to have sex with her?
Engh—He may have. I don't think he did. He may have while they were on the other side of the car, or at least attempted, but I'm not sure.

Bustamante even used Betty Lee's autopsy report from Dr. Patricia McFeely to back up his contentions. It stated in part that while the body of the victim was found unclothed, there was no bruising or trauma to the genital or anal areas.

Despite Bustamante's best efforts, the judge eventually allowed the state's contention of both aggravating circumstances—murder in the course of a kidnapping, and murder in the course of an attempt to commit criminal sexual penetration—to stand. Both allegations, if agreed upon by the jury, could give Robert Fry the death penalty.

By April 3, 2002, the jury selection was winding down in Albuquerque. As Michelle Abbot wrote in the *Farmington Daily Times,* "Defense attorneys and prosecutors continued a delicate dance as jury selection completed its fifth day in the death penalty trial of Robert Fry." Abbot went on to say that the prosecutor and defense attorney carefully questioned each of the prospective jurors from a pool that included 245 individuals. She wrote, "The trick for both sides is to keep every potential juror walking a fine line of impartiality."

One dangerous point of contention arose in one instance, when a prospective juror thought he might have seen Robert Fry being brought from a holding cell. Just that image alone proved that Fry was already a prisoner, and Bustamante said that this juror might have tainted the others in the jury pool by discussing it with them. Bustamante wanted an entire new jury empaneled, but Judge Birdsall excused this potential juror and said that the others had not been tainted by what the juror in question had seen.

The fact of the matter was, prospective jurors did not see Robert Fry in jail garb each day in court as he sat beside his lawyers taking notes. Fry wore a suit coat and tie, and it was hard to tell him from any of the other defense attorneys. He had trimmed his hair and looked very neat and presentable. Fry often scribbled on a yellow legal pad, just like a lawyer, as the parade of prospective jurors moved through, and he often conferred with his defense attorneys, Ed Bustamante and Eric Hannum.

Meanwhile, Prosecutor Michael Cox and ADA Joe Gribble ran through a mind-numbing number of prospective jurors. Cox estimated that they would go through 140 or 150 before finally being able to empanel a jury with two substitute jurors. He was pretty close to the mark. By late Thursday afternoon the field was narrowed from 139 to 43. And then it was time to exercise their preemptory strikes of jurors among these 43. Ed Bustamante was allowed to strike 9 prospective jurors, and the prosecution was allowed to strike 7. Each side did make several strikes, and finally agreed that they had done all they wanted. When the final strike was exercised, Judge Birdsall declared, "We have a jury." He also added, "This was educational, long and tiring."

In fact, no one in the San Juan County judicial system could remember a process quite like it, but then this wasn't your average murder trial. The jury may not have known of all the charges against Robert Fry, besides the Betty Lee case, but everyone in the system certainly did. There was sure to be emotional testimony on the stand by witnesses, courtroom challenges and lengthy sidebars with the judge as the actual trial commenced.

ADA Joe Gribble told reporters at the time of empaneling, "I'm delighted that we're getting started. Seven days of jury selection was getting tedious." When asked how long he thought the prosecution side would take, he answered, "Who knows? It could be a week, a week and a half. Two weeks." In fact, all of this was uncharted water, in a courtroom out of the San Juan County prosecutor's jurisdiction and the challenge of getting witnesses, more than 180 miles from the Farmington area.

Not far away from the courthouse, Detective Tyler Truby was in Albuquerque with over two hundred pieces of evidence and photos, stored in the state attorney general's office. Truby was itching for the trial to begin. It was now nearly two years since he and Detective Bob Melton had arrived on the incredibly bloody crime scene on CR 6480 near Kirtland and saw the dead woman's body in the brush.

On April 8, 2002, the jury trial of Robert Fry for the murder of Betty Lee finally began. In an opening statement Joe Gribble said, "Betty Lee screamed in terror. Robert Fry had already bragged, 'I'm going to stick someone tonight.' " He went on to describe the incredible brutality of her death.

In the courtroom's gallery Betty Lee's teenage children bowed their heads and cried.

Ed Bustamante, on the other hand, blamed the whole incident on Les Engh. He said, "Even though Robert Fry was behind the wheel that night, he was only an accomplice to the murder. Betty Lee died at the hands of Les Engh. Even though Robert weighed ninety-nine more pounds than Engh, regrettably he did nothing to stop it."

Joe Gribble began his long list of witnesses for the prosecution by introducing the tow truck drivers on the scene during the early-morning hours of June 9, 2000. Floyd Robinson told of trying to extricate the Fry vehicles and bogging down himself in the soft sand. Charley Bergin, owner/operator of Bloomfield Towing, related how he had pulled all the other vehicles out, but had become frustrated by a cell phone that wasn't working properly. Frustrated, he threw it to the ground.

Next on the stand was Deputy Matt Wilcox, who discovered Bergin's cell phone in the dirt. Wilcox told how it was a little over a mile away from Betty Lee's body, amidst a lot of tire tracks. Wilcox was followed by Detective Terry Eagle, crime scene technician, who led the jury through a host of crime scene photos and aerial photos of the terrain. Then Eagle discussed the actual bowie knife and sledgehammer, which were presented to the jurors for inspection.

Norman Lee, Betty Lee's brother, gave a narrative of her life, and pointed out Betty in a Christmas photo. Other crime photos were much more disturbing and Judge Birdsall would not allow one in particular to be projected onto an overhead screen. Instead, it was passed from hand to hand among the jurors. The photo was graphic in the extreme, a view of Betty Lee's head, with blood and brain matter exposed. It was too much for one juror. A twenty-five-minute recess had to be called while the juror regained her composure.

The next day, Detective Terry Eagle returned to the stand. Wearing white gloves, he handled evidence and photos, which were displayed to the jury. Amongst these were several pairs of shoes, pants and shirts that had belonged to Robert Fry. The most damning one was a black T-shirt with a white skull on the front and the word "Misfits" on the back. Down near the bottom of the skull was a tiny drop of blood. Eagle told the jury that it was Betty Lee's blood.

ADA Dustin O'Brien led Terry Eagle through these exhibits for two hours, including photos of tire and shoe plaster casts. The tires were important because they had tread marks similar to those of Robert Fry's car. And the shoe prints were, of course, important because they were similar in size to shoes owned by Robert Fry.

Defense attorney Ed Bustamante hit back with an admission from Eagle that there had been many shoe prints out at the crime scene, not just Robert Fry's. Bustamante then wanted to know why only seven plaster casts of shoe prints had been taken when there were literally dozens of shoe prints at the scene. Some prints belonged to Fry, some to Engh, others to Betty Lee and still others to unidentified individuals. Bustamante also got Eagle to admit that he had only been a crime scene technician for a few months when he first began to work on the Betty Lee case.

Bustamante was on the offensive with sheriff's deputies and particularly Detective Bob Melton during cross-examination. He asked Melton three times if he had taken written notes or audio recordings during Les Engh's initial interviews. Melton answered three times that he had not, but then it was not his habit to do so. A videotape had finally been shot during Les Engh's third interview.

Detective Melton was calm and collected on the stand, and he presented an aura of competence. He had been on the witness stand in many previous cases giving testimony, and he had a long background in law enforcement to back up his contentions and way of handling crimes. It was quite apparent that Melton wasn't some rookie who had inadvertently messed up at the Betty Lee crime scene or in later interviews of suspects.

Phillip Wareheim, a crime lab supervisor for the Department of Public Safety, took the stand next. For over an hour he compared Robert Fry's shoe sizes and tire marks to crime scene plaster casts. Based on his comparisons, Wareheim put Les Engh, Betty Lee and Robert Fry all at the crime scene.

The jurors then watched a forty-five-minute black-and-white videotape of Robert Fry's first interview at the sheriff's office in June 2000. It depicted Fry and his mother sitting in an interview room with Detective Melton. During this tape Fry said he and Engh had given a ride to a man named Ryan out to the Kirtland area on June 9, 2000. Fry told Melton that Ryan was too drunk to give good directions, so they lost their way on the dirt roads, and because of this, Fry's car eventually became stuck in the sand. Fry added that Ryan had then walked off into the night and had not been heard from since.

Gloria Fry was also heard on the tape, explaining how she had gone to pick up Robert and Les Engh out on the dirt road. Detective Melton explained to the jury that Gloria Fry was in the interview room because she and Robert had insisted that she be present as he was questioned. For the first time jurors saw Fry out of a suit and tie and with his hair longer. In the video he wore a T-shirt, dark pants and shoulder-length hair.

April 10, 2002, was the day that Robert Fry's friends and former friends began to testify for the prosecution. Steve Lavery said that on the night of June 8, 2000, at The Kettle restaurant, "Fry was very, very agitated. Really off the wall that night. He was running his mouth off and going to kick ass." Then Lavery spoke of the argument and near fight that Fry had instigated with another patron named CC at The Kettle. Lavery said that he and others had to intervene.

At that point, Lavery recalled, Fry went out to his car. Lavery said that Fry came back in a few minutes later wearing a jacket, which covered something at his side. "I thought maybe it was a gun," he added. "I couldn't say. I just saw something."

Telani Sokolowski had also seen the disturbance that night at the restaurant. She told the jury, "He (Fry) sat down across from me, but when I asked him, 'Bobby, what's going on?' he wouldn't talk to me. Then he got up and went outside. When he returned, he was wearing a jacket."

Sokolowski said she thought Fry might have a weapon there. At this point Fry told her, "Someone's going to die."

David Johnson was at The Kettle as well. He testified that Fry said, "I'm wearing an eight-inch bowie knife and I'm going to stick somebody tonight."

Following Johnson was a clerk from the Apache Y convenience store who remembered Engh's being there and he could see Fry's vehicle out front.

The next witness was much more powerful, it was none other than Gloria Fry. She told the jurors that her son had used a cell phone that she had given him, which belonged to the probation department, to call her in the early-morning hours of June 9, 2000. She had driven out to the dirt road when Robert indicated he was stuck, and gave both Les Engh and Robert a ride. They dropped Engh off at his residence and then went home.

Gloria continued and said that she and her husband and Robert returned in two vehicles to try and extricate Robert's car, but that her husband's pickup became stuck in the sand. She returned home, got dressed for work and grabbed some old rugs for James's and Robert's vehicles. The rugs were to be placed beneath the tires to try and give them some traction. Shortly after 8:00 A.M., she returned to the area and described what happened next.

"I came upon someone standing on a rock. I got curious and drove over there. I saw police cars and encountered authorities who said there had been a homicide. Then [later] I told my son about the investigation. I told him he was real lucky. Somebody got killed over there and you're lucky you weren't one of them."

Asked by Michael Cox why she hadn't asked her son what he was doing in that area, she said it hadn't occurred to her that he might be useful to the authorities. She said she didn't connect him being stuck on the dirt road with a body that was a little more than a mile away. "It never entered my mind," she said.

Gloria Fry also stated that Robert had phoned her after being arrested, admitting to being at the murder scene, but by then he was blaming the murder on Les Engh. She said, "He (Robert) called and he was afraid for our safety. He said Les had threatened us if he told. He said we should not go home."

Just how Les Engh was a threat to them at that point, Robert Fry didn't say. After all, Les Engh was behind bars, just as he was. The prosecution added that this was the first time Gloria Fry had related this story to anyone.

Detective Tyler Truby was called next as a witness and said that this was the first time he'd ever heard of Robert Fry admitting to being at the murder scene. Fry certainly hadn't done so when being videotaped in June 2000. Truby also said this was the first time he'd ever heard about any threat from Les Engh. Then Truby told of sifting through the immense pile of clothing scattered in Robert Fry's room on June 10, 2000. He had rummaged through the pile of clothing, looking for items that appeared to have blood on them. Truby said he eventually selected several pants, shirts and shoes to be analyzed. Especially noteworthy was a black T-shirt with a white skull on the front. It had what appeared to be a tiny drop of blood on the bottom of the skull, and Robert Fry had admitted to wearing that T-shirt on June 8 and 9, 2000. Even Gloria Fry backed her son up on that account. When the blood spot was later analyzed, it proved to have come from Betty Lee.

April 11 was a day of testimony from the medical examiners and tech experts. Dr. Ross Zumwalt, the state's chief medical investigator, noted that he had found a nine-by-three-inch wound in the back of Betty Lee's head. He said, "It gaped open widely, revealing multiple skull fractures and brain lacerations—evidence of at least three, and more likely four or five, blows probably inflicted by a ten pound sledgehammer."

Zumwalt also stated that Betty Lee had sustained a 1½-inch stab wound through the breastbone that stopped just short of her heart. He said the knife had to have been "a very sturdy knife" to inflict a wound through a bony area more than an inch thick. And it had to have been wielded with great force.

This brought Johnny Ausburn to the stand. Ausburn stated that he had sharpened a bowie knife for Robert Fry one week before Betty Lee's murder. He said it had an eight-inch blade. In fact, he identified the knife that officers found at the scene as being the same knife that he had sharpened for Fry.

One thing the jury did not hear was a comment the prosecution wanted admitted. While the jury was out of hearing, there was a sidebar about a comment Ausburn made. The comment was: "Fry was so fond of the weapon, he nicknamed it Bubba the Butcher Knife." Judge Birdsall said this was too prejudicial and the comment did not get in.

The next witness on the stand was exceedingly important for the prosecution. He was Rod Englert, a prominent criminologist and expert in blood pattern analysis. Englert was a thirty-eight-year veteran of the sheriff's office in Multonamah County, Oregon. By 2002, he had given five hundred lectures and seminars in thirty-five states, Canada, Russia and Great Britain. He gave training seminars in unsolved crimes and crime scene recon-

struction. His premier area of expertise was blood
spatter analysis. Englert had been a consultant in
250 cases throughout the United States and was a
graduate of the FBI National Academy.

The reason Englert was so important to the Betty
Lee case was that two men had been there at the time
of the murder—Robert Fry and Les Engh. Both men
were now pointing their fingers at the other one as
being the killer, each said he was merely a witness
to the murder. The prosecution could bring forth
lots of witnesses about Fry's comments and actions
at the restaurant before the crime, but in a death
penalty trial, they had to have someone besides
Engh say that Robert Fry had wielded the sledgehammer that delivered the deathblows. That man,
they hoped, was Rod Englert.

Englert gave the jury a twenty-minute tutorial in
blood spatters. He told them there are about six
quarts of blood in a human adult body. From the
position of the spatters and stains, an expert can
determine the movement or position of the victim
in relation to his or her assailant. It is also possible
to ascertain from which direction the assault
came.

Traditional old-style investigations of this sort
involved using strings from the source of the blood
to the central point of the spatter pattern. By the
late 1990s, a computer software program called
BackTrack created the string effect digitally. The
investigator could enter width, length, direction and
position of each blood droplet or stain and the
software would determine the angle of attack and
flight pattern of the blood.

As Anne Wingate pointed out in her book *Scene
of the Crime,* "The type of spatter pattern is determined by the force with which the blood falls, the

distance it falls, and the type of surface it lands on and whether it lands vertically or at an angle."

Englert then described specific blood spatter patterns found on Robert Fry's shoes that were consistent with his being the one who wielded the sledgehammer. The most damning evidence of all was the blood found on Robert Fry's Misfits T-shirt. The blood had already been proved to be that of Betty Lee by DNA testing, and Englert said, "In my opinion, the blood source is Betty Lee on the ground, and she has been hit a number of times by the person who wore this shirt."

Even though Les Engh's clothes also had blood on them, they were not consistent with blood spatters. According to Englert, the bloodstains were consistent with someone dragging a bloody body, which Engh said he had done.

During a break in the trial, a very interesting note came up later while the jury was out of hearing. The prosecutors told the judge that they believed the knife (Bubba) had also been used in The Eclectic murders. Even though they very much wished to have evidence of Robert Fry's involvement in that case admitted, it was not allowed in by Judge Birdsall.

April 12 was dramatic to say the least. Les Engh was on the stand and the jury at last had an eyewitness account of the murder of Betty Lee. For three hours Engh gave a recitation of the events of June 8 and 9, 2000, starting at The Top Deck Lounge, and then the later altercation at The Kettle. Engh said, "I asked Robert to give me a ride home, just to get him out of there." It was this ride that led them to the convenience store on the edge of town and Betty Lee standing alone outside at a phone booth.

Engh was very self-possessed on the stand, answering all the questions in a matter-of-fact tone. Some observers thought he was cold and distant, others found him to be frank and believable. He didn't flinch from anything.

Engh said that Betty Lee became nervous almost as soon as they drove off onto the dirt road outside of Kirtland. "I guess she was getting scared because we had gone kinda far off the highway."

Engh told of her getting out of the car and corroborated the police report of Fry driving alongside her as she walked in sandals. Somehow Fry managed to talk Betty Lee back into the car. Engh stated that they hadn't driven far when Fry stopped the car for a second time. "He (Fry) got out, came around to the passenger side and opened the door and pulled her out by the hair. She was hollering a little and started fighting. He (Fry) told me to grab her legs. Then Robert pushed her shirt and bra up around her neck. He pulled out his knife and stabbed her in the chest. She continued to struggle, kicked free and knocked the knife away into the sagebrush. She started to run away, but we caught up with her in a matter of seconds. He (Fry) was holding her and I pulled her pants off. She was still kicking and yelling and screaming and kicked free and started running again.

"Robert handed me a flashlight from inside the vehicle and told me to look for the knife. He took a sledgehammer from among the tools in his car. She was on the ground fifteen or thirty feet away from where I was looking for the knife. I saw Robert raise the sledgehammer. I saw him swing it. I didn't see him hit her, the car was in the way. She was yelling and screaming. She kept saying things like, 'Why are you doing this to me?' I saw him swing again."

Joe Gribble asked Engh, "Did the screaming stop?"

"Yes," Engh answered.

After Fry had killed Betty Lee, Engh said, they each grabbed one of her wrists and dragged her facedown through the dirt away from the road. Her bloody trail was later measured at being 120 feet from the spot Fry killed her to the spot they tossed her into the brush.

When it was his turn, Ed Bustamante grilled Engh for more than an hour on cross-examination. He repeatedly stressed that Engh had lied to authorities when he was first questioned. Bustamante said that it was only when he reached a plea agreement with the authorities that he began to finger Robert Fry as the killer. Bustamante kept pounding on the point of Les Engh as a liar—someone who made up stories to save his own skin.

There was a weekend recess of the trial after Les Engh's testimony and it didn't resume again until April 16, when prosecutors wrapped up their case. By this point the prosecution had called more than twenty witnesses and presented fifty photos and pieces of evidence. To cap everything off, the prosecution presented a thirty-minute videotape of Les Engh's confession to police a few days after the murder of Betty Lee. It was a heavily edited tape, deleting all references to Donald Tsosie and that murder. The jury had not heard a word about Donald Tsosie during the entire trial, and they weren't about to hear any now.

After the prosecution rested, the courtroom was cleared so that Robert Fry and his parents could consult with his lawyers. Nearly twenty of Betty Lee's relatives, who had faithfully attended the trial, were escorted from the courtroom. What happened next was perhaps the most important forty-five minutes of Robert Fry's life. His attorneys approached the prosecutors with the possibility of a deal in what they termed a "soft offer." They wanted to know what Robert Fry would get in return if he confessed to the murder of Betty Lee.

The prosecution reiterated their bargain of a year before: Fry would have to plead guilty to the murders of Betty Lee, Donald Tsosie, Joseph Fleming and Matthew Trecker. In exchange, the death penalty would be removed, but he would have to serve a life sentence. For forty-five minutes Robert Fry and his parents mulled this over. Gloria Fry seemed to have quite a bit of input into the conversation, according to reporter Debra Mayeux.

Robert Fry decided in the end to take his chances with the jury. He knew that all it took was one person to hold out against a conviction, and New Mexico juries were very skittish in death penalty cases. Robert Fry had gambled with other people's lives in the past—now he gambled with his own. He told his lawyers that the trial would go forward. In a very real sense it was now liberty or death.

A very somber Ed Bustamante approached the prosecution team and said, "Let's proceed."

After this crucial conference the jury and Betty Lee's relatives returned to the courtroom. Ed Bustamante called his first witness for the defense, bloodstain pattern analyst Norman Reeves. Just like Rod Englert, Reeves had a long tenure in law enforcement. He had been on a police force in New Jersey for twenty-five years, then moved to Tucson, Arizona, and went into a private consulting business. Over the years he helped both prosecutors and defense attorneys on their cases. He had even helped the Royal Thai Police on a case in Bangkok, Thailand. Reeves was a member of the American College of Forensic Examiners.

Reeves, unlike Englert, said there was not enough blood evidence to determine as to who was standing where when Betty Lee was hit by the sledgehammer. Reeves said the bloodstains on Engh's clothing could have come from dragging Lee through the dirt, or from the sledgehammer blows. Engh could not be excluded as the killer. As for Robert Fry's clothes, especially the T-shirt with the skull, in his opinion, there was not enough of a spatter mark there to say for sure that Fry was the killer.

The next person on the stand was meant to damage Les Engh's credibility. She was Sonya Duke, an employee of the Pre-Prosecution Diversion Program. Duke admitted that Engh had lied to her in the past on a different case concerning a forgery (the forgery of Pastor Fleming's signature). It was Bustamante's claim that Engh was a habitual liar who could not be trusted then and could not be trusted now—especially when his life had been on the line before making a deal with the authorities.

The third defense witness was a handful for both sides. He was convicted felon Shawn Nolan. Nolan had shared a jail cell with Les Engh during the previous year at the San Juan County Detention Center. In November 2001, he contacted Gloria Fry and said he had some information about Engh. Supposedly, when Gloria Fry talked to Nolan, he said that Engh had admitted to him that he was the killer of Betty Lee, not Robert.

Now on the stand, however, Nolan totally changed his story. He told Bustamante that Engh never admitted to stabbing or hitting Betty Lee with the sledgehammer. Even worse, on cross-examination,

Nolan told Michael Cox that he had invented the story after having a fight with Engh. He had initially contacted Gloria Fry as a way of getting even with Engh.

Closing arguments were basically a reiteration of the case as both the prosecution and defense saw it. Judge Birdsall once again gave the jury instructions as to how they were to proceed in the jury room as they debated on guilt or innocence. They were not to consider the death penalty and all its ramifications at this point. That would come later if they found that Robert Fry was guilty of first-degree murder. Now they were to concentrate on only the task at hand: was he guilty of killing Betty Lee in the early-morning hours of June 9, 2000?

The jury deliberated for seven hours, working right through lunch without a break. During the deliberations Robert Fry seemed relaxed and upbeat. He chatted with his attorneys and scribbled on notepads, even when the jury members filed back into the courtroom. Long deliberations usually boded well for the defendant. They are often a sign the jury is having trouble reaching a unanimous decision.

As Fry stood at the defense table with his lawyers, his demeanor immediately changed as the verdict was read. To his astonishment, he heard the word "guilty" ring forth from the foreman on the first-degree murder charge. Fry trembled and dropped his head into his hands. Before long he was sobbing, as were his mother and sister.

According to a reporter for the *Albuquerque Tribune*, the entire family "was absolutely wailing."

In some ways, even worse than the guilty verdict for first-degree murder, were the guilty verdicts for kidnapping and attempted rape. It was these additions to murder that could get Fry the death penalty.

Fry was still sobbing as he was led from the courtroom by United States marshals. Members of the prosecution, law enforcement personnel and court staff made a barrier between him and Betty Lee's family in the audience, who hugged each other upon hearing the verdict. Robert's mother and sister called out encouragement to him as he was led away.

The rest of April 18 was left to the attorneys on both sides and the judge to clarify about aggravating and mitigating circumstances that would be allowed in the penalty phase. Under New Mexico law, only a very select set of circumstances could garner the death penalty, and by Judge Birdsall's decision, Robert Fry fell within the scope of the law.

The next day, April 19, was important because the jury was to determine how it viewed the act of kidnapping. "The facts are obvious," Michael Cox said. "Fry said on the night of the crime, 'Someone's going to die,' and that he intended to stick someone with an eight-inch bowie knife. Robert Fry said he wanted to kill. He armed himself with a deadly weapon and stabbed Betty Lee. When that didn't kill her, he armed himself with an even more deadly weapon. His intent was evident when he struck Betty Lee in the back of the head with the weapon."

Cox argued that the string of events began at The Kettle when Fry told others he intended to kill someone that night. According to Cox, once Fry lured Betty Lee into his car for a supposed ride home, the kidnapping began to take place, since Fry had no intention of taking her there. What he did intend to do was either rape her or kill her. Fry may not have raped her, but he certainly killed her. It didn't matter that at first Betty Lee didn't know she was being kidnapped. Fry had formed the intent to kidnap, according to Cox.

Ed Bustamante vehemently disagreed with this assessment and said that once Fry decided to kill, there was no kidnapping involved. And he argued once again that anyone who didn't run away when their life was threatened by a person could be deemed to be kidnapped under this interpretation. He said this made no logical sense. Bustamante told the jurors, "It is your duty to consult at this point. You are under no obligation to reach a decision on this matter."

The jury did reach a decision, however, and they sided with the prosecution as to the matter of kidnapping. Even though this was very damaging, Robert Fry took their judgment calmly, unlike his outburst of crying on the murder's guilty verdict.

At this point Ed Bustamante tried a very interesting legal gambit. It's possible he did so to deflect the jury from believing Fry would get off too easily if he only received prison time, rather than a death sentence. With Fry's permission, Bustamante asked Judge Birdsall to give Fry the maximum sentence on each of the remaining charges—that is, for kidnapping, attempted rape and tampering with evidence.

Bustamante said, "We are asking the court to aggravate each sentence and run them consecutive to a life sentence." In New Mexico, a life sentence was not quite what the name implied. With good behavior an inmate could be released after a number of years served if the parole board recommended that he was suitable for release back into society. What Bustamante was intending to do was make sure the jury knew that Fry would probably spend the rest of his life in prison if they voted to let him live. The prosecutors gave no objections to this. Bustamante's hope seemed to be that the jurors would think this sentencing was so harsh, they would not feel the need to impose the death penalty.

Judge Birdsall replied, "Having had the luxury of sifting through all the evidence during the course of the trial, I find it highly appropriate to follow counsel's stipulations as to aggravating circumstances."

Judge Birdsall then sentenced Fry to twenty-four years on the kidnapping charge, twenty years on the attempted rape charge and two years for evidence tampering. Because of the personal injury involved, New Mexico's law stated that Fry would have to serve at least 85 percent of this time before he was eligible for release. Of course, all of this was moot if the jury decided on the death penalty in the first-degree murder charge.

On April 22, the jury began to hear from witnesses for and against the death penalty in the sentencing phase. Among those speaking of aggravating circumstances were members of Betty Lee's family. Her sister Evelyn got on the stand and often referred to Betty in the present tense. She said, "Betty is into plants. You watch your plants grow and it's like watching your children grow."

Another sister, Margaret, also picked up on this theme. She said, "Betty had such a love of the environment. Of loving things. She understood the value of life."

Margaret then recalled how she and Betty had spoken two weeks prior to her death about the coming of spring to the high desert. They spoke of the renewal of plants and life. Margaret said that Betty indicated that they would have many memories of this year, because it was the year 2000.

Then she added that she and Betty Lee were always their father's favorite. "We were daddy's girls," she said.

Margaret spoke of a road sign on the outskirts of Shiprock that was written in the Navajo language. Its translation was: "Take care of yourself. Travel in beauty."

She added, "Now when I see that sign, I wonder if my little sister ever looked up at it."

One of Betty Lee's daughters, Roxanne, a high-school sophomore, described her mother as strict, but with a sense of humor. She said that her mother was busy getting a degree at Diné College so that she could help the family financially. Her mother was planning to get a business degree. Roxanne recounted how she and her mom had been at a park on the afternoon on the day before the murder. She said, "Now I have nobody to talk to."

After Roxanne, it was time for those on the defense side who spoke of mitigating circumstances in an attempt to win Robert Fry his life—even if it was a life behind bars. The first for the defense was Mark Cunningham, a clinical forensic psychologist. Cunningham cited statistics about convicted murderers, stating that by a large margin, they did not kill again after receiving life in prison. Michael Cox challenged Cunningham on this issue by stating his statistics did not take into account someone with Robert Fry's psychological profile, and Cox's arguments aimed straight at the heart of what should and shouldn't be considered scientific evidence by the jury. He asked Cunningham, "How many in your study were convicted for the murder of women? For a particularly heinous murder?"

Cunningham answered that all murders were heinous by definition.

"Then have you gone back and seen how accurate you are in your predictions?" Cox asked.

Cunningham replied about these cases, "Some were sealed. I couldn't say how all the studies have turned out."

Cox shot back, "So we have no way of knowing how well you are doing, do we?"

At this point there was a break for a conference between the attorneys and the judge. Cox wanted to ask about the numbers and how accurate Cunningham was in his estimations about convicted and imprisoned murderers killing again. He cited the case of Andrew Martinez, who had been part of Cunningham's study. Martinez murdered another inmate after he was incarcerated. Cunningham explained that the method he used was akin to an insurance company actuary who predicted how likely it was that a car owner would have an accident and priced car insurance rates accordingly.

Cox countered this with, "If the insurance agencies underestimate a risk, they lose money. If you underestimate a risk, someone may lose their life." Then he said, "You indicated that you are in the forefront of doing actuarial studies, but in fact you don't know what an actuary does to become certified, do you?"

"No, sir," Cunningham replied.

The next day, Cunningham was still present, with the jury out of hearing, and Judge Birdsall said to Cox, "Mr. Cox, you were in some zealous questioning yesterday (in regards to Cunningham). Please ask the court if you may approach the witness." This was a polite way for Birdsall to say, tone it down.

Then Judge Birdsall told the prosecution and defense attorneys that Cunningham had to tap-dance around certain numbers pertaining to Robert Fry because if he didn't, they were going to get into Donald Tsosie and Eclectic case territory and he was not going to allow that to happen. Judge Birdsall added that because Cunningham couldn't answer certain questions specifically, it made him look to the jury as if he were trying to hide something about Robert Fry. So there were essentially two choices now, according to Judge Birdsall, the questioning of Cunningham could go on the way it was, or there could be an expanded questioning, which was going to open up a whole can of worms.

Defense attorney Hannum jumped into this argument stating that Cox had already presented to the jury that Cunningham had done a specific study of Robert Fry, but the jury wasn't hearing about it. And Hannum contended the jury would think that the study had been so negative that Cunningham and the defense didn't want them to hear about it, when just the opposite was true.

Judge Birdsall asked, "What would his answer (as to Fry's percentage rate of committing another felony while in prison) be?"

Hannum answered, "Nine percent chance for any violence in the future and .2 to 1 peercent to kill again."

Judge Birdsall said, "Yes, the state stepped into it. I just don't think they stepped into it deeply." Judge Birdsall was very worried that if Cunningham read his report on Robert Fry, then the state would be allowed to provide its own expert witness in this area. That might take weeks, and he shuddered to think what would happen to the jury by that point. Some jurors might become restless and not care about the case anymore, while others might inadvertently speak to the media about the case.

Cox, for his part, was not about to let Cunningham

just blithely report about Robert Fry's evaluation without an extensive cross-examination. He indicated it would take a lot of time accumulating discovery and rounding up an expert witness. Cox also said that in the report were statements by Fry's parents, and all those issues were going to come into play, including Robert's past history of lying and stealing.

Whether Judge Birdsall liked it or not, he did have a can of worms on his hands. In the end he opened a window that would allow both sides to follow through without kicking the door wide open. His idea was that Hannum could ask Cunningham about very specific numbers as to Fry's likelihood of violence in prison, and Cunningham would only give the numbers and not expand on what the numbers meant.

Both the prosecutors and defense attorneys agreed to this stipulation, and before the jury was brought back into the courtroom, the lawyers, judge and Cunningham all ran through a dress rehearsal of what would be asked and what would be answered. Judge Birdsall told Cunningham, "Sometimes you tend to want to explain things very thoroughly. Sometimes that makes attorneys very nervous. Sometimes it makes judges very nervous. We're just going to be talking about the numbers. Is that very clear?"

Cunningham answered, "Yes, sir."

Then Hannum asked him, "Dr. Cunningham, Mr. Cox asked you if you had done an evaluation of Robert Fry, or assessment of his likelihood of future violence. Did you do that?"

Cunningham answered, "Yes, I did."

Hannum asked, "And what is your assessment of his future risk of violence?"

Cunningham answered, "If in the general population—across a life term, his likelihood of a serious assault of any sort at all is 9.4 percent. His likelihood of an aggravated assault on a staff member, like a guard, is .5 to one percent. Likelihood of killing an inmate is .2 to one percent. And nationwide the likelihood of killing a guard is one in one million per year."

With all of the wrangling about numbers and assessments, the next witness for Fry was straightforward by comparison. It was his pastor, Connie Hill, of the United Methodist Church in Farmington. She had first met Robert Fry in 2000 and had been working with him since the time of his arrest. Initially she had begun talking to him in prison on the request of family members. He told her of his life in prison and events leading up to the murder of Betty Lee. She said he was afraid for his life in prison and the life of his family on the outside. "He was afraid they would be killed," she said.

This brought an immediate objection from Cox and it was sustained. The judge told the jury to disregard the last statement.

Pastor Hill said that there had been a fear among his family members that Robert Fry was becoming suicidal in prison. This aspect brought up a line of questioning from Ed Bustamante.

Bustamante —You understand that Mr. Fry will probably die in prison, no matter what happens?
Hill —Yes.
Bustamante—Would you like to continue to see Mr. Fry in prison?
Hill—Yes.
Bustamante—If you have that opportunity, how often would you see him?
Hill—It depends on where he was located. We have worked primarily on his spiritual issues. That is what would we would continue to work on.

Bustamante—Do you feel you've made progress on these issues?

Hill—Absolutely.

Bustamante—What kind of progress are you making?

Hill—I've seen Robert grow tremendously, spiritually. To the point where he not only has learned a great deal about Scripture, but he prays on a regular basis.

At this point Connie Hill began reading a letter from Robert Fry's older sister Vickie Rogers. It began by stating how badly she felt for Betty Lee's family and was sorry for their loss. Then Vickie said that no matter what, she was still proud to be Robert's older sister. She wrote, "I've had to sit here and whisper, 'I love you,' so now I'm just going to take some time to say it out loud. I love you Bob."

She wrote that the jury needed to see another side of him. She said he had been strong and strong-hearted and wanted everyone to love him as a person and a friend. For her, however, he would always be the little boy out playing in the yard and asking her for a ride to go and get some candy at the store. She said she had a husband and children who believed in Robert—not as an inmate, but a man who had played ball in the yard with them. "So you the jury must see that also," she wrote. "Bob, I love you with all my heart."

Connie Hill next read a letter by Jeanne Winchell, Robert's other sister. Jeanne wrote that she, too, was proud to be Robert's sister. She said she loved him more today than ever, even though she and her entire family were sorry for the death of Betty Lee. She wrote that Betty Lee's family were also a strong and caring family. "He was a very happy, loving little boy, that enjoyed playing cars outside and watching my dad build things. Watching mom plant things. Lying on the floor with me, watching Scooby-Doo."

She said that Bob was also a great friend to people. "He lost jobs, gave up opportunities, and lost parts of himself to help his friends, or anyone who asked. He was caring and loving."

Then she wrote to the jury, "May God be with you in your deliberations and peace be with you."

The next person to speak for Robert Fry was his mother, Gloria. She took the stand and told the jury, "I've always thought that Bob was special, but then I think that all my children are. As one of Betty Lee's family said, they came from a blended family. So did we. My husband was married before and had Vickie and Jimmie. There's seven years between them and the younger two. And when you're a stepmom, that's kind of a hard moniker to hang on somebody. But I learned to love the older two as though they were mine as well. The children are all ours."

Gloria talked about Robert playing in the yard with his cars and building roads. Hannum asked her if at some point Robert's contact with certain people caused him problems. Gloria answered, "They and he became involved in alcohol and drug use. I'm not blaming other people for what Bob got involved with, but his need to belong, and their willingness to take from him, hurt. He would give rides or money, whatever it took to be part of that group. I think it took a terrible toll on him."

Hannum wanted to know if alcohol caused a problem for Robert. Gloria said, "Yes, it did. Bob at this time is a recovering alcoholic."

Hannum asked what her relationship was with Robert since his incarceration in 2000. Gloria said,

"It's been very hard. Even in this courtroom, to see him sitting at a table and be disallowed talking to him. We try to do sign language to him. In many respects I haven't had my son for two years. And yet, the parts I've had, I desperately want to continue having. We saw him every Tuesday and Thursday (at the detention center). Fifteen minutes each time, through glass. We write letters.

"I've watched Bob become more responsible. To understand more about who he is and how he got involved with those people, and how he became the person he was. He's finding his way back to the Bob that we knew, and has always been there.

"I think Bob has a lot to give to people. Should the jury choose life, he's going to be ninety-eight years old, but in that time I believe he can help people. He loves to help people. He's willing to help people academically. He's willing to help people with their addiction problems or any other kind of problems. He's been working on his addiction problems in prison. I think Bob can be a benefit to the people in the prison system."

Hannum asked, "Will you continue to keep up your relationship with Bob if his life is spared?"

Gloria responded, "Oh, absolutely. He's my son. I love him."

The next person on the stand was James Fry, Robert's father, and he was very emotional the whole time. Ed Bustamante asked him a series of questions.

Bustamante—Do you love your son?
James Fry—Very much.
Bustamante—Can you tell the jury why you love him?

James Fry—Bob and I were buddies ever since he was born. All through his growing up, we did things together. There was camping, fishing and hunting. The picture you saw a while ago, he and I made the frame for it.

Bustamante—What kind of things would you do when Bob was young?

James Fry—Like I said, we went fishing, went hunting. We played ball. He was always pretty good at playing ball. One time he was supposed to go camping with the Scouts, but it rained up there (in the mountains), so we stayed in a building down at Brookside Park.

Bustamante—Do you remember Robert when he was a baby? Do you remember the first time you held him?

James Fry—(cries) Yep. It made me feel good then and I still think he's a good man.

Bustamante—Have you continued to speak with Bob in jail?

James Fry—Yes, sir, every chance we had.

Bustamante—Before he went to jail, did Bob enrich your life?

James Fry—Yep. I was always proud of the things he did. Like all kids, you'd get upset on some things, but you'd bust your shirt with pride on other things.

Bustamante—After Bob went to jail, did he continue to enrich your life?

James Fry—Yep. I never could have suspected he would do something like this. My father taught me to always respect women, and I taught my children the same thing. I never saw at any time when he wasn't nice to women or people in general.

Bustamante—Mr. Fry, if the jury says they'll allow him to live—he'll probably die in prison. Do you

*wish to have the opportunity to still see him in
prison?*
James Fry—Yes, sir. I sure do. He's still my son.

After James Fry's presence, the jury watched a
short video about the cell Robert Fry would have
to spend the rest of his life in at Santa Fe Detention
Center. It was obviously very small and cramped
and not someplace that anyone would want to spend
their life in.

After this five-minute video, the most potent of
all the witnesses took the stand—it was Robert Fry
himself. He said to the jury in a strong and steady
voice, "Ladies and gentlemen, my name is Robert
Fry. I am the defendant in this case. I'd like to start
off by saying to Ms. Lee's family how truly sorry I
am for the loss of their loved one. I want you to
know I have great remorse over what has happened to her. I will carry the guilt of her death
with me for the rest of my natural life. I am truly
sorry for what happened.

"You heard from my parents, my pastor, two letters from my sisters about me. I'd like you to know
a little about me. My mom and dad come from two
large families. My father is the youngest of seven.
My mother has five brothers and a sister—so seven
once again. I'd like to thank them for standing by
me, through all of this. I love them very much.

"You heard from the letters from my sisters. I also
have a brother, who lives in Kansas City, Missouri,
who has three children. My sister Vickie and her husband live in Dallas. My sister Jeanne and her husband
live in Farmington, with their two sons, who I love
very much. I want to thank them for standing by
me throughout all of this. And for the love I have
for them and their love for me. My best friend in

the world is probably a two-year-old little boy, my nephew Adam."

Then Robert Fry brought up a person whose existence had not been mentioned in any context up until this point. He said, "One person you did not get to hear about is my son. He's two and a half years old. I've seen him five times in my life since my arrest. I won't get to see him grow up, because I will spend the rest of my life in prison."

Just what his son's name was, or even who the mother was, Robert Fry didn't say. However, there had been rumors and talk amongst his friends for years that he did have a child, though even they never said who the mother was. It was all in the realm of supposition rather than fact.

Robert Fry continued, "My father and mother raised me in a very loving house. My father was a heavy-construction operator for thirty-three years, and probably the main reason why I went into construction and why I have a great love of building things. As a child he'd take me into his shop and teach me how to work his tools. Show me how to do things that I need to know in life."

Once Robert Fry began talking about his father, he became very emotional. His steady voice now cracked often, and he was on the verge of tears. He said, "I can remember my father taking me on camping trips. Teaching me how to fish, teaching me how to swim. When all the other kids were running around screaming about Rambo or Conan the Barbarian—well, they were those kids' heroes. My dad was my hero. Because no matter what happened, he was always there. He always did whatever he had to do to make sure he would make it to my baseball game or football game, or whatever. My dad wasn't into sports. Didn't watch them on TV.

But whenever I took up a sport, he took the time out of his life, not knowing anything about it, to try and work with me.

"When my sister had a project in school to build a suit of armor, my father sat down and built one for my sister. He used me as a guide for it. It's one of the fondest memories I have of my dad. He was always willing to be with us. I've idealized my dad since I was a little kid, and he's the most loving, caring man I've known my whole life.

"My mother is probably the one person in the world to give me my love for music. She was always singing. Learning how to play the keyboard. My mother was a police officer in Albuquerque when she and my dad met. She quit the force to marry my father—to become a wife and mother. She ran the family crisis center in Farmington and helped start the domestic violence counseling unit. She even lobbied all over the state to have laws changed. Even as busy as she was, she always had the time for one of our famous talks. She'd talk about everything and anything, from the time I was little. She taught me how to cook, how to sew, to make me into a well-rounded person.

"My dad taught me how to be a boy. (He cracks up crying.) My mom taught me how to . . ." (He never finished the sentence as he cried.)

"Ladies and gentlemen, when you go back in to make your deliberations, it's not me you've got to consider, because one way or the other, my life is over. They're the ones you've got to think of, because giving me the death sentence isn't going to affect me one way or the other. Once I'm executed, I'll be past caring. But they'll have to live with my death, and that I can't . . . (He breaks down again.)

"I've seen my dad cry three times in my entire life. Once when [his] sister passed away, once the day I was found guilty and today when he talked about me. They're the ones you have to consider, not me. Thank you."

Robert Fry's entire family was crying by this point. On the other side of the aisle, Betty Lee's friends and family sat in absolute silence.

The judge reiterated instructions to the jury on how they should proceed in the penalty phase. Basically they had ten items they could use as mitigating factors to choose life imprisonment over death:

1. An understanding that Robert Fry would serve at least sixty-seven years before he even had a chance at release.
2. They appreciated the enormity of being confined in prison for that amount of time.
3. There was the possibility that Robert Fry would be rehabilitated at some point.
4. Robert Fry's former military service.
5. Robert Fry's strong support structure, including family and friends.
6. Robert Fry had a possibility of being rehabilitated by religious beliefs.
7. Robert Fry's age.
8. There was a codefendant who was serving a life sentence for the same crime, and was not eligible for a death penalty.
9. Robert Fry had no similar history for similar crimes. (Of course, the jury didn't know about Joseph Fleming, Matt Trecker or Donald Tsosie.)
10. Anything else that would make the juror believe that life imprisonment was more satisfactory than the death penalty.

The jurors would have to weigh all these mitigating factors against the enormity of the crimes Robert Fry had imposed on Betty Lee in her heinous murder.

At this point the prosecution and defense got one last shot to persuade the jury in their diametrically opposed opinion on what should happen to Robert Fry. Prosecutor O'Brien began by saying to the jury, " 'Why me? Why are you doing this to me?' Those are Betty Lee's last words as she pleaded with Robert Fry right before he stabbed her in the chest and opened up her skull with a sledgehammer. By his own choice he took away forever, a mother, a friend, a daughter and a sister. Ladies and gentlemen, you're now faced with your final decision, a decision to determine what is right for the murder of Betty Lee.

"What weight should you give Dr. Cunningham? He wants to quantify the probability that someone who is convicted might kill again in a prison setting. He says it's a low risk, by using studies that tend to support his theories, disregarding other studies that don't support his theories. He boiled it down to a few simple statistics. Said there's a 9.4 percent chance that Robert Fry will assault someone in prison. He said that between .5 and one percent chance that he will kill another inmate. And one in one million that he would kill a guard. He categorized all of this as a low risk. But we're not talking about fender benders or insurance company profits. We're talking about violence and murder. Talking about a killer. The risk of violence and murder is never a low risk, it's always a terrible risk, no matter what.

"You heard from Robert Fry's mother and she told you he was a good boy. She showed you a picture of him when he was ten years old. But we're not here about a ten-year-old Robert Fry. We're here about a twenty-eight-year-old grown man. That grown man is a convicted killer, who killed an innocent woman.

"You heard from his sisters as well. And what did they talk about? They talked about a little boy. They described having good times as children. They had good memories of him as a child. You didn't hear that Robert Fry is no child today.

"Along with mitigating circumstances, you can consider the crime. You've already heard the brutal facts. About how Betty Lee's life was taken. The knife driven through her chest. The sledgehammer swinging into her head by Robert Fry. You know the terror and hopelessness Betty Lee must have felt as she pleaded with Robert Fry, 'Why me? Why are you doing this to me?'

"He responded to her by killing her. And you saw how he left her bloody body at the side of a road. We saw how he blatantly told Detective Melton the day after he kidnapped and murdered her that he had a great night until he got stuck.

"It was a cold, brutal, decisive murder. Fry did not even know her. Until today you haven't heard much about Betty Lee. Now you know a little about her. You know who she was. You know who she loved. You know who loved her. You know what hopes she had for the future.

"You heard about her children. Robert Fry took away a mother of five children forever. Mother of Roxanne, Tashina, Eli, Natasha and Nicholas. Five kids who will never again know their mother. Five kids who will never have a mother get excited when they bring home a good report card. To be proud when they graduate from school. To teach them what's right from wrong. To put a Band-Aid on scraped knees. Robert Fry made a decision that night. He took all that away and a lot more. He took it away forever.

"Robert Fry also took away a sister. A sister who made her brothers and sisters laugh. Made them proud. Was there to give support when they needed her. Always would come by to see them. Remembered all their birthdays.

"Robert Fry also took away a daughter. He caused a mother to outlive her own daughter. And he took away a part of the future of all these families as well as friends who Betty Lee touched. He took away Betty Lee's future. He took her plans to finish school, to get a house, watch her children grow up. It was all taken away by Robert Fry when he decided to take away the innocent trust of a woman who just needed a ride home.

"It's time for him to be punished for what he did on that night of June 9, 2000. For all that he took away from Betty Lee. All that he took away from her family.

"Ladies and gentlemen, when you consider this crime, this victim, and you weigh the aggravating circumstances against the mitigating circumstances, you will find the defendant, Robert Fry, should be sent to death row. It's a fair and proper sentence and just punishment for the crime that he committed. Thank you."

Fry's defense lawyer Ed Bustamante was just as adamant for an opposite course, for leniency, and much more emotional in his delivery than O'Brien had been. Bustamante said, "Good afternoon, folks. The first thing I want to say from the defense is— we offer our condolences to Betty Lee's family. You heard them speak this morning. They have so much class, so much strength, that I'm embarrassed to see how much strength they have, because I feel they have more than I have known. They talked about their family and what their beliefs are. Their core beliefs were that they valued life and they respect life. And I'm asking you to translate that into this hearing.

"When a wrong is done, in our society, especially a terrible wrong as in this case, we mobilize lots of parts of our society. We do that to find out who the wrongdoer is, we do that to avenge the victim, to separate the victim from the perpetrator. We mobilize police, prosecutors, defense attorneys and members of the community. You guys come in at the very last of this. You sat through a month of sometimes heartbreaking, painful, tough testimony.

"We do all that, because we value life. That is a basic function of every person who grows up in a proper way. So when Mr. Cox talks about the rights of Betty Lee, and when we come to finally acknowledge those rights, I think he is wrong. I think everything we did in this case, the police investigators, through Mr. Fry's arrest, we did all that in honor of Betty Lee. At the same time, because we're a society of laws, we safeguard the rights of the accused, because to wrongly convict someone would dishonor Ms. Lee's memory.

"So safeguarding the rights of someone does not in anyway dishonor Ms. Lee's memory. What we're asking from the defense is that you affirm why we're here. And that's because we value life above everything else. We value Ms. Lee's life and we recognize and are sorrowful about the way she died. We affirm the value of her life, as someone who never appeared here, who never spoke, but whose presence overwhelms this courtroom. It is the reason Robert Fry will do a life sentence. Essentially Robert

Fry is going to die in prison. And that is exactly what he deserves.

"Members of the jury, I ask you to think of Robert Fry in prison and realize that we value life so much, let's put Robert Fry away where he can live out his life in prison, behind bars in a small cell. He can truly reflect on the enormity of what he did. I ask you to give Robert Fry a chance to grow old and recognize what he's done to his family. And what he's done to the Lee family.

"We're not talking about the relative worth of Betty Lee and Robert Fry. Betty Lee, her loss and suffering is beyond measure. But what I'm asking you to do is look at what is proper punishment with a little bit of mercy and realize that Robert Fry, for all the terrible things he's done, has some worth in his life.

"In recognizing that, you'll force Mr. Fry to suffer for his misdeeds. We're asking you, members of the jury, to dole out severe punishment and realize that for at least the next sixty years, Robert Fry will be in prison in a brutal place with brutal people. When he ends that life's sentence, his parents will be gone. In forty years Mr. Fry will be an old man sitting in the same cell, with no one around to support him. I have no doubt when the years go on, Mr. Fry will die alone. I'm not asking you to feel sorry for Mr. Fry. He doesn't deserve it. He will lead a caged life, like a caged animal. It will be a lonely life until the day he dies.

"Consider where we live. We live in New Mexico. We're a unique place for lots of reasons. Next door we have Texas. We're not Texas. In New Mexico we hesitate to impose the death sentence. It's even more rare when we actually execute someone. We have a perfect example here of why a life sentence is tougher than a death sentence. Terry Clark was recently put to death. The fact is, he volunteered for the death penalty. He thought that a life sentence was worse than death.

"I am asking you to come back and say to Robert Fry, 'Mr. Fry, you need to live with what you did, in that terrible place for the rest of your life. And if not for him, I ask that you do it for Gloria and Jim and Vickie and Jeanne. They are good people and lead good lives, and for some awful reason, their son did a terrible thing.

"By granting some measure of mercy, you are not elevating Robert Fry's life over Betty Lee's. For any of you who want to give a life sentence, I ask you and beg you to cling to that belief. Look to your own background and remember the time you chose life. For me it's something I don't regret. There is something I regretted . . . (cries). No, I don't want to do this. I'm sorry.

"If you make Robert Fry die in prison, I think you grant dignity to the life of Betty Lee. You all affirm everything her family said this morning. That they value life, they enjoy life and life is important. Thank you."

The state responded with just a few more words to the jury. "You're here for one reason. Betty Lee. Betty Lee, without question, was brutally and viciously murdered by Robert Fry. The question is punishment and responsibility to answer for the actions of June 9, 2000."

The Betty Lee murder trial for weeks had been the realm of prosecutors, defense attorneys and witnesses. Now, nine men and three women sat in one of the deliberation rooms of the United States Courthouse in Albuquerque. In the streets down below, the pace of everyday life swirled around the downtown area, but within the antiseptic interior of the conference room, the jury wrestled with a decision that was the most difficult for any jury. They deliberated for five hours and then sent a query to Judge Birdsall. They asked if he would make them announce how they voted individually. Judge Birdsall sent back a reply that he would not. It would be a group statement.

This bit of information augured well for Robert Fry. It seemed to indicate that one or more jurors was holding out for life imprisonment, and there was no unanimity amongst them. Joe Gribble leaned over and whispered to one of the reporters that he now thought the jury would go for life plus forty-six years.

Finally, after 5½ hours of debate, the jurors filed back into the courtroom. The only person they looked at was Judge Birdsall. None of them looked at Robert Fry or Betty Lee's family.

Judge Birdsall asked if the jurors had reached a decision. "We have, Your Honor," the jury foreperson said.

"How do you find on sentencing?" Judge Birdsall asked.

The words coming out of the foreperson's mouth stunned almost everyone. The jury decided on death for Robert Fry.

Unlike his outburst of sobs at the guilty verdict, Robert Fry showed almost no emotion now. He raised his eyebrows to his family members sitting in the courtroom and gestured with his hand to his heart.

Judge Birdsall asked the entire jury if the vote was unanimous. They responded that it was.

Robert Fry was led away by United States marshals as his mother, father and sister Jeanne looked on in disbelief. They had nothing to say to the reporters as they left the courtroom; nor did any of the jurors as they were led out in a phalanx by law enforcement personnel.

Most of Betty Lee's family were just as silent, except for her brother Norman. He told reporters, "I believe justice was served. He should never have done what he did to my sister."

Ed Bustamante and Eric Hannum were close-lipped to the media, but the prosecutors had plenty to say. ADA Joe Gribble stated that in a way he was surprised, because New Mexico juries hardly ever gave out death penalty sentences. Then he added almost in amazement, "Fry turned down a plea agreement offered last year that would have required him to plead guilty to first-degree murder, kidnapping, attempted rape and tampering with evidence. Had he chosen the deal, he would have been given less time than the life sentence and forty-six years the jury could have imposed."

The headline in the *Albuquerque Tribune* was: FRY LOSES GAMBLE ON DEATH PENALTY.

Michael Cox told reporters it would have been a lot easier for the jury to vote for death if they'd known everything about Fry that the prosecution knew. This jury had no idea that Fry had also allegedly killed Donald Tsosie, Joseph Fleming and Matthew Trecker. Cox said, "We thought if they heard everything that we knew, they would opt for death, but they didn't, and they still came back with a good verdict. I'm really impressed with this jury."

Cox surmised that the appeals process on the case would take at least two or three years. In the meantime, the state and San Juan County were going forward in the prosecution of Robert Fry for the murders of Tsosie, Fleming and Trecker. The reasoning was that Fry might be able to overturn one death penalty conviction, but it would be a lot harder to overturn two or more.

Gribble said, "At this point we're still going to trial (on the other cases)."

And Cox added, "The additional prosecution isn't overkill until all the appeals are done. He's a dangerous man."

Chapter 9

... Tribulations

As expected, Robert Fry and his lawyers began the appeals process on the Betty Lee case almost immediately. It was far from a hopeless case. In the recent past there had been another murderer in New Mexico who had gotten his sentence reduced. Appellate courts tended to look at things in a very different light than a jury of twelve citizens did.

The next order of business for the prosecution was to decide which case would come first—Donald Tsosie's murder or The Eclectic case. Originally they were going to go with The Eclectic, but eventually decided that Donald Tsosie would be first in line.

In the summer of 2002, Leslie Engh was on board to give evidence against Robert Fry in Donald Tsosie's murder, just as he had done in Betty Lee's case. ADA Dustin O'Brien told the *Farmington Daily Times*, "We would have had no way to solve that murder (Betty Lee's) if he hadn't told us." Engh's cooperation, however, was not giving him a get-out-of-jail-free card. In fact, even with a plea bargain, he still received a very stiff sentence for his actions in Betty Lee's murder and Donald Tsosie's murder.

Displaying little emotion, Engh was sentenced in District Judge George Harrison's court to two life terms plus ten years for two counts of first-degree murder and one count of kidnapping resulting in death. Engh's attorney, Gary Mitchell, asked that the sentences run concurrently, which meant, under New Mexico law, that Engh was eligible for parole in thirty years. ADA O'Brien agreed to the request. He said, "This was a horrible crime, but he did cooperate and testify."

Betty Lee's family was in court for the sentencing of Les Engh and they chimed in on the matter as well. Lee's sister, Jessie Charleston, told reporter Debra Mayeux, "It was a fair sentence, since he helped out."

Betty's brother, William Lee, agreed. "It helps with the grieving process. We agree with the sentencing because had it not been for Engh's cooperation, the Betty Lee case would not have been solved."

William Lee added that he was glad that Engh chose to plead guilty rather than go through a trial on the Betty Lee case. He said the family had suffered enough already and didn't want the process to drag on. "There would have been a lot of painful memories," he said.

Les Engh's father was at the sentencing as well, and he was not as pleased with the outcome as the others. He told Debra Mayeux, "You guys convicted him before it even went to trial. Why the hell should I say anything to you?"

Before there could even be a Donald Tsosie trial, it had to pass review with the state court of appeals in Santa Fe over a matter of jurisdiction.

This was a serious problem, since it had to be proved beyond a reasonable doubt that Donald Tsosie's body had been found on county land, not the Navajo Reservation. Tsosie had been killed in a location very close to the borderline, and if it was found he was on the reservation, then the federal court, not San Juan County, would be handling the matter.

San Juan County district judge George Harrison had already ruled in July 2001 that the crime scene was not in "Indian Country," as he put it. But the defense team for Fry had appealed this decision to the higher court in October 2001, and since then it had been in limbo as the Betty Lee case proceeded. Even San Juan County's new district attorney, Greg Tucker, wanted a clear ruling of jurisdiction. He told reporters, "If the defense hadn't asked for a ruling from the higher court, we would have. Jurisdiction is a legal issue that's never waived. We wouldn't want to invest all the time and money in prosecuting Robert Fry for Donald Tsosie's murder and then have him turn around and appeal the conviction on jurisdictional issues."

Finally, on October 11, 2002, the state court of appeals ruled on jurisdiction. They said in part, "It is clear that the crime scene was not in Indian Country." San Juan County could go ahead with its case against Robert Fry in the murder of Donald Tsosie. Heading the prosecution team was a young ADA named Eric Morrow. Sandra Price, who had been the district attorney only months before, would now be his second.

Right from the start, nothing would go smoothly on the Donald Tsosie case—not for the prosecution and not for the defense. In the actual trial the proceedings would veer to the brink of a mistrial on three occasions.

The first problems came for Fry's defense team, Ed Bustamante and Eric Hannum, who were suddenly removed from the case. The exact reason why was never stated in public. All Hannum would tell reporters was: "There are things that came up that made it necessary for us to get off the case."

Just what those "things" were, he didn't elaborate, and Ed Bustamante kept mum about the matter. The state's defenders' office stepped in and began to negotiate a contract with Santa Fe lawyer Stephen Aarons. Steve Aarons had a long and colorful career as an attorney. He had attended George Washington University, Saint Louis University and Oxford University. He was a lieutenent colonel in the Judge Advocate General's (JAG) Corps of the Army, and he had prosecuted fifty court martial cases between 1980 and 1983 and was special defense counsel in a Nürnberg, Germany, murder trial. He spoke Spanish and German.

Aarons opened his own law office in Santa Fe in 1992, and he had been practicing as a defense lawyer since then, handling over thirty murder cases. One very interesting case that he was involved in just before the Fry/Tsosie trial was that of Judge Charles Maestas, of Esponala, New Mexico. Four women accused Maestas of propositioning them. They said that Maestas had promised to reduce their citations if they had sex with him. Suzetta Salazar actually went ahead and had sex with Maestas—but she audiotaped their sexual encounter.

At Maestas's trial, Aarons acknowledged that the man did have sex with Salazar, but he said the sex was consensual. Aarons told *Court TV,* "It's not illegal to have sex. Evidence will be presented that at least three of the four women did not tell the truth about their allegations."

Things took an even more bizarre turn when the lead investigator for the state, Karen Yontz, was shot dead while allegedly trying to rob an Albuquerque bank. Aarons contended that Yontz had set up the whole scheme to discredit Maestas in the first place. Just before the Robert Fry trial began, Judge Maestas was found guilty and sentenced to three years in prison. It was a victory of sorts for Aarons because the sentence was very light compared to the fifty years that Maestas could have received.

As far as the Fry/Tsosie case went, a new wrinkle appeared when Darrell Hare and Alexis Diego went to the authorities just before jury selection began. For the first time they told them what Fry had said while watching *America's Funniest Home Videos*. Fry had said he'd killed an Indian up on the Bluffs and then threw the man's boots down at him. This fit with where Tsosie's boots were eventually discovered—a fact never published in any newspaper. And it seemed to be in line with the story that Larry Hudson had told on the same matter. Diego and Hare even mentioned the use of a shovel in the crime.

Change of venue on the Fry/Tsosie case once again became an issue, and the forthcoming trial was eventually moved out of San Juan County and back to Bernalillo County and Albuquerque. It was to take place in the brand-new high-rise federal court in Albuquerque. The multistoried building had an elegant lobby and plush new courtrooms, and presiding judge Thomas Hynes would later quip to jurors, "Folks, here's your federal tax dollars at work." Thomas Hynes, who had been a Deputy District Attorney during the "Chokecherry Massacre" trial, was now a superior court judge.

On the upper floors, you could see beautiful views

of the Sandia Mountains and the tree-lined Rio Grande River. A revitalized downtown district encompassed the surrounding area with restaurants and businesses. On the fourth floor of the federal court was a courtroom slated for the Donald Tsosie trial. The building had wood-paneled conference rooms and a large courtroom filled with natural light from large windows. It was a long, long way from the dusty murder scene along the Bluffs above the San Juan River.

Despite the plush surroundings, it was all business in Judge Hynes's courtroom in August 2003 as the jury selection began on the Tsosie case. The charges against Robert Fry in the case were:

Count One
Did kill Donald Tsosie, a human being, without justification or excuse, by any of the means with which death may be caused (capital felony).
Count Two
Did unlawfully take, restrain, transport or confine Donald Tsosie, by force, intimidation or deception, against Donald Tsosie's will, with intent to inflict death, physical injury or sexual offense on Donald Tsosie, and the defendant did not free Donald Tsosie in a safe place or did inflict great bodily harm upon Donald Tsosie (first-degree felony).
Count Three
Did attempt to steal property, to wit: money from the person of Donald Tsosie by use or threatened use of force or violence, while armed with a deadly weapon, to wit: a wooden stick, shovel or hammer (a third-degree felony).
Count Four
Did destroy, change, hide, place or fabricate physical evidence, to wit: a body, stick, shovel, hammer, clothing, with the intent to prevent apprehension,

prosecution, or conviction of himself or another or to throw suspicion of the crime upon another (a fourth-degree felony).

The jury selection for the Tsosie trial in Albuquerque for the first time brought together all the new legal participants who had not been involved in the Betty Lee trial. Judge Thomas Hynes presided, Eric Morrow was the lead prosecutor and Sandra Price was his second. On the defense side were lead attorney Steve Aarons, his second, Jeff Jones, and defense investigator Robert Sandoval. This jury selection was incredibly speedy in comparison to the Betty Lee trial. Within two days Judge Hynes had impaneled a jury. It was indicative of his style, and several times during the jury selection process, he was heard to say to a prosecutor or defense attorney, "Let's move along."

Hynes had a learned but folksy style, and the jury appreciated his frank and understandable jury instructions. He imparted the serious nature of the work they were doing, and often thanked them for their cooperation. It did instill a sense of respect and cooperation within the jury.

Judge Thomas Hynes was a graduate of Farmington High School, where Robert Fry would also be a student many years later. Hynes had been a marine in Vietnam and later a boxer at Notre Dame University. Deciding to go into law, he attended Georgetown Law School. Once he'd passed the bar, Hynes returned to the Four Corners Region to practice law. In fact, he had been a young ADA when the Chokecherry Massacre occurred. Hynes and a police officer were the first ones to hear the boys' confessions. The Fry/Tsosie case was in some regards like déjà vu for Hynes. In the first interview with the boys on the Chokecherry case, they admitted these facts that were related in abbreviated form: "Offered ride to Indian. Hit with rocks. Hit with sticks. No personal effects. Pushed Indian off mountain." It sounded eerily like what Robert Fry and Les Engh had done to Donald Tsosie.

The jurors chosen for the Tsosie trial were once again a good cross section of Albuquerque and New Mexico society. There was a clean-cut young Anglo, a middle-aged African American, an Anglo housewife and a young Hispanic woman. There was also a Native American woman, an older gentleman with a white beard and a large young white man with long hair, who had the appearance of a biker. In another setting it was easy to imagine him being a drinking buddy of Robert Fry's. Yet, this man was just as attentive and cooperative as all the rest of the jurors.

Perhaps the most remarkable person in the courtroom was Robert Fry himself. He had lost a lot of weight in prison and now appeared almost muscular and trim, wearing a nice tailored suit and tie. He also wore a pair of dark-framed glasses. If no one knew any better, they could have easily mistaken him for one of the defense lawyers. In fact, at one point, Jeff Jones asked the prospective jurors, "Does this man look like a murderer?" The general consensus from them was that he did not.

To add to the illusion that he was a defense attorney, Fry constantly took notes on a yellow legal pad as the jury selection process went on. He chatted casually with his defense team and seemed to like Robert Sandoval a lot. Sandoval was also a big man, with a dark full head of hair and trim goatee. Never far away from Robert Fry were his parents, Gloria and James, who sat in the gallery. Interestingly enough, on the other side of the courtroom were Jeff and Christina Trecker. They were not only there to see the man they accused of killing their son, Matt, they were also there to give support to the Tsosie family. It was a hardship for them, being so far away from Farmington, but they came every day nonetheless. Because of her bad back, Christina had to bring a pillow into court to use on the hard spectators' benches. Even this was too much at times, and she had to go out of the courtroom to sit on more comfortable chairs in the lobby once in a while. But she was determined to be there, pain or not. She wanted Robert Fry to know that her presence and, by extension, that of her son, Matt, was always there, watching him and listening to him and the evidence against him.

The opening arguments for the Donald Tsosie case began on August 23, 2003. Eric Morrow told the jurors, "It was all about 'rollin' an Indian.' " Morrow took the jury through the entire episode on the night of March 31, 1998, and early-morning hours of April 1, 1998. It began when Fry and Engh left The Kettle and picked up Donald Tsosie at the Turn Around Bar, because he appeared to have more money than the other Native Americans there. Morrow's story continued with the fight between Robert Fry and Tsosie in the car, and Les Engh choking Tsosie with a belt. It reached its crescendo as Robert Fry beat Tsosie with a shovel and jabbed him in the face and eye with a sharpened stick, only to throw his battered body over the cliff near Scorpion Point. Fry's final bit of contempt for Tsosie was when he threw the man's boots down at him, and hit Tsosie in the head with one of them.

Defense attorney Steve Aarons had a very different take on all of the events leading up to the death of Donald Tsosie. He rhetorically asked the jurors, "Is this trial a crossword puzzle? No. It's more like a house of cards. A house of cards built by Leslie Engh's lies. And he's put some jokers into the deck."

Aarons said he would prove that Les Engh was a habitual liar, who blamed Robert Fry for the murder of Donald Tsosie to save his own neck. Engh had taken advantage of Fry's predilection for bragging. In fact, Aarons himself called Fry a braggart who invented violent stories to impress his friends, and this had gotten him into trouble about the Tsosie murder. He said that Engh had heard Fry's bragging and lies, and now intended to frame him for the murder of Donald Tsosie; according to Aarons, though, it was Engh who was responsible for Tsosie's death.

Aarons said that Fry had learned what Engh and his buddies had done to Tsosie, and made it seem that he had done the deed—when, in fact, he had not even been up on the Bluffs on March 31 or April 1, 1998. Aarons said Fry's stories were so outrageous that he had even claimed to be a Navy SEAL, when nothing was further from the truth. Most of Fry's stories were wild, but harmless, Aarons said, but in this case he had unwittingly snared himself in a trap. Aarons said when Engh was questioned about the murder of Donald Tsosie, he began to look around for a fall guy, and the obvious one was Robert Fry. Aarons said that to save himself, Engh had made a deal with the prosecution and the deal was to hand over Robert Fry, who was innocent of the crime, on a silver platter.

Genevieve Chee, Donald Tsosie's girlfriend, was the first witness called by the prosecution. When she looked for the first time at a photo of Donald's body being hauled up from the canyon, she gasped and cried. It was almost as if they had just laid his body out before her in the courtroom.

Genevieve told of letting him off at BCI Biological Laboratories on March 31, and that he couldn't give blood that day, so he wanted to stay over in Farmington and visit friends. She agreed to pick him up at their usual location, the Safeway store on Main. She said, "But when I got there, he wasn't there."

"Did you look for him?" Eric Morrow asked.

"Yes, I looked all over town. I even went to the Turn Around Bar. I couldn't find him anywhere. Finally I went home," she cried.

Steve Aarons zeroed in on a letter that Donald Tsosie had supposedly written to Genevieve Chee sometime in the spring of 1998. This letter was later found in a black duffel bag that Chee had given to one of Tsosie's sisters. The letter indicated that Donald Tsosie was leaving her for a white woman. Aarons asked if Chee had ever seen this letter.

She emphatically said that she hadn't.

"Did you take that duffel bag to Donald's sister?" he asked.

"Yes," she answered.

"So, what did you think when you couldn't find him?"

After a long pause she answered, "I thought he was with another woman."

Kenneth Jose was the next on the stand, telling of how he discovered Donald Tsosie's body. He had walked along the edge of the Bluffs and saw what he thought was someone sleeping or passed out down in a canyon. He yelled at him, until he saw blood. Then he got scared because he was sure the man was dead. He did admit to picking up a watch there, but he eventually got rid of it.

Judge Hynes spoke up and asked Jose, "How far from the body were you?"

Jose answered, "About from here (the witness stand) to that table (about five feet away)."

Aarons picked on the fact that Jose could not remember what day he had found the body. Jose thought it had been there about a month after the person had died. But a month from when?

Detective Black, as a witness, spoke of the scuffle zone, finding the bloody broken sticks and photographing the area. He also mentioned taking plaster casts of tire impressions there. Black did admit that the crime scene had not been well protected. He also surmised a great deal of time had passed between the time when Donald Tsosie died until the officers came on the scene.

Aarons asked Black why he had found four sets of footprints at the scuffle area not three. Four sets of prints would indicate there were more people there at the time than just Donald Tsosie, Robert Fry and Les Engh. Black had no answer for that.

Aarons also keyed in on beer cans that had been ripped open in a certain manner and tossed on the ground. These beer cans were found near the scuffle area and also near the end of the dirt road at Scorpion Point. Aarons tried to make it look as if Les Engh had been there with two other buddies for a while, and not sitting in the backseat of Robert Fry's car, choking Tsosie. Aarons indicated that the second crime area had never been adequately analyzed.

In fact, Aarons alluded to an even darker possibility when he pointed out a photo to Detective Black where a set of footprints had seemingly been wiped out on purpose. Or "swiped by hand," as he put it. In one set of police photos, the footprints are distinct and untouched. In a later photo they have been swiped and obscured. This indicated either bad crime-scene integrity, or even worse, a police cover-up.

Detective Black looked at the photos in question and said, "It doesn't look like a hand rubbed it out to me. Besides, it's not linked to the crime scene."

Black did, however, admit that the crime scene area was not as pristine as it could have been. He said by the time he got there, there had been a lot of foot traffic by BLM officers and sheriff's officers all over the area.

Asked about the watch that Kenneth Jose had picked up, and that was later taken by police, Aarons wanted to know why it had not been introduced as evidence.

Detective Black replied, "No blood was found on it. And it had passed through too many hands by the time we got it."

Crime lab forensic scientist Noreen Purcell said that she had examined the boots, the cowboy hat and blood on sticks that had come from the crime scene. She admitted that no DNA profiles were extracted from the boots or blood on the hat of Donald Tsosie. She said that she had tried to find blood from Robert Fry and Leslie Engh in the collected material but couldn't find any. She also related that there was no DNA matching Donald Tsosie found in Robert Fry's vehicle, but she noted that Fry's vehicle had been seized and searched two years after the death of Donald Tsosie.

Steve Aarons told Purcell that according to Engh, Robert Fry and Donald Tsosie had struggled violently in Fry's car. Then he asked her, "So why was there no blood from Fry or Tsosie in that vehicle?"

Purcell answered that unless the participants actually bled onto surfaces of the vehicle at the time, there would be no blood evidence to extract later. She explained they could have bled on their faces and clothes, but not on or inside the car.

Phillip Wareheim, who had testified against Fry in the Betty Lee trial, was back on the stand again. He told the jury that he studied the bloody sticks that had been collected at the crime scene. Wareheim noted that all the sticks at some time had been part of a single item, and he believed that item to have been a broom handle. It was a broom handle consistent with the one Les Engh described.

A group of Robert Fry's old friends began to take the stand, including his boyhood chum Larry Hudson. Hudson recounted how they had been friends since grade school and how he considered Fry's parents as his own. He also told of all the wild tales that Robert Fry had regaled him with over the years. It was one of the reasons he didn't believe Fry's story of rolling an Indian up at the Bluffs in 1998. When this story was recounted to him on their fishing trip to Navajo Lake, Hudson didn't want to listen to it a second time.

When Fry was arrested for the Betty Lee murder, however, Hudson began to take the story seriously. It was his call to the San Juan County Sheriff's Office, telling them to speak to Les Engh, that had led directly into the Donald Tsosie/Robert Fry investigation.

Sandra Price asked Hudson how he felt testifying against his old friend. Hudson replied, "This is not pleasant. I see his parents scowl at me."

Steve Aarons asked Husdson if he ever got any money for turning in information on Fry. Hudson admitted that he eventually did, but he had turned it down twice before finally accepting it. "I did not want that thousand-dollar reward," he said.

Then Steve Aarons told Hudson that a future witness, Michelle Hearn, would contradict Hudson's story of going to Navajo Lake on May 6, 2000—the date Robert Fry supposedly told him the tale of the Indian on the Bluffs. Aarons said Hearn would say that she and Fry and Hudson had all gone to a Dwight Yoakam concert that weekend. Hudson adamantly denied this and stuck to his Navajo Lake timeline.

It was during this exchange that the trial first veered close to a mistrial. Since the door had been opened about dates and concerts, Sandra Price, on redirect, asked Hudson if the concert was close to the time of The Eclectic incident. This was the first time The Eclectic had been mentioned.

A recess was called and Aarons asked the judge to declare a mistrial because any information about The Eclectic murders was not supposed to be presented before the jury. Sandra Price and Eric Morrow argued that the defense had opened the door to such questioning when they brought up the date of the Dwight Yoakam concert. Price and Morrow contended the actual Yoakam concert had been in 1996, not 1998. Judge Hynes mulled everything over and decided not a great deal of damage had been done. He didn't think a jury in Bernalillo County would tie the Donald Tsosie case to The Eclectic case, something they may not even have heard about. He did caution everyone, though, not to mention The Eclectic again.

Steve Aarons's next tack against Larry Hudson took nearly everyone by surprise. Aarons said that Robert Fry had had an affair with Hudson's ex-wife, and that was why Hudson was getting even now. Hudson denied this was the case, though he admitted his ex-wife had affairs. In fact, on redirect he said that even his own brother had an affair with his ex-wife, and apparently so had many other men. He didn't care whether Bobby Fry had an affair with her or not. He was glad to be rid of her and had even shown Fry his divorce papers in 1995, saying, "I'm rid of her. Now I'm free!"

To back up the story of Robert Fry and Larry Hudson fishing at Navajo Lake, Sandra Price got fish-and-game warden Patrick Block on the stand. Block proved that Robert Fry had bought a fishing license on May 6, 2000, at the Kmart on Main Street in Farmington.

Albuquerque area medical examiner Marcus Majowsky said that he had examined the body of Donald Tsosie on May 1, 1998. Even though it was in a state of decomposition, he was able to discern that several of Tsosie's ribs had been fractured and two crescent-shaped wounds on his back could have been from a shovel. Majowsky originally said that he thought the cause of death was from fractures to Tsosie's neck; he later amended this and said that cause of death could also have been from hypothermia. He said because of extensive wounds Tsosie received, he could have not gone far after being pummeled. Majowsky determined that Tsosie had been dead for about a month before the police came upon his body.

On cross-examination Aarons had Majowsky admit several things detrimental to the prosecution's contentions. Majowsky said that Tsosie could have been killed on April 12, 1998, not April 1, as Les Engh claimed. The injuries could also have been inflicted by one person, not two, or three people and not two, and manual strangulation could have been the cause of death, not blows from a shovel or jabs from a sharpened stick. Even Engh had admitted he was the only one to use a belt around Donald Tsosie's neck.

As far as physical evidence went, Majowsky admitted that there were no shovel nicks on Tsosie's ribs, nor evidence that his genitals had been jabbed with a stick—things that Engh said Fry had done to Tsosie. Even more specifically, Majowsky could find no hammer blows to Tsosie's head. This story had occurred in one of Fry's tales to Larry Hudson. Aarons said this outlandish detail proved that Fry had not even been there, but only heard Engh's tales about the murder, and then made the story his own with embellishments added later.

Darrell Hare recited for the state the stories Robert Fry had told him after the murder when Fry had met him at an all-night restaurant on April 1, 1998. Fry had sat down at his table and told him that he'd just rolled an Indian. Hare added, "Fry said, 'I pulled him out of the car and hit him. I told Les to grab the shovel. Les hit the guy in the neck with the shovel. I think we killed him. We pushed him off a cliff.' "

Then Hare related the time that Fry had gone up to Durango in May 2000. He and Fry and Alexis Diego had all been watching *America's Funniest Home Videos* when someone on the show threw a shoe and hit another person. According to Hare, "Fry said, 'I threw a boot down and hit an Indian in the head. It was so funny.' " After that, Fry reiterated the story he had told Hare on the night of April 1, 1998, in the restaurant.

On cross, Aarons had Hare admit that when he saw Fry at the restaurant in the early-morning hours of April 1, 1998, that Fry did not look bloody or that he had even been in a fight. He was excited, yes, but then he often was when telling these kinds of tales. Hare had even related to Detective Tyler Truby on March 7, 2002, "I thought Fry was just talking big. He was always talking about beating up people."

Aarons also had Hare admit that he hadn't told any authorities until June 2003 about Fry's supposed visit to Durango—the visit where they all watched *America's Funniest Home Videos* and Fry laughed at the shoe being thrown, saying he had done that to an Indian up on the Bluffs.

Aarons poked a lot of holes in Hare's recitation, but when Sandra Price had Hare draw a shovel on a large piece of paper, his drawing matched almost exactly the type that Engh said Fry had used on Donald Tsosie. It had a short handle with a crossbar at the top. And the shovel part was spade-shaped, not a flat edge.

On the stand Alexis Diego told of Robert Fry's story in Durango about the boots and the Indian. And fireworks immediately erupted when Steve Aarons started to cross-examine her. Aarons said, "You don't like Bobby Fry, do you?"

She answered, "I looked up to him as a big brother."

Aarons then questioned: "Didn't you say to the DA he tried to rape you?"

Diego emotionally responded, "He did rape me when I was sixteen. I forgave him."

No one had seen this coming, and the line of questioning blew right up in Aarons's face. Not only did the jury wonder if Fry had killed Donald Tsosie, now they wondered if he was a rapist as well.

Eric Morrow pounced on this opening on redirect and questioned Diego a little more about the alleged rape. She said it had happened when she'd passed out from drinking. She woke up later and knew that Fry had raped her.

This line of questioning didn't go on for long. Judge Hynes told Morrow, "Okay, that's enough. We're not going down this road."

After the startling revelation by Alexis Diego, came the physical evidence testimony of experts. By comparison, it seemed cold and clinical. However, the prosecutors knew that it could be vital. Many agreed that the expert testimony of Rod Englert in the Betty Lee case seemed to guarantee that the jurors saw Robert Fry as her killer, not Les Engh. They hoped to score big again with tire tread expert Dwayne Hildebrand. Nothing, however, would go smoothly in this trial, and Hildebrand's presentation almost blew up in the prosecutor's face. In fact, it was the second incident that nearly caused a mistrial.

Dwayne Hildebrand had been a forensic specialist for the Scottsdale, Arizona, Police Department. By now, he had a private consulting firm that dealt with crime scene analysis, especially where footprints and tire tread marks were concerned. Hildebrand had been an expert witness in trials in half of the United States, helped on FBI cases, and had even won international awards from Finland and Switzerland.

Yet before he even took the stand, there was trouble brewing for ADA Eric Morrow. Outside the presence of the jury, Morrow told Judge Hynes that he wanted to admit into evidence photos for Hildebrand to look at that concerned tire tread marks of Robert Fry's car and photos from the crime scene. But Hildebrand had not taken these photos, Detective Terry Eagle had, and they had never been admitted into evidence when Eagle was on the stand. In fact, these photos as yet were not part of the court record.

Judge Hynes gave Morrow a stern lecture on admissibility. "The witness (Hildebrand) doesn't know they were pictures of the vehicle. Since Eagle had taken the pictures, they should have been admitted into evidence then, not now. I will give you three days to get Terry Eagle back on the stand with those photos." Otherwise, the judge cautioned, he might be compelled to call a mistrial.

It was a rattled and chagrined Eric Morrow who preceded with witness Hildebrand on the stand in front of the jury. Judge Hynes let Hildebrand testify about the photos in question after Steve Aarons said he would not object. Aarons had a pretty good idea what Hildebrand would say, and he intended to use it to his own advantage.

Hildebrand started out by saying that Terry Eagle had sent him tire photos and he got a possible "hit" off Robert Fry's front passenger tire. The tire casts from the crime scene were not good, however, and one was totally flawed, while the other was just barely okay. From these tire casts, the best Hildebrand could do was use them for elimination purposes only. He could say what tires had not been there, and only possibilities of the ones that had been there.

Hildebrand said that the tire cast probably came from a Dean Celestial tire manufactured between 1998 and 2000. It seemed to have two grooves and two ribs, the same as Robert Fry's front passenger tire. The best photo match to Robert Fry's tires was at police marker #9 from the Bluffs area. Hildebrand said the tire mark left there probably occurred because the driver had pulled quickly into that spot. This matched Engh's statement of Fry suddenly stopping near the fight location. As far as the time period when the tire tread was left at the Bluffs, Hildebrand stated, "You cannot look at a tire impression and say when it was left there. Not even an expert tracker can do that. There are too many variables." He added that wind, rain and heat can make changes and no one can scientifically say how and when the changes occurred, unless they were photographing the site constantly.

Hildebrand didn't help Morrow's cause any by admitting that the police photographs he received were flawed because a tripod had not been used when the photography had been done. This caused distortions in the photographs. Worst of all, a wide-angle lens had been used, which caused even further distortions. The best Hidlebrand could do is say that Robert Fry's car might have been there on March 31 or April 1, 1998.

Steve Aarons had a field day with Hildebrand concerning the distorted police photographs and flawed tire casts. He also elicited testimony that Hildebrand had never gone to the actual crime scene. All Hildebrand had to go on were these less-than-perfect photos and flawed plaster casts.

Aarons asked, "You don't know how many tires with this similar design are out there on the road, do you?"

Hildebrand answered that all he could say was that seven manufacturers made that type of tire in the 1990s and one of Fry's tires was similar.

Aarons asked, "But anyone could buy this type of tire, let's say at a tire store in Farmington."

Hildebrand answered, "That's right."

Aarons really hit upon the photography used in many evidence shots of tire marks and shoe prints, and was particularly adamant about one shoe print that had obviously been swiped. He asked Hildebrand to look at photos of the shoe print before it had been swiped and after. In the "before" photo, Hildebrand said, it did not appear to be a policeman's shoe. Then about the swipe mark, he said, "I don't know if it was done intentionally or not."

Perhaps worst of all, Aarons had an e-mail that

Hildebrand had sent to Eric Morrow before the trial began. In it Hildebrand stated to Morrow about his findings: "I don't think [my work] helps much."

He was right. The prosecution had hoped to hit a home run with Dwayne Hildebrand's testimony, and instead they had nearly struck out. The best Morrow could do after this fiasco was to get Terry Eagle back on the stand to say that the shoe print that was swiped had belonged to Detective Black. At least he could prove there was no police cover-up involved at the crime scene.

If the questioning of Hildebrand had been a disaster for Eric Morrow, he rebounded admirably the next day with his star witness, Les Engh. As in the Betty Lee case, Engh was unemotional, matter-of-fact and thorough. For nearly two hours he took the jurors back, step by step, to the night of March 31 into April 1, 1998. Through the witness's eyes, the jurors saw Donald Tsosie being picked up at the Turn Around Bar, the fight between Fry and Tsosie in the car, and Tsosie's death struggle as he was pounded and stabbed by Fry. It was graphic, believable and brutal.

After Engh was through, Sandra Price asked him, "Are you making any of this up today?"

"No, ma'am," he replied.

"What do you hope to get out of this (testimony)?" she asked.

Engh answered, "I hope for anything I can get. Hope for the best. Expect the worst. It's terrible where I'm at. Now I have trouble sleeping. Depression. I feel bad."

On cross-examination Aarons tried to portray Les Engh as a liar who would do anything to save his own neck, including framing Robert Fry for the murder of Donald Tsosie. Aarons got Engh to admit he had lied about a firearm he had once owned, lied about his service in the military and had even forged a document to the probation department about his community service.

Aarons zeroed in about the period Engh went AWOL from the military, which was around the time that Donald Tsosie had been murdered. Aarons said that Engh had family and friends up in Wyoming. Hadn't he gone there with friends in March or April 1998, Aarons asked.

Engh said no.

"Didn't you go there in a white pickup with Wyoming license plates?" Aarons asked.

"No," Engh replied.

Aarons kept coming back to this white pickup truck with Wyoming plates that Donald Tsosie's half brother Paul James had supposedly seen at a Safeway in Farmington in either March or April 1998. James claimed that one of the men in that pickup looked like Les Engh, and he had been giving Donald Tsosie a bad time. James said that the man was particularly mad at Tsosie because he was with a white woman in the parking lot and she owned a purple Neon.

A heated exchange broke out between Aarons and Engh:

> *Aarons—You told lies today, didn't you? You weren't with Robert Fry. You were mad at the Indian because he was with a white woman.*
> *Engh—No.*
> *Aarons—You weren't with two other guys in a white pickup truck?*
> *Engh—No.*
> *Aarons—You went all the way to the end of the road with them at Scorpion Point, didn't you?*
> *Engh—No.*

Aarons—You had some beers there?
Engh—No.
*Aarons—You claim that Robert Fry went out there
a few days later to check about a body?*
Engh—Right.
*Aarons—You sure thought it would help (about
Engh's interview with Detective Bob Melton), didn't
you, telling about Fry.*
Engh—(angry) It didn't do any good!
*Aarons —You weren't trying to protect your friends
from Wyoming?*
Engh—No.
Aarons —Make Robert Fry the fall guy?
Engh—No!

On redirect Les Engh told Sandra Price how
helping the prosecution had affected his life in
prison. He said other inmates called him a rat and
made a slicing motion across their throats when
they saw him. He had to be kept in protective custody. Fingering Robert Fry as the killer had not
made his life easy.

Engh also helped the prosecution by drawing a
shovel on a piece of paper that the jury could see.
From memory he drew a shovel that looked almost
exactly like the one Darrell Hare had drawn. Engh
said it was the shovel that Fry had used to beat
Donald Tsosie. The shovel that Fry always kept in
his car. A shovel with a short handle and crossbar
on the grip.

During most of Engh's testimony Robert Fry fu-
riously scribbled on his yellow legal notepad. He
seemed to be very irritated at his former friend
and killing partner. At one point Fry looked over
at his mother and crossed himself.

As the trial wore on, it veered toward a mistrial
once again. Paul James was supposed to be on hand

to be a witness, but he was nowhere to be found. It was already known that James had a drinking problem, but just how pronounced this problem was would soon be known to one and all. Judge Hynes was not amused by James's absence and had harsh words for both the prosecution and the defense. He told Eric Morrow that the state should have known how severe James's drinking problem was and kept better track of him, even if they had to keep him in custody overnight to make sure that he would be available for trial. In fact, Paul James had been in a detox center 212 times by September 2003.

At this point Steve Aarons wanted a mistrial, saying that James was crucial for his defense, but Hynes gave Aarons a lecture about subpoenas on Indian land. He told him that he should know that the state of New Mexico had no legal means of compelling the Navajo Nation to bring James in, and that if James was so important to his case, he should have taken steps to ensure the man would be in court. Hynes said that both the prosecution and the defense knew very well about James's drinking problem.

Then Judge Hynes said, "Mr. Aarons, you can pick your poison." He told him that he could either start questioning defense witnesses other than Paul James or let the prosecution start their closing arguments. One thing Judge Hynes was not going to allow was valuable time to be wasted.

Aarons decided to start his list of witnesses while sheriff's officers in other counties were out looking for Paul James. Aarons called firearms, tool marks and tire track expert Nelson Welch to the stand. Welch had a master's degree in physics and had been with the New Mexico State Police. He also had crime lab training in tire print and shoe

print identification. In fact, Welch had been used
by prosecutor Eric Morrow as an expert only a few
years before on a different case.

Welch had received all 182 photos that the sheriff's office provided on tire tracks and shoe prints
related to the Tsosie murder site, and he'd also
gone to the location to survey the ground himself.
From the evidence he gathered, Welch related it
was virtually impossible to say that Robert Fry's
tires had caused the tire tread marks up on the
Bluffs.

Aarons next had a hostile witness in Sonya
Duke. She had already spoken about Les Engh in
other matters and worked for the San Juan County
DA's office in the pre-prosecution unit. Asked
what type of report she had given on Engh, she responded, "Average."

Aarons asked, "Did you become aware that he
forged a document?"

She answered, "Yes."

Aarons queried point-blank, "Would you call
him a liar?"

Duke replied, "I wouldn't say that."

Aarons's next witness was Robert Fry's father,
James. James Fry said he had lived in Farmington
for thirty-five years and was now retired. At one
time he had worked as an animal control officer
for the city of Farmington. A long-handled shovel
was displayed by Steve Aarons in the courtroom
and he asked James Fry if he recognized it. James
said that he did and related that is was a shovel he
had purchased back in 1997 and it used to have a
short handle. Then he said, "But I was digging up
roots and broke the handle. So I replaced it with a
longer one."

Asked who had the shovel in March and April

1998, he said that Robert had borrowed it then. "He kept a lot of stuff in his car," James said.

The point of all this was that James Fry declared that this was the same shovel that Les Engh was trying to say that he and Robert Fry had thrown into the San Juan River after killing Donald Tsosie. Obviously, if it was in the courtroom, it couldn't have been thrown away. It was one more instance where Steve Aarons tried to portray Les Engh as a liar who invented details as he went along.

Michelle Hearn, twenty-eight, took the stand next and was perhaps Robert Fry's biggest fan. She said that at one point she and Robert had planned to get married. She said, "I loved him a lot. I still do. He's always been there for me."

She told Jeff Jones that while on the way to a concert in Farmington to hear Dwight Yoakam, she was riding with Robert Fry and Larry Hudson. During the ride, she said, Robert Fry told her that Les Engh and two of his buddies had killed an Indian up at the Bluffs. Hearn said that Fry made no mention of himself being there. Then she added that the conversation had taken place between March 1998 and Robert's arrest for a different matter in June 2000. She didn't mention that the different matter was for the murder of Betty Lee. She seemed to think the event had been on May 6, the same time that Hudson and Fry had supposedly gone fishing at Navajo Lake.

During cross-examination Sandra Price immediately dug into Michelle Hearn's story. She brought up a 1994 incident when Hearn was involved in a scheme to steal a vehicle and duplicate its key. Hearn replied that wasn't true. She said she had only intended to take the car out for a test-drive.

Price, however, said, "You told Robert Fry's father that you would lie for him, isn't that right?"

Hearn answered, "I never told anyone I would lie for him."

Then Sandra Price asked, "Was the concert you went to around the time of The Eclectic?"

Heads popped up all over the courtroom on that one. Hearn answered, "I don't remember."

Judge Hynes, and everyone else, let the remark about The Eclectic pass without comment. Yet he and the defense listened very closely to what might come next.

Sandra Price did not go down that dangerous road any more. Instead, she mentioned a statement that Michelle Hearn had once made about the way Robert Fry fought. Hearn admitted, "He often said, 'He who hits hardest and first, with a sucker punch, wins.' "

By late afternoon on that day, Paul James was still missing and Judge Hynes was getting very irritated. There was a chance that a lot of good hours of testimony were going to be missed if James did not show up. Frustrated, Hynes finally instructed Steve Aarons and Jeff Jones to read from James's interview with a sheriff's detective about his sighting of Donald Tsosie back in 1998. Aarons was to play the part of the detective and Jeff Jones was to play James.

Aarons was concerned about this presentation, and he said that he couldn't question an interview statement or show it photographs to refresh its memory—the way he could a live witness. Judge Hynes countered that under the circumstances, this was the best he could do, and that if James was found later, Aarons could question him. In the meantime, he and Jones were to read the transcript.

Suddenly, like two actors in a rehearsal, Steve Aarons and Jeff Jones began reading the interview transcript as if they were preparing for a play. Aarons played the part of the detective while Jones played the part of Paul James. All of this was relevant to the time frame of Tsosie's disappearance. Genevieve Chee had said the last time she saw Donald Tsosie alive was on March 31, 1998, the same day that Les Engh said that he and Robert Fry had picked him up to be rolled. On the other hand, Paul James said that he saw Donald Tsosie alive on Easter Sunday, April 12, 1998.

Detective—Take us back to April 1998.

James—Yep. I want to know who killed my brother. I left him there in Farmington. There were three guys.

Detective—(He shows James a photo of Robert Fry and Les Engh with short hair—not the long hair he had then.)

James—They weren't there.

Detective—You saw him (Tsosie) get into the car with a white girl?

James—Yeah, I did. It was on Easter. My daughter's birthday was around then. (Actually, his daughter's birthday is September 16.) The reason I left, I had a hangover. I was drinking. I had a liter of vodka that day. I said to Donald, "Come on, brother, I don't trust this town." He turned around and said, "Leave me alone. Do your own business." Them guys were giving Donald a problem. They were driving a "dualie" (a pickup with four back tires). I was just sittin' around the corner. One guy pushed the lady that was with Donald.

When asked why he didn't call 911 at the time, James said that he didn't want to get involved.

Then he said that one of the guys wore a floppy hat, not a baseball cap or a cowboy hat. Also, he said that the pickup the guys drove had a license plate on the back with a horse on it.

"Like a bucking horse?" the detective had asked.

"Yeah," James had replied.

"Those are Wyoming plates," the detective had concluded.

James's statement became more erratic and incoherent as it went on. He appeared to be intoxicated as he gave the interview. He talked of owning some bulldogs and he would give a pup to the detective if they found Tsosie's killer. Then he did add one coherent thing: "I don't like Farmington anymore because of what they did to my brother."

The rest of it tailed off into incomprehensible statements. Judge Hynes raised his eyebrows after the recitation and commented, "Sounded to me like a bunch of gibberish."

Several jurors nodded their heads in agreement.

Aarons's next witness was defense investigator Robert Sandoval. He had sent Sandoval to talk with Paul James only a few days before the present trial. James was so taken with Sandoval's tough-guy looks that he called him a "big wicked-looking Mexican."

"Are you a big, wicked Mexican?" Aarons joked to Sandoval on the stand.

"I guess so," he laughed.

Sandoval had shown James several photos. One was of Robert Fry. James said he had never seen him. Sandoval showed him one of Les Engh with short hair. James said he didn't know him. But when Sandoval showed him one of Les Engh with long hair, James said, "I think this guy was there." In other words, Engh had been with the two other guys who were giving Donald Tsosie and the white woman a bad time at the Safeway parking lot on Easter Sunday, April 12, 1998—a date, by which, Les Engh was saying Tsosie was already dead.

On cross Sandra Price said to Sandoval, "You've been through the police academy. Why didn't you show James a photo lineup?"

Sandoval answered he wasn't a police investigator and wasn't required to do so. Besides, he only had those particular photos with him.

Finally, by the next court session, the ever-elusive Paul James was discovered lying in a ditch near Gallup, New Mexico, nearly 120 miles from the courthouse in Albuquerque. He was once again intoxicated. When he was cleaned up and brought to the court, he hardly became a star witness for Aarons. He rambled on and often contradicted his own statements. It was nearly as disjointed as his original statement had been.

Judge Hynes had moved the trial along at a brisk pace, and both sides were ready for closing arguments. At the beginning of the trial, many predicted that it would last for at least three weeks. It lasted less than two.

Steve Aarons attempted to initiate damage control on Paul James's commentary by saying, "The prosecution tried to discredit his testimony by bringing up his alcoholism. But he held his own. Yes, maybe he is an alcoholic, but all of these people (Fry and associates) seemed to have a problem with alcohol."

Aarons then portrayed Robert Fry as an outlandish storyteller. "Bob brags about things and he can't back up what he's said. He is a BS artist. Nobody believed him. His stories were like a game of telephone. The tale always gets taller after it circulates among friends. I know these stories are disturbing, because most people tell a story and the fish gets a little bigger. But Fry and his friends talked about fights and killings."

Aarons said that Les Engh used Fry's penchant for bragging to frame him for the killing of Donald Tsosie. "Engh is not a stupid person, but he is a liar," Aarons said. Then he added that when Engh was brought into the sheriff's office for an interview, he started concocting a story about Robert Fry to save himself. If the jury was to believe Engh, they would have to believe that Fry had killed Tsosie in the early-morning hours of April 1, 1998. According to Paul James, however, he said he saw Donald Tsosie alive on April 12, 1998.

Aarons said that even the physical evidence did not back up Les Engh's story, and he listed the reasons.

1. An expert said that Robert Fry's Ford Aspire couldn't have driven over the dirt road on the Bluffs at a high rate of speed as Les Engh indicated, especially if Fry and Tsosie were fighting at the time.

2. There were two evidence scenes at the Bluffs, not one. One was at the scuffle zone, and the other was near the end of the road at Scorpion Point. Robert Fry never mentioned this area in his story, and Engh didn't want to, because it would implicate him and his Wyoming buddies.

3. There were similar torn-apart beer cans at the scuffle zone and near Scorpion Point. The sheriff's officers had processed cans from both areas, but they had never brought them into evidence against Fry.

4. There was a large discrepancy about the size of the shovel.

5. Engh said that he and Fry had thrown the shovel away in the San Juan River after beating up

Donald Tsosie. Yet, Aarons said, the shovel was in the courtroom at this very moment.

6. There were no indications that Donald Tsosie had been stabbed in the genital area, as Engh claimed that Robert Fry had done.

7. There were four sets of shoe prints at the scuffle area, not three. This would indicate that Les Engh, two buddies and Donald Tsosie had been there.

Aarons wrapped it all up by saying, "There is no actual evidence to tie Robert Fry to the crime scene, only his stories about murder."

Sandra Price gave the summation for the prosecution and pointed out that so many things that Robert Fry had boasted about to friends were backed up by evidence. There was the use of a broom handle that broke and the bloody sticks from it that were in evidence. Those sticks had Donald Tsosie's blood on them. The time frame that Fry boasted about did fit into the period that Tsosie died. A lot of time had gone by between Donald Tsosie's death and the discovery of his body, but when officers searched the scene, they found a tire tread mark that was similar to one made by the front passenger tire of Robert Fry's car. And, most of all, Fry had bragged about throwing boots down at the Indian. That item had never been released by police, and yet that is exactly what happened. One of Donald Tsosie's boots was found to be lying down by his head in the canyon.

She said that Les Engh had been a good witness, and had given the jurors a blow-by-blow account of what had happened on the night of March 31 to April 1, 1998. It began at the Turn Around Bar and ended up with a dead or dying Tsosie thrown over the cliff by Robert Fry. She characterized Engh as a man with nothing to gain by framing

Robert Fry. He was already serving a life sentence for the murder. She said of Engh, "He is simply trying to do the right thing."

Price said that Fry was even a good witness against himself. "He has bragged and bragged and bragged. He bragged to four separate people about the crime. We have Donald Tsosie's body to back up what Fry was bragging about."

Then she quoted a lyric from a Bob Dylan song. It spoke of hunger being ugly when the soul is forgotten. Price said, "Fry had a hunger, a hunger for violence, a hunger for alcohol, and because of that hunger, he forgot the soul of Donald Tsosie. The walls of this courthouse protect the rights of the victim. Donald Tsosie had the right to a long and fruitful life."

The jury deliberation on the Donald Tsosie case, unlike at the Betty Lee trial, was swift and to the point. In less than an hour, they filed back into the courtroom and everyone rose. As Robert Fry stood by the defense table, the verdict was read. The jury found him guilty on all charges. Robert Fry listened to the verdict with his head hung and his arms at his sides. He did not utter a word, nor did he look at his parents as he was led from the courtroom by U.S. marshals.

Fry's parents hugged each other and shook their heads. Donald Tsosie's family members were just as silent as Robert Fry had been. Whatever emotions they felt, they kept to themselves. Robert Fry had just become the first person in New Mexico history to be twice eligible for the death penalty.

On September 4, 2003, there was once again a list of people asking the jury to spare Robert Fry's life during the sentencing phase, as they had done at the Betty Lee trial. Fry's sister Vickie told them, "He was happy. Always happy. A good kid. He had a big imagination. He wanted to be a movie star or rocket scientist."

His sister Jeanne said, "He had an innocence about him as a child. A carefree attitude. He was good with other children. He didn't like to fight."

Jeanne told the jury how he had made a complete turnaround in prison. He was now sober and respectful. She said his motto now was "Trust in yourself. Believe in God and believe in your family." She said that he read the Bible in prison and that she and her family started going back to church because of him.

Robert's mother, Gloria, was very emotional and told the jury, "He was always an entertainer. A storyteller. He sang in his church choir and put on performances for the family. At three years old he used a tennis racket for a guitar and sang 'Rhinestone Cowboy' for his grandmother.

"He wasn't angry at the world. He wanted to help the world. Bob always was a good friend. But he picked some lousy friends."

Gloria Fry told of how Robert now encouraged his nieces and nephews to lead good lives. He gave them advice about picking good friends and staying away from trouble. And he warned them about alcohol.

Ex-fiancée Michelle Hearn said, "I think without Robert Fry in my life, my life would be a lot harder. He's always been there for me when no one else was." She said that when she had family problems, he had always helped out.

Dr. Roy Jacob Matthew, a psychologist at Texas Tech University, had studied Robert Fry's school, military and alcohol treatment records. He also had interviewed Robert Fry in prison. Matthew told the jury, "There is no question whatsoever that Fry is an alcoholic. He has been in treatment five times. When you go through that history, you can see the total devastation it has had in his life. Yet he was unable to stop."

Matthew told the jury that Fry had used marijuana, methamphetamine, LSD, cocaine and mushrooms. "There is that aura of a thirst that cannot be quenched."

Matthew also delved into Fry's military record. He said, "Fry had a tendency to become very difficult and mean when he was drinking. There were problems with him showing up late and with oversleeping." He even got so drunk on one shore leave in Guam that he had broken the nose of another man in a fight.

Matthew said that as long as Fry remained in prison, he wouldn't be able to drink or cause problems for himself or others.

Isolde Waite, a counselor at Robert Fry's maximum-security facility, tended to agree with Matthew's assessment of Fry. She said, "Everybody likes to deal with him because he doesn't give anybody any problems. He doesn't like being a violent person."

She said that Fry came to her seeking help with substance abuse and anger management problems. "The change in this man's behavior came about after he [was incarcerated]. He had an epiphany."

Perhaps the most important person in front of the jury in Fry's case for leniency was Robert Fry himself. He spoke with emotion and at least the outward appearance of sincerity. He told the jurors, "There was no damn excuse for what happened to him (Donald Tsosie). I've come to know who Robert Fry was. He was an out-and-out bastard who would get drunk and didn't know how to act in society."

Then Robert Fry turned toward the members of

Tsosie's family in the audience and said, "I pray [to] God you can find peace in your life and move forward."

Fry said, "I had a whole separate life. The drinking, the drugs. The things I was doing. Now I got to know myself, sitting in a small cell, staring at the walls day after day. You can't hide from who you are there."

Fry said before his arrest, he liked to go into the woods to hunt and fish. Now he had to find pleasure in the most simple of things. He said, "The little bit of joy I have is in a bag of potato chips."

He looked directly at the jury members and sobbed: "I ask you today, God, please don't kill me! I don't want to die!"

Of this comment, Joline Gutierrez Kruger, a reporter for the *Albuquerque Tribune*, wrote, "Fry sputtered and wailed as a chorus of howls burst from his red-faced family."

During all of Robert Fry's pleas for his life, reporter Debra Mayeux heard sighs and moans from members of Donald Tsosie's family. She also said that she heard whispered words from them. The words were "Kill him."

The Tsosie family were traditional and shy of the spotlight and media. Only Regina Dennison, Donald Tsosie's niece, spoke up on his behalf. She told the jurors, "My uncle's death has made a big impact on our family. He wasn't there for my high-school graduation. He cannot support his children. My mother and aunt suffer from nightmares where they see my uncle. He tells them how angry he is. He doesn't like where he is. He wasn't ready to leave."

Though she left it unsaid, Regina Dennison indicated that what had become of her uncle Donald was one of the worst fates that could befall a Navajo after death. He became a ghost who had to wander through the afterlife, angry and unsettled. He had not attained *hozro*. He had not been able to finish his life as the Holy People had instructed: "To go with beauty all around him."

Eric Morrow was also not buying any of Robert Fry's contrition. He pushed for the death penalty and told the jurors, "His allocution is about me, me, me. His real remorse is about himself. He left Donald Tsosie's mutilated body on a cliff for scorpions and maggots. Left to rot. He is a vulture who took off Donald's boots and tried to rob him.

"This case is not about the Fry family, although I feel sorrow for them. The case is about an innocent man—Donald Tsosie. Robert Fry was not innocent. He made choices that led to Tsosie's death."

The very last shot at the jurors to ask for leniency was left up to defense attorney Jeff Jones. He apologized on Fry's behalf to the Tsosie family sitting in the court and said, "First-degree murder is never pretty, but the death penalty is for the worst of the worst. Someone who kidnaps a child, who rapes and murders that child.

"You have to find that there is no room for Fry to live . . . yet [find] something that you feel inside yourself that he has to live.

"Imagine Robert Fry sitting on a gurney, a needle is put in his arm. His eyes shut and he's gone. Fry is more than an animal. He's funny sometimes. He brings joy to his family.

"We pray that you will give him a chance to breathe. I and Steve Aarons, Robert Fry and the Fry family, will pray for you in your decision-making process."

The jury was out for only a few hours and then returned. The quick return of a jury does not usually bode well for the defendant, indicating that they have probably reached a unanimous vote in favor of the prosecution. Yet, nothing on the Tsosie trial went as planned for the prosecution or defense. As Robert Fry stood silently at the defense table along with his lawyers, the decision was read: the jury could not unanimously decide for death. The most Robert Fry would get would be life in prison for the murder of Donald Tsosie.

When he heard the verdict, Fry clutched the edge of the table and looked as if he would collapse. He started crying and so did his family members. The Tsosie family members were stunned. They had been sure that a death penalty conviction would be read. They had nothing to say to reporters as they left the courtroom.

Judge Hynes, however, had plenty to say, and he took the dramatic step of telling the jury information about Fry that the jurors had never heard during the trial. He filled them in about his conviction on the murder of Betty Lee. He said, "When you look into these cases, what you are going to find is there's a lot more going on."

Eric Morrow was naturally disappointed with the decision. He told Debra Mayeux of the *Farmington Daily Times,* "He is unsalvageable. He has not changed. He will not change."

Steve Aarons was delighted with the decision. He told Mayeux, "We're relieved that a life sentence was imposed. I think [Fry] deserves to live. He is a good person when kept away from alcohol."

The most pleased person, of course, was Robert Fry. He was no fool, and he understood that overturning one death penalty conviction would be much easier than overturning two. Yet his trials and tribulations were not yet over. Two people were determined to make sure of that. They were Jeff and Christina Trecker, and they never forgot or forgave Robert Fry or Harold Pollock for what they had done to their son, Matthew. The Treckers were the driving force, making sure that the San Juan County District Attorney's Office would go forward on The Eclectic Murders case. For them it was never a matter of choice—it was a matter of justice.

Chapter 10

End Game at The Eclectic

Even before the Donald Tsosie trial was under way, new evidence regarding The Eclectic case kept percolating to the surface. As with all things concerning Robert Fry, the unexpected was the norm.

In October 2002, Detective Tyler Truby was once again on a long journey to seek out the truth about Robert Fry. In this case it didn't concern Betty Lee, but rather the connection between Robert Fry, Harold Pollock and The Eclectic. As Truby wrote in his report, "I went to Tempe, Arizona, where I made contact with Harold Pollock. I advised Pollock that I needed to ask him some specific things about the crime scene at The Eclectic. Pollock agreed to speak with me and requested that his girlfriend, Karianne Grey, be present. During our conversation, I indicated to Pollock that I had spoken with a crime scene reconstructionist about this case. I advised Pollock that the reconstructionist believed two or more persons were involved in the death of Matt Trecker."

Truby asked Pollock to name who was at The

Eclectic on the night of the murders. Pollock told him that it was just himself, Fry, Fleming and Trecker. Truby then asked if Pollock thought he might have been involved in the death of Matt Trecker. Pollock answered that it was possible, but that he couldn't remember. Pollock then told him that he had a therapist in Farmington, and that if he went back to Farmington, the therapist might be able to assist him in recalling his involvement. Truby agreed to take Pollock and Grey to Farmington on the following day. He told Pollock to think about what had happened at The Eclectic and they could discuss it on the drive back from Arizona.

On October 24, 2002, Truby picked up Pollock and Grey from Grey's mother's residence. As they returned to Farmington, Truby asked Pollock if he could remember any more about the murders at The Eclectic. Pollock responded that he couldn't. When they arrived at Farmington, Truby dropped Pollock and Grey off at a friend's house, then asked Pollock to contact him the following morning.

At 9:30 A.M. on October 25, Pollock phoned Detective Truby. He said that he'd tried contacting his therapist, but the phone line was busy. Truby agreed that Pollock should call him back as soon as an appointment had been made with the therapist. Then about five minutes later, Truby phoned Pollock and asked if it would be all right if he went with him to the therapist's office. He told Pollock, "I could discuss the case and the therapist could be there for any painful feelings that you experience."

Detective Truby contacted the therapist, who agreed to allow him to conduct the interview at his office and that he'd be there to assist Pollock with emotional issues. A time was set for 1:30 P.M. Truby phoned Pollock once again, and Pollock agreed to meet him at the therapist's office at the appointed time.

Harold Pollock, however, made a fateful decision at 11:00 A.M. He phoned Truby and said that he just wanted to meet him and not the therapist. He said that he could talk to the therapist later if he felt like it. Truby agreed to meet Pollock at Gem's restaurant at noon. When they arrived there, however, the restaurant was very busy. Not wanting to talk with so many people around, Pollock asked Detective Truby if they could go someplace more private. They agreed upon meeting at Señor Peppers Restaurant. Karianne Grey would accompany Pollock.

At Señor Peppers, Pollock told Detective Truby that he had remembered more about his involvement in the murder of Matt Trecker. He said that his memory had partially returned two to three months previously. He had awakened one night in a sweat and was very upset. He told Karianne about his involvement, and sometime thereafter tried to commit suicide, but failed. He showed Detective Truby a scar on his wrist from a cut that had been self-inflicted.

Pollock said that it was still somewhat vague to him, but he remembered being in the bathroom at The Eclectic and hearing what sounded like a fight in the front part of the store. When he left the bathroom and walked down the hall to the showroom portion of the store, he saw Robert Fry standing on Jospeh Fleming's throat. He said that Fry pushed hard on Fleming's throat and then approached Matt Trecker.

"He hit Trecker in the face," Pollock said. "I had

never seen anybody hit that hard before. Trecker immediately fell to the floor and didn't move. Robert then returned to Fleming. I could see Robert's face and it appeared like he was possessed. He pulled out a knife from a sheath on his belt. Then he slit Fleming's throat. That's when I began to yell at him."

Pollock said that Fry looked up at him and then at Trecker, who was lying on the floor. Pollock said that Fry knelt down beside Trecker, lifted up Trecker's shirt and began to say, "We can do this! We can be each other's alibi. Come on, Harley, I need your help in this."

Pollock said that Fry waved him over, and then stabbed Trecker in the left side of the chest with the knife. Then he handed Pollock the knife.

Pollock said, "I stabbed Matt in the chest three or four times. Fry smiled and took the knife. Then he wanted to cut off Matt's head. He used the knife and made several slices on his throat. Then he stood up. I looked at Matt's throat. It made me feel sick, so I went to the rest room and vomited. When I came back to the showroom, Robert was holding a sword with a wavy blade and a samurai sword. He gave me the samurai sword. We began to hit Matt's neck with the swords. It was like trying to cut firewood. But for some reason the swords wouldn't cut very deep and we couldn't get Matt's head to come off completely."

Pollock said that Fry then put the sword down and walked away. When Fry did, Pollock gathered up the knife and swords to wipe them off. He noticed that Fry had a key for the door and Pollock began walking toward it. He started to follow Fry, but Robert Fry turned around and laughed. He said that the key had broken off in the lock. After some discussion they picked up a computer monitor and threw it through the front window. Pollock couldn't remember if it was he or Fry who threw the monitor through the window. By this time he was in a daze. Once the window was broken, they escaped by that route.

After throwing away the weapons into Farmington Lake, they went to a convenience store. Fry started laughing when they got out of the car and he told Pollock about the blood on his face, "Look, I've got on war paint."

Harold Pollock's conversation with Detective Tyler Truby was one of the worst mistakes he ever made. Perhaps he thought that coming clean about what happened at The Eclectic in November 1996 would help him. Obviously, he forgot that his immunity deal required that he not be part of the murders, and there was also a clause that he not leave the state of New Mexico. Harold Pollock had broken both demands of the immunity deal and was now vulnerable to being arrested.

The arrest came very quickly, in fact, on that very same day, October 25, 2002. The list of charges against him were numerous:

Count 1
On or about November 29, 1996, Harold Pollock did kill Matthew Trecker, a human being (a capital felony).
Count 2
Harold Pollock did knowingly combine with Robert Fry for the purpose of committing murder (a second-degree felony).
Count 3
Harold Pollock did steal property, to wit: weapons belonging to Alex Seifert (a third-degree felony).

Count 4
Harold Pollock did combine with Robert Fry for the
purpose of committing larceny (a fourth-degree
felony).
Count 5
Harold Pollock did destroy, change, hide, place or
fabricate evidence, to wit: stolen weapons (a fourth-
degree felony).
Count 6
Harold Pollock did destroy, change, hide, place or
fabricate physical evidence, to wit: weapons used to
commit murder (a fourth-degree felony).
Count 7
Harold Pollock did destroy, change, hide, place or
fabricate physical evidence, to wit: blood evidence
(a fourth-degree felony).

There were three other, lesser charges as well.

The headlines in the *Farmington Daily Times* the next day announced, POLLOCK ADMITS TO HELPING FRY IN ECLECTIC KILLINGS. Reporter Debra Mayeux wrote, "The Eclectic homicide case broke wide open Friday." She then reported all the details of Tyler Truby's report. San Juan County district attorney Greg Tucker told her, "Pollock's statements are consistent with the office of the medical investigator's findings."

Harold Pollock was held in the San Juan County Detention Center without bond. By October 28, 2002, he was in magistrate Carla Vescovi-Dial's courtroom for a preliminary hearing. With a forlorn expression, Harold Pollock waived his rights to a reading of the charges. Then through his court-appointed attorney, Overziena Ojuri, Pollock requested a short visit with family members in the courtroom. Special prosecutor Rick Tedrow objected, but Ojuri said, "A lot of the state's evidence against Mr. Fry is from statements made by Mr. Pollock. His statements strengthen the case against Fry. He has given his admission and is helping to bring some closure. He is not a threat. Mr. Pollock wants to let his family know he will be in jail for a while."

The judge granted Pollock's request for four minutes. Pollock went and sat with his family members and Karianne Grey in the jury box. He smiled and talked with them for a while and his eyes misted over when he had to tell them good-bye.

Matthew Trecker's parents, Jeff and Christina, were also in the courtroom that day. They told reporter Mayeux that they had a sense of relief that Pollock had come forward with his story of what had happened at The Eclectic in November 1996. Jeff Trecker said, "We're pleased. God bless their (the San Juan County Sheriff's Office and district attorney's) efforts."

Between the time of Harold Pollock's preliminary hearing and his next court date, some significant changes occurred in San Juan County. Detective Bob Melton ran for sheriff of the county and won. The headline in the *Farmington Daily Times* announced, THERE'S A NEW SHERIFF IN TOWN.

Reporter Laura Banish quoted Melton as saying, "Anyone who wants to be in a public position needs to be open and responsive. I can't think of a better place to be elected sheriff. I understand the tremendous trust that has been placed in me, and I will do everything to ensure that I keep that trust in my personal and professional activities."

The voters of San Juan County apparently trusted Bob Melton as well. A great degree of that trust came from his untiring efforts to discover the truth about who had murdered Betty Lee, Donald Tsosie, Joseph Fleming and Matt Trecker.

On January 5, 2003, Harold Pollock found himself in the courtroom of Judge William Birdsall—the same judge who had sentenced Robert Fry to death for the murder of Betty Lee. Pollock's defense attorney by now was Cosme Ripol, of the New Mexico Public Defenders' Office. Ripol told Judge Birdsall that he was deep into discovery and needed more time. Then he asked that Pollock be released on bond from the San Juan County Detention Center.

Judge Birdsall replied, "It's going to be a waste of time, because I handled the Fry preliminary hearing of The Eclectic case, where Mr. Pollock testified, and as long as it's up to me, Mr. Pollock isn't going anywhere."

Harold Pollock took issue with Judge Birdsall's decision, and soon thereafter he sent a jailhouse letter to the court system. The letter stated, "I, Harold Pollock, wish to excuse Judge William Birdsall. He was the judge that oversaw my arraignment on my current charges. I believe he has a preconceived opinion of me that could influence his judgement."

The request was denied, but Pollock was not yet done asking favors of the court. Through his attorney, he asked for an interview with Danyelle Miller, Lyle Miller, Mary Kazlauskas and John Bloomquist. All of these people had connections to The Eclectic case. Tyler Truby had already interviewed them and Pollock wanted to be able to do the same.

In February 2003, Pollock presented an even more unusual request—he wanted a furlough so that he could get married. His lawyer, Cosme Ripol, wrote, "Harold Pollock would like to have a furlough to get married. Pollock prays the court grant him a furlough for February 21, 2003, from 8 A.M. to 5 P.M."

Then Ripol noted, "Sandra Price attorney for the state does object to the motion."

This marriage furlough proposal was judicially discussed all through the rest of February and March 2003. Judge Thomas Hynes, who was handling this aspect, kept refusing each new proposal, citing the seriousness of the crime in which Pollock was involved. Judge Hynes also denied a request for an in-jail ceremony. Finally, out of frustration, Harold Pollock and Karianne Grey decided to take the matter into their own hands.

As Debra Mayeux later reported, Karianne's recently ordained friend, Alisha Shafer, along with Karianne, another adult and six children, went to visit Harold Pollock at the San Juan County Detention Center. Mayeux wrote, "A special family visit Wednesday at the center led to wedding bells. Instead of you may kiss the bride, they said you may kiss the glass."

Karianne explained to Mayeux that she and Pollock had been living together for 2½ years prior to his arrest and had planned to get married in December 2002. Then Pollock had been arrested and it prevented them from having a ceremony. Karianne told Mayeux she would take the last name Grey-Pollock.

Detention center lieutenant Jim Calhoun confirmed that a special visit of three adults and six children had occurred, but "to the best of my knowledge, we had no idea of a marriage. If it was done, it was private." He then explained that jailhouse guards do not enter the room during a visit, so they were not privy to what went on. He added that the detention center never allowed conjugal visits.

As May 2003 rolled along, Harold Pollock became increasingly dissatisfied with his attorney, Cosme Ripol. Apparently, Ripol was not enthused about his client, either, and he asked to be removed as Pollock's attorney. He stated, "The relationship has been irrevocably broken." His request was granted.

In Ripol's place, Gerald Baca, of Las Vegas, New Mexico, became Pollock's attorney. Baca said he was happy to have Pollock as a client. He also told the new presiding judge, John Dean, "I haven't had a chance to scratch the surface of the case yet. There are motions to be considered as well as a hearing date, but nothing has been set in concrete."

Perhaps because of this change in counsel, the Donald Tsosie trial preceded The Eclectic Murder case. Robert Fry, who was charged in The Eclectic Murders, had a somewhat different set of charges against him than those of Pollock:

Count 1
Robert Fry did kill Joseph Fleming . . . indicating a depraved mind regardless of human life (a capital felony).
Count 2
Robert Fry did kill Matthew Trecker . . . indicating a depraved mind regardless of human life (a capital felony).
Count 3
Robert Fry did steal property, to wit: knives, swords, assorted weapons belonging to Alex Seifert (a fourth-degree felony).
Count 4
Robert Fry did destroy, change, hide physical evidence, to wit: weapons (a fourth-degree felony).

Count 5
Robert Fry did destroy, change, hide physical evidence, to wit: clothing and shoes (a fourth-degree felony).
Count 6
Robert Fry did knowingly intimidate or threaten Harold Pollock (a third-degree felony).
Count 7
Robert Fry did knowingly intimidate or threaten Jae Willliams (a third-degree felony).
Count 8
Robert Fry did knowingly intimidate or threaten Leslie Engh (a third-degree felony).

One of defense attorney Baca's initial tasks was to get Harold Pollock's trial severed from that of Robert Fry's, and he was successful in this regard. Even then, every case concerning Robert Fry always seemed to have minefields on the road to justice, and The Eclectic Murders case was no exception. Fry's defense attorney spotted one potential minefield and wanted it to explode in the face of the prosecution. It concerned Harold Pollock's retention of lawyer Randall Roberts in November 2000, when he first spoke with Detective Bob Melton.

Fry's attorney filed a motion with the court bearing a lengthy title: "Motion to Disqualify Office of the District Attorney and Suppress All Statements of Harold Pollock." The motion contended that prior to Robert Fry being charged on The Eclectic Murders case, he had been represented by Randall Roberts. Then along came Harold Pollock and his interview with Detective Bob Melton on November 29, 2000. Pollock wanted Randall Roberts to be his attorney at the interview. That same day Melton sat down with Pollock, Roberts, Tyler Truby, DA Sandra Price and Farmington police detective

Cordell. After the interview Roberts negotiated an immunity deal with Sandra Price for Pollock in The Eclectic Murders. In exchange for immunity, Pollock had to tell everything he knew about Robert Fry's participation in the murders. It was during this interview that Pollock gave a fair assessment of the murders, leaving out his own participation in stabbing Trecker. In fact, Pollock blamed everything on Fry at that time and mentioned nothing about his own involvement.

The real bone of contention with Robert Fry's attorney in 2003 was that, in his estimation, Randall Roberts should not have been making any immunity deals for Pollock, if he was still representing Fry. As the motion stated, "Randall Roberts had a clear ethical obligation to not undertake the representation of a client whose interests conflict with those of a preexisting client, namely Robert Fry. Robert Fry did not give Randall Roberts permission to represent a party whose interests were adverse to his own. The office of the District Attorney paid lip service to the ethical obligation of Mr. Roberts and endorsed an agreement wherein Mr. Roberts violated the most basic of ethical obligations.

"Rather than seek justice for Mr. Fry along with all citizens of New Mexico, as is their duty, and rather than safeguard Mr. Fry's rights to due process and effective assistance of counsel, the office of District Attorney instead chose to go into an agreement fraught with error and subject to collateral attack at its inception."

The DA's office shot back to the court a memo-
 n of their own on this issue. It spoke of
ve Melton's initial interview with Harold
 and Pollock's request for Randall Roberts

to represent him. At that point Detective Melton went to Ms. Price's office and told her of the conversation with Pollock. Ms. Price then called Mr. Roberts.

"Ms. Price put the call on speaker phone with Detective Melton present, and spoke with Mr. Roberts about whether he could represent Pollock. Ms. Price told Mr. Roberts that she believed that Pollock's statement might implicate Robert Fry in the murders because law enforcement believed that Pollock and Fry were the last two people to have seen the victims at The Eclectic alive. Ms. Price asked Mr. Roberts if he might have a conflict of interest representing Pollock because Mr. Roberts previously represented Mr. Fry in an unrelated case or given the fact that Mr. Roberts and Fry's mother were friends. Mr. Roberts indicated that he did not feel that there would be anything that would preclude him from representing Pollock in the matter."

The memorandum went on to discuss the meeting attended by Pollock, Detective Melton and all the others. It stated that during that time, Randall Roberts was not Fry's attorney on anything related to The Eclectic. The judge took both arguments into consideration and came down on the side of the prosecution. The prosecutors would not be taken off The Eclectic case and everything that Pollock had said would stay in the judicial process.

The next real bump in The Eclectic Murders case made this matter seem like a tempest in a teapot by comparison. Trouble fell literally out of the sky to almost demolish the prosecution's case. On January 22, 2004, Farmington firefighter and student pilot Jeff Lewis took off from the Farmington airport in a small plane. Within minutes his Beechcraft Bonanza A-36 was having trouble. At 7:15

P.M., SWAT Sergeant Darin Hardy happened to look up from the parking lot of the Farmington Police Department. He told reporters later, "I didn't believe it was happening at first. I saw the plane veer straight up and come down on the north end of the Farmington Police [Department] building."

In fact, the plane came down right on top of Detective Pat Cordell's office—the very office where all his years of material on The Eclectic was stored. The plane smashed on the roof, spreading bits of wreckage and aviation fuel everywhere. It was incredible that no one except the pilot was hurt, and even he survived the crash and was taken to the hospital.

Farmington fire marshal Herb Veazy told the *Farmington Daily Times,* "I think it's a miracle the building didn't burst into flames. The aviation fuel is quite volatile."

Sergeant Pat Cordell experienced a miracle of his own. He was not at his office at the time, but he was certain all his documents and tapes on three different murder cases, including The Eclectic, were all destroyed. When he arrived at his office, he couldn't believe his eyes—all of the records had survived. As he told reporters later, "That was my major concern, that all that stuff for the trials would be gone."

A closed-door negotiation among Judge John Dean, ADA Arlon Stoker and Robert Fry's attorney Steve Aarons occurred on March 23, 2004. Stoker told a *Farmington Daily Times* reporter, "We were just setting up for a trial." As it turned out, they were setting up for a trial once again in Albuquerque's federal courthouse where the Donald Tsosie trial had taken place. Steve Aarons was quite satisfied that jurors from Albuquerque would give his client a fair hearing. Initially the trial was going to take place in Santa Fe, but then Albuquerque was deemed to be more appropriate.

On the other hand, Harold Pollock's attorney Gerald Baca wanted nothing to do with a trial in Albuquerque. He feared that prospective jurors there had been tainted by what they'd already heard and read about Robert Fry and Pollock's connection to him. Baca stuck to his request for a trial in Grants, New Mexico, to begin on April 6, 2004.

Once again, nothing would go exactly as planned when it came to anything concerning Fry and his friends. On the day before jury selection was to begin, Harold Pollock put forth that he wanted to make an Alford Plea; then he changed his mind, and changed it back again at the last minute. With their heads almost spinning from all the changes, the judge, defense attorney, prosecutor and Harold Pollock all sat down on April 5 to hammer out the Alford Plea.

In essence, an Alford Plea stemmed from a court ruling in a 1963 case called *North Carolina* v. *Alford.* Mr. Alford was indicted for first-degree murder, and at the time, in North Carolina, if a jury found a person guilty, the default punishment was death. The jurors had to go out of their way to grant a life sentence for that crime. In Alford's trial, things did not appear to be going well for him. A police officer had incriminating evidence and two witnesses said that before killing the victim, Alford had taken a gun from his house, stated his intentions to kill the victim, then returned to his house with a declaration that he had killed the victim.

After the prosecution presented their case,

Alford took the stand and testified that he had not committed the murder, but that he wanted to plead guilty because he feared the jury would find him guilty and he'd be faced with a death sentence. He wanted to plead guilty to second-degree murder, even though he still claimed he was innocent. A second-degree murder plea would get him life in prison.

Alford told the court, "I plead guilty, from the circumstances that he (my lawyer) told me. I plead guilty on a second-degree murder charge because they said, there is too much evidence, but I ain't shot the man. We (me and the victim) had no argument in our life. I just plead guilty because they (the prosecution) would gas me for it, and that is all."

Before sentencing, the judge asked Alford about his prior convictions. Alford said that he had served six years of a ten-year sentence on another murder, had been convicted five times for robbery, and had been convicted for trespassing, stolen goods, forgery and carrying a concealed weapon.

All of this eventually went to the United States Supreme Court. The dissenting judges said that an Alford Plea was just an excuse to escape the death penalty when defendants knew that they were guilty but didn't want to say so. But the majority opinion let *North Carolina* v. *Alford* stand. They cited many other cases to back them up in this regard, including one from fifteenth-century English law. In that case it was said that a defendant paid a fine to the king rather than face possibly very serious charges. As part of that law, "he put himself on the grace of our Lord, the King, and asked that he might be allowed to pay a fine—*petit se admittit per finem.*"

Harold Pollock decided to follow in Alford's shoes.

He stated that even though he thought he was not guilty for either murder at The Eclectic, he agreed that the state of New Mexico probably had enough evidence to find him guilty of first-degree murder. Instead, he would plead to being an accessory to murder. Such a plea would give him a life sentence with the possibility of parole in thirty years.

After Harold Pollock indicated what he wanted to do, both Christina and Jeff Trecker had a chance to express their opinions before the court. Christina went to the podium wearing a photo of Matt on her blouse. She began to read from a notepaper, but before she got very far, she broke down and said, "I can't do it."

Instead, someone else had to read from her statement. The statement described what a kind and loving son Matt had been and that he'd earned a two-year scholarship to San Juan College. Her declaration stated, "He never gave me a day of grief until he discovered The Eclectic." Then she added about Harold Pollock, "He chose to kill. I'll never forget what he did to Matt. I hope he never does either. What goes around, comes around."

Jeff Trecker spoke next directly to Pollock. He said, "Matt was the heart and soul of our family. It was a true honor and privilege to be called Dad by him. [Pollock] doesn't deserve the plea because Matthew was shown no mercy that night at The Eclectic. I have to try to forgive him. But it's going to take a long, long time."

At that point Jeff broke down and, through his tears, said, "God have mercy on you, Harold."

Harold Pollock also took his turn to speak. He once again denied having killed either Matt Trecker or Joseph Fleming. Instead, he said, "What I did that night, I'm not proud of it. But I didn't kill Matt."

He reiterated that he was afraid that Robert Fry would kill him that night at The Eclectic if he didn't use a sword on Trecker. But he contended that Matt was already dead when he chopped on his neck with a sword.

Prosecutor Arlon Stoker disputed this contention of Pollock's. Stoker said that evidence proved Fry could not have committed both murders at The Eclectic by himself. Stoker did not elaborate on what the evidence was, but he did say, "We believe Pollock was the one who initially was involved in restraining and stabbing Matthew Trecker. We had evidence he had a much more direct involvement."

Finally Judge John Dean handed down the sentence on Harold Pollock. Dean said, "There's no way to make this right. The plea agreement is a way to settle this case, but there are no winners."

Harold Pollock was talking to his lawyer during Judge Dean's pronouncement, and Dean became irked by Pollock's lack of attention. Judge Dean spoke directly to Pollock and said, "Mr. Pollock, did you hear me? I sentence you to life in prison."

After the verdict Stoker said, "Pollock had an easier time pleading to accessory to murder than out-and-out murder." Then Stoker added that because of the heinous nature of the crime, he didn't believe Harold Pollock would ever be getting out of prison. Stoker told the *Farmington Daily Times,* "The guy's going to die in jail. He's going to serve a life in prison and he's not coming out."

After it was all over, Christina Trecker added one bit of incredible magnanimity to the proceedings. She told reporters, "I forgive him for what he did. Matthew would have wanted it that way."

Then she quickly added that the case against Robert Fry on The Eclectic Murders was the big one, as far as she and Jeff were concerned. "We're ready for it," she said.

Epilogue

Black God to the People:
The ghost of Big-Monster-who-wanders-alone planned to become chief. . . . For these reasons I am entrusting to you that which I contribute to the ritual of the War Ceremony, so that it may be a means of defense and hope for you for the future.

In the spring of 2004, a Navajo ceremonial dancer in full regalia performed an Enemy Way dance in central New Mexico. To the north of him was Dibéntsaa, Sacred Mountain of the North, below him the Rio Grande. In the distance a hawk soared majestically in a turquoise sky. As he danced, he demonstrated how the Navajo took strength from the stories of the Hero Twins as they confronted good and evil—a recitation of how to ward off the deadly intrigues of enemies. By chanting and dancing and reciting the right prayers, he displayed how evil could be overcome and justice prevail.

Many miles away, in Albuquerque, defense lawyers and prosecutors geared up once more for the presence of Robert Fry. The last stage of the drama that had begun in the occult-strewn halls of The

Eclectic on Thanksgiving 1996 was about to unfold. As of this writing, Robert Fry's trial for his part in The Eclectic Murders is scheduled for the fall of 2004. But like everything else concerning him and his murderous days, nothing is carved in stone.

Many miles to the north of the Navajo dancer, Robert Fry's family waited with a mixture of hope and dread for the upcoming trial. And across town, near the San Juan River, Jeff and Christina Trecker waited with the same feelings of hope and dread. In a sense many things had come full circle. It was now thirty years since three Farmington boys had killed and mutilated three Navajo men in Chokecherry Canyon. As Farmington's mayor during 1974 said in April 2004, "I think there are lessons to be learned from any event, good or bad, and we would be fools not to learn from what happened and move forward from there."

Sheriff Bob Melton agreed, saying, "When I first came to law enforcement, cultural awareness or diversity training was nonexistent. Today it's just part of not only basic training for new recruits, but part of our ongoing training."

For many Navajos of the region, the events of the Chokecherry Massacre still cast a long shadow. As Vern Lee, a Navajo from Kirtland, told Laura Banish of the *Farmington Daily Times*, "I held a lot of anger toward white people because of what happened." Then he admitted, "The Navajos are also a racist people. One of the words we use describes whites as *ana'i*, which means enemy."

In its own odd way, the trials of Robert Fry for the murders of Betty Lee and Donald Tsosie helped the healing process concerning the Chokecherry Massacre. A Navajo woman named Pauline told a reporter for the *Farmington Daily Times*, "I think the Navajos were really upset when the three boys were not brought to justice. With Fry, I think the court did something about it this time. Law enforcement did a better job of bringing him to trial and not just sweeping it under the rug."

When Sheriff Bob Melton and Detective Tyler Truby finally enter the federal courthouse in Albuquerque for the Robert Fry/Eclectic trial, if they look out the windows to the west, they could possibly visualize over the horizon the outline of thirteen-thousand-foot Mount Taylor—Tsodzil—the Sacred Mountain of the South. For the Navajos, it is fastened to the earth by a great stone knife. Its symbolic colors are the blue sky and blue horizon light of dusk. At its base the Hero Twins deposited the heads of monsters, as a warning to evildoers. And it was here that Turkey Buzzard promised the Hero Twins, "Wherever monsters are killed and decay, I will be present as a scavenger. My evil attitude will become one of responsibility. I will help mankind."

No matter what happens to Robert Fry at The Eclectic trial, he will die in prison either by lethal injection or as an old man. His only moments of happiness may be the small things he mentioned, such as a bag of potato chips and a glimpse of the sky when he is let outside, one hour a day. Perhaps when Robert Fry's last trial is over, those who died and the family members who survived their deaths can reach that synthesis of Anglo and Navajo serenity—closure, *hozro,* harmony.

For the victims—Joseph Fleming, Matthew Trecker, Donald Tsosie and Betty Lee—their spirits may, as Irvin Morris wrote in his story "The Blood Stone," be "rising on a sunbeam, traveling on a rainbow."

HORRIFYING TRUE CRIME
FROM PINNACLE BOOKS

MORE MUST-READ TRUE CRIME FROM PINNACLE

BOOK YOUR PLACE ON OUR WEBSITE AND MAKE THE READING CONNECTION!

We've created a customized website just for our very special readers, where you can get the inside scoop on everything that's going on with Zebra, Pinnacle and Kensington books.

When you come online, you'll have the exciting opportunity to:

- View covers of upcoming books

- Read sample chapters

- Learn about our future publishing schedule (listed by publication month *and author*)

- Find out when your favorite authors will be visiting a city near you

- Search for and order backlist books from our online catalog

- Check out author bios and background information

- Send e-mail to your favorite authors

- Meet the Kensington staff online

- Join us in weekly chats with authors, readers and other guests

- Get writing guidelines

- AND MUCH MORE!

Visit our website at
http://www.kensingtonbooks.com